Mixing and Mastering In the Box

The Guide to Making Great Mixes and
Final Masters on Your Computer

Steve Savage

With diagrams by Iain Fergusson

OXFORD
UNIVERSITY PRESS

OXFORD
UNIVERSITY PRESS

Oxford University Press is a department of the University of Oxford. It furthers the University's objective of excellence in research, scholarship, and education by publishing worldwide.

Oxford   New York
Auckland   Cape Town   Dar es Salaam   Hong Kong   Karachi
Kuala Lumpur   Madrid   Melbourne   Mexico City   Nairobi
New Delhi   Shanghai   Taipei   Toronto

With offices in
Argentina   Austria   Brazil   Chile   Czech Republic   France   Greece
Guatemala   Hungary   Italy   Japan   Poland   Portugal   Singapore
South Korea   Switzerland   Thailand   Turkey   Ukraine   Vietnam

Oxford is a registered trade mark of Oxford University Press in the UK and certain other countries.

Published in the United States of America by
Oxford University Press
198 Madison Avenue, New York, NY 10016

Library of Congress Cataloging-in-Publication Data
Savage, Steve, 1948–
Mixing and mastering in the box : the guide to making great mixes and final masters on your computer / Steve Savage.
   pages cm
Includes bibliographical references and index.
ISBN 978-0-19-992930-6 (cloth) — ISBN 978-0-19-992932-0 (paper) 1. Sound—Recording and reproducing—Digital techniques. 2. Mastering (Sound recordings)—Data processing. 3. Sound recordings—Remixing—Data processing. 4. Computer sound processing. 5. Digital audio editors.   I. Title.
TK7881.4.S3824 2014
781.460285—dc23   2013042817

Mixing and Mastering In the Box

For my family—where the rumpus begins!

Acknowledgments

The greatest influences on this book have come from the many artists and musicians whom I have worked with over the years. As should be clear from the content here, making recordings is a collaborative process. For all the technical details involved—all the strategies and critical listening elements—the work itself must reflect the spirit of the artists and musicians. So while the book is steeped in the techniques of mixing and mastering, my primary goal is to serve the creative process—the musicians and their work.

I want to thank my editor, Norm Hirschy, for his enthusiasm for this project; he has been a critical link in support of my writing. My gratitude also goes to my family and friends who put up with my obsession about how things sound. Finally to my students—even though you can read the book now—you'll still have to listen to me talk endlessly about all this stuff!

Contents

About the Companion Website

www.oup.com/us/mixingandmasteringinthebox

A companion website has been created to accompany this book, and the reader is encouraged to use it to supplement the material presented here.

The website contains 65 audio clips that provide concrete examples for many of the mixing and mastering concepts discussed in the text. Each example comes from a project that the author worked on, and the artist name and track title are listed in the book and at the website. They are marked with the icon ⏵.

The author wishes to thank the artists and record companies for generously agreeing to have their work used for these educational purposes, and to Oxford University Press for preparing and maintaining this site. Access the website using username Music1 and password Book5983.

Introduction

Mixing and mastering represent the final challenges in creating great recordings. This book opens with a guide to mixing and mastering that provides an overview on how to succeed in taking your recordings through the final stages that prepare them for release. I define and describe mixing and mastering in detail, and I also pinpoint the essential similarities and differences between the two processes. In the course of the book, I then explore the tools and creative processes involved in creating great mixes and final masters, working completely within a Digital Audio Workstation (DAW) on a computer ("in the box"). For many of the chapters, you will find audio examples available at the companion website, allowing you to hear what the results of the processes being discussed actually sound like.

Making great mixes requires creativity in combination with a practical understanding of the process of building a mix. Initial recording and editing work tends to be less complicated because the practical aspect of recording can often be separated from the creative process (e.g., once the signal path is set, the vocal recording proceeds without concern for technical elements). Mixing represents the process whereby the musical vision and the audio reality come together. Students ask me how to approach mixing—how to know if a mix is "right," and how to know if a mix is "finished." There are no easy answers to these questions, in part because there are no "right" answers. But the path for the aspiring mixer is clear, and this is the approach that *Mixing and Mastering in the Box* takes—detailing the process necessary to becoming a good music mixer.

Making final masters requires understanding the goals of mastering and developing a specialized ear for achieving those goals. The function of mastering is often not clearly understood, and the process is often considered beyond the capabilities of a home or project studio. Indeed, until fairly recently audio mastering required a lot of specialized and expensive equipment. But the ability to create and deliver final masters via the computer has made mastering accessible on a wide scale. *Mixing and Mastering in the Box* describes what is needed for effective mastering and explains the process in both technical and creative terms.

Although much of the information presented in *Mixing and Mastering in the Box* is applicable to those using analog mixing gear, or a hybrid of digital and analog tools, the book focuses directly on working completely within the Digital Audio Workstation (DAW)—that is, "in the box." This approach to mixing and mastering has become increasingly common on all levels (including many multi-platinum recordings). It has many creative and practical advantages, and because the capabilities have become so advanced and the practice so widespread, it is the focus of this book.

This book represents both a continuation and an expansion of the material presented in my previous book, *The Art of Digital Audio Recording*. In some cases I refer the reader to that book for information that may provide a helpful context for the topics discussed here. There is a small amount of information repeated, but it is presented differently and significantly expanded to provide greater insight into the specialized jobs of mixing and mastering.

Over the course of writing this book, and as a result of some projects I had during that time, I came to realize the profound shift that has taken place in the relationship between mixing and mastering, largely a result of the use of brick-wall limiting. This is a processing technique that has created what has been termed the "loudness war." It has caused me to write the piece presented here as appendix B: "Why Mixing and Mastering Can No Longer Be Separated." In fact, this is so key to understanding the implications for creating great mixes and final masters that I toyed with the idea of presenting the piece as a foreword rather than an appendix. In the end, it seemed that the full implications of these ideas could be grasped best with a broader understanding of much of the material in the body of the book. I mention this appendix here because the reader may wish to read this short section early in the process of exploring the book, and then return to it after absorbing more of the previous material. In any event, it is my hope that this appendix will add clarity to your understanding as you delve deeper into the joys and challenges of creating great mixes and final masters.

MIXING AND MASTERING

I am not here to claim that mixing or mastering is easy, or that everyone should be doing it for himself or herself. I make my living primarily mixing and mastering for others, so I certainly believe that hiring an experienced mixing and/ or mastering engineer might be the best production decision you can make. Nonetheless, I believe that effective mixing and mastering are not beyond the capabilities of anyone seriously interested in doing these things themselves— and of course, the luxury of working for oneself and the benefits in financial savings (sometimes essential) make it an adventure worth pursuing for many.

Part I of this book has two goals: to present some introductory material that bridges both mixing and mastering, and to provide "quick guide" chapters to jump-start the process for those who may not initially want to go through the entire book but, rather, want to use it as a reference when problems present themselves. I begin by defining the basic terms. While I think most readers are likely to have a pretty good idea about what constitutes *mixing*, this may be less true for the more elusive process called *mastering*. In any event, a short description of each follows.

What Is Mixing?

Mixing refers to the final stage in the production of a single audio program— typically a song, but can also relate to a radio show, TV show, movie, commercial, webcast, or any other audio program material. In this final stage, all of the audio elements are combined to create the final version of the audio program in its intended format. Typically, that format is a stereo audio file, but it might be surround sound (requiring several files) or even mono, and it may be analog tape or some other storage media.

You are no doubt aware that most music is created from multiple sources that occupy many tracks in a typical DAW. All of these elements need to be set for level, panning, and processing (EQ, compression, reverb, etc.). Mixing, thus, is creating the final placement and sound of each element over the course of the musical time line, and then transferring the musical piece to its intended file and/or media format. The creative imagination must serve the mixer's sonic vision of the final audio.

What Is Mastering?

Mastering most often refers to the final stage in the production of multiple audio programs—typically, a group of songs or pieces of music. In this final stage, all of the individual pieces of music, which have already been mixed down to their final format, are balanced to sound good together and a final master is created. The final master is the source to be used for duplication—for a CD this is a typically a CD-R that is exactly the same as what is desired for the final CD that is to be manufactured. There is another kind of processing that refers to the creation of a single piece of audio for a particular format, such as for download from iTunes or streaming on Pandora or Spotify. This has also come to be called mastering (such as "Mastered for iTunes"), but it isn't actually mastering in the traditional sense (more on this in chapter 12).

The typical rationale for changes made in the course of creating a final master that contains multiple audio files is as follows. Each element is mixed to sound as good as possible, but mixing may occur over several days, weeks, or even months yet the musical pieces will be played one right after the other on a CD or other format; all of the pieces need to be balanced for level and overall sound so that they sound good played together as a group. The first task of mastering, then, is to adjust the level of each musical piece so that they all sound like they are essentially the same volume (much more on this in part III).

Beyond that, it may be helpful to adjust the frequency balance of some songs so that they all sound relatively similar. For example, one song may sound like it has more bottom end than another. Taken individually this may not be a problem—both songs sound great—but when they are played one right after the other, one song may suffer in contrast to the other. So, the mastering engineer will adjust the low frequencies of one of the songs (more on the song that has less low end, or less on the song that has more—or a little bit of each). It isn't that either song really needed the adjustment if it were playing on its own, but when it's sitting with the other songs it fits better with the adjustment. All elements of the sound: level, frequency balance, dynamic range, ambience, and effects are considered in the mastering process.

While mastering is primarily the time when adjustments are made to provide the best compatibility between different audio materials, it may also be when the overall sound of the program material is enhanced. It can be difficult to differentiate between changes made to increase compatibility and changes made to enhance the overall sound—both considerations often enter into the final decision making.

Mastering may also be used to try to "fix" perceived problems with the mix, because it is either impossible or impractical to return to the mix stage to make those changes. Clearly, because mastering occurs with material that is already mixed—typically, stereo program material— it is much more difficult to change the relationship between individual elements (this is the task of mixing). Nonetheless, it may be possible to subtly alter relationships that would be better accomplished through mixing, but can be addressed in certain ways through mastering (again, much more on this in part III).

Larger productions such as TV shows or movies don't go through a separate mastering phase over the whole audio program material, though much of the processing associated with mastering may be integrated into the final mixing process, and various of the individual elements such as music cues or sound FX may get mastered separately before they go for the final mix. Music soundtracks from films released on CD and/or for download will be mastered just as any other group of music material is.

Finally, mastering is when the overall level of the program material is set. Not only does the mastering engineer set the relative level between each of the individual pieces of music, she or he must also decide on the overall level of all of the pieces (e.g., how "loud" the entire CD will be). While this was as true back in the analog days of the LP record as it is today, in the age of the CD and mp3, the issues involved in this decision have changed dramatically (covered in part III).

The setting of the overall program level is something that needs to be considered when mixing if the audio is not going to go to a final mastering stage. If it's a one-off song or piece of music, then there's no real reason for a formal mastering, but the mixing engineer will likely want to use one or more of what are traditionally mastering techniques to set the overall level of the one musical piece. Whether or not that is actually "mastering" may be debated— a master for that one element may be created as a CD-R or in some other format—but it doesn't really fit the typical mastering process because it doesn't bear a direct relationship to other associated material. Often, with a single piece of audio, what is created is a premaster that is a high-quality final version (including overall level processing) but that has not been converted to its final format (which would be the actual master). In many cases the final conversion to a master is handled by the downloading or streaming service that will deliver the audio.

All of the issues touched upon here will be dealt with thoroughly in later parts of this book. This part I introduction is intended to give those who may not have been thoroughly clear on mixing and (especially) mastering a better sense of what the roles of these functions are and where the discussion is headed.

Chapter 1

The Starting Point
Fundamentals of Mixing and Mastering

1.1 Preparing to Mix and Master

Now that most recording, editing, mixing, and mastering are all done in the same or similar computer-based DAW environments, the lines between these various functions has become increasingly blurred. There are various tactics on the road to creating great mixes and final masters. Some people are beginning to create final mixes from early in the recording process and some don't think about the mix until the recording and editing are complete and the DAW file is optimized for mixing. Some people include some mastering functions as a part of the mixing process and some don't. There will be more about these techniques discussed in later chapters, but here I will outline what must be done before any mix can be completed and before any mastering can be started.

Am I Mixing Yet?

In the introduction to part I, I define mixing as the process of creating the final placement and sound of each element over the course of the musical time line, and transferring the musical piece to its intended file and/or media format. This suggests that each individual element is in its final form and this is, strictly speaking, a requirement of the mix stage. Final mixing can only occur once all of the recording and editing (and fixing and tuning) are completed. However, because all of these functions are housed together in the DAW and are easily accessible, and because all of the mixing functions (including advanced ones) may be housed in the DAW in the same file, it is very easy to transition from one mode of work to another. This is particularly true in the case of editing, fixing,

6

and tuning because these might be small tweaks that don't significantly interrupt the flow of the mixing process.

When I take on a new mixing project I always ask if all the editing, tuning, and fixing are completed. If it's not, then I suggest that it should be before I start mixing. If they want me to work on these elements I will be happy to, but that isn't mixing and will need to be billed (and hours calculated) separate from mixing. While I am often told that those things are done and that the music is ready to be mixed, I am almost always also told that "if you happen to hear anything that needs to be fixed, please go ahead and fix it—just use your judgment" (or something to that effect). That said, please note that this book is about mixing and mastering, so editing, tuning, and fixing are not covered here (editing is covered thoroughly and tuning and fixing are discussed in my previous book, *The Art of Digital Audio Recording*).

The capabilities of the DAW have created the ability to transition easily between functions, so you may find yourself doing a fair amount of mixing well before all of the recording or editing is completed, and you also may find yourself stepping back to do a bit of editing (or even recording) when you're supposed to be in the middle of a mix. There are advantages and disadvantages to these changes in workflow.

Doing too much mixing before you're really ready to mix may create problems when you do have everything in place for mixing. If you EQ compress and/or add effects to a track before you're really in mix mode, it is essential that you review those decisions when you focus completely on the final mix. *Whatever you do to one sound affects how it is working with all the other sounds, so you shouldn't make any final decisions about sounds until the context is complete.*

Alternatively, mixing requires special kinds of focus and listening skills that are different from those used for recording or editing. If you do too much bouncing back and forth between functions, something (or everything) will likely suffer. It is best to stay focused on mixing when you're mixing, editing when you're editing, and so on. That said, if you are mixing in the box at your own facility, with the ease and speed of total recall and the luxury of schedule flexibility, you may allow yourself to get sidetracked into other things, such as editing or recording, and then simply take a break and return to mixing when you're feeling fresh again, remembering that whatever you've done to your music may mean that you need to reconsider some elements of your mix.

Am I Mastering Yet?

Mastering is the final step—the completion of your audio project. Most mastering is focused on the relationship between multiple, complete audio elements (such as songs) and the creation of the final delivery materials. These may be CD-R for CD manufacturing, an mp3 for downloading or streaming, or some other format. Because mastering is the setting of all the relative relationships between these distinct elements it is necessary for the program material to be complete before beginning. That means that final mixes must be done and bounced to a final mix file (typically a stereo file) before you begin mastering.

In most cases, mastering is going to require a new file to where you import all of your material and then undertake the mastering process. There are some dedicated mastering programs, but mastering can also be done in most of the same programs using for recording and mixing. If you discover something that you want to change that requires remixing you will need to go back to your multi-track mix file and make the changes, bounce that into a new final mix file, and then import that back into your mastering file for mastering. Details on file preparation and the mastering process, including various options when changes are desired and remixing is not possible, are covered in part III.

As mentioned in the introduction to part I, there are a number of mastering functions that may end up getting applied in the mix situation—especially if it's standalone program material that won't be combined with other material in a traditional kind of CD environment. Over the course of the book I will cover the ways in which mastering and mixing cross paths and why it might be desirable to include certain mastering functions as a part of the mixing process.

1.2 Where to Mix and Master

Recordings can be made in a wide variety of environments (close miking can alleviate a lot of room acoustic issues), but mixing and mastering require a more controlled acoustic condition. Mastering is the most demanding of all audio practices in regard to monitoring environment, but it is still within the range of small studios. I will cover the fundamentals of acoustics that promote effective mixing and mastering and also address practical solutions for those who don't have the space or the budget to create the ultimate mixing or mastering environment.

Acoustics

It's easy to say that you should mix and master in an acoustically neutral environment, but that's very difficult (really impossible) to achieve. I will briefly consider the technical issues regarding acoustics as they specifically relate to mixing and mastering, but I suggest that you look to the many other resources that deal much more extensively with room acoustics for recording studios if you require greater detail. The reality is that there is only so much you can do to alter your room acoustics without very expensive remodeling, which is beyond the budget of many. Understanding some basics about acoustic environments will allow you to maximize your room's potential with the minimum expense. I will cover the three critical areas regarding room acoustics here: isolation, frequency response, and ambient characteristics. In the following section, I point to three principles regarding setting up your mixing and mastering environment that are within just about everyone's reach.

Isolation is only important if there are issues regarding intrusion of sound from the outside that makes it difficult to work, or transmission of sound from your studio that causes problems for others. Small reductions in transmission are achievable relatively easily by using weather stripping to seal doors and heavy curtains over windows. The only solution for more difficult transmission problems is applying mass. Soft material such as rugs or acoustic panels will alter the sound in the room, but will do little or nothing to change transmission through the walls—only significant mass actually stops low frequencies from traveling through walls, doors, and windows. Some studios have actually resorted to installing lead in the walls to deal with transmission problems. If remodeling, or building from scratch, you can use a variety of construction techniques to reduce transmission, but for existing spaces, severe transmission problems are not going to be solvable without large expenditure, so choose your workspace accordingly.

Frequency response within a room, on the other hand, is something that you can control, often without major expense. Frequency response refers to the effect the room environment has on the range of frequencies, from low to high. Soft material such as rugs and curtains will reduce the high-frequency content of sound in a room but have little effect on bass frequencies. Parallel walls and 90° angles are the biggest enemies of sound because they create standing waves and phase problems that translate into unnatural bass frequency buildup. Because almost every room that wasn't designed and built to be a studio is made of mostly parallel walls and 90° angles, most of us need to try to address these problems. Standing waves can be contained by putting materials in the corners, along parallel walls, and between the walls and the ceiling. These "bass traps" vary in design and price, and you're not likely to be able to eliminate all parallel walls and right angles in your room, but whatever you can afford to do will improve the overall sound of your room (see diagram 1.1).

The *ambient characteristics* of your room refer to the extent and quality of the reflections that create reverberation. High-frequency reflections create the

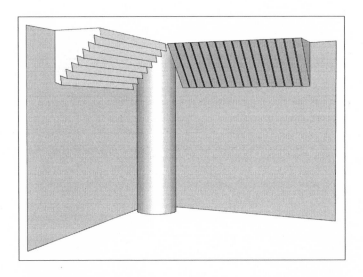

DIAGRAM 1.1

Several bass trap designs.

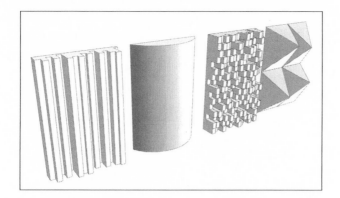

bulk of the audible reverberation and can be responsible for some of the most undesirable kinds of room reverberation (such as that boingy sound that you sometimes hear when you clap in a room with a lot of hard services that are either parallel or at right angles). Too much reverberation (and especially strong early reflections) can seriously compromise the accuracy of your monitoring. See the principles below for some specifics on room setup that can help balance the frequencies and control the ambience in your room.

While absorption can help with frequency balance and control ambience as well, it can also create an unpleasant listening environment that is so dead as to suck the life out of the music. A certain amount of room ambience across the frequency range is needed for a natural-sounding environment that is pleasing to the ear. For this reason the use of diffusers has become a popular and important element in controlling room acoustics. By using uneven surfaces to break up the frequencies, diffusers reflect sound that is more evenly balanced across the frequency spectrum. This maintains a certain "liveness" to the acoustic environment while helping to create a neutral listening environment without excessive frequency nodes (specific frequencies that are emphasized by poor room acoustics).

Diffusers scatter the frequencies by using small reflective surfaces of different depths. The deeper the portions of the diffuser panel, the lower the frequencies that will be affected. Too much diffusion will create the opposite problem from too much absorption; the room will sound very "live"—open and airy— but that sound probably isn't accurately reflecting the recording that is being worked on. More diffusion can be great for a room that is used to record in, but for mixing and mastering a room balanced with absorption and diffusion will be best (see diagram 1.2).

Principles

By principles I mean the specific guidelines about mixing and mastering environments that you can probably control without too great of expense and regardless of the technical challenges you may have with your room acoustics.

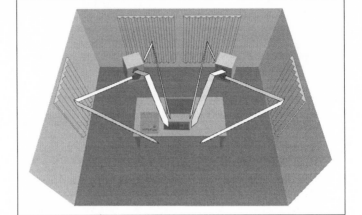

DIAGRAM 1.3

Dampening speaker
reflections.

1. *Dampen the immediate reflections from your speakers to your mix position.*
Wherever the closest walls to your speaker are you will want to place some dampening material to reduce reflections to the mix position (see diagram 1.3). You can use a mirror to determine where the material needs to go—ask someone to hold the mirror at the wall or ceiling while you sit in the mix position. When you see the speaker in the mirror, that is the general area that needs dampening material. There are many relatively low-cost acoustic panels that can be purchased that provide proper absorption—search "acoustic treatment" to find options.

2. *Use a combination of absorption and diffusion to treat your room and use Internet resources to help design your room treatment within your budget.* There are several companies that sell acoustic treatment for studios (wall panels, bass traps, etc.) and they will offer free advice regarding your room. You can send them your room dimensions and they will suggest a strategy for how to treat your room (along with a list of the products you should buy from them to accomplish this, of course). You may decide to execute the strategy in stages (depending on budget) and/or you may decide to acquire some of the treatment options from other sources or build them yourself. There are designs for absorbing panels and diffusers that are easy to obtain over the Internet so if you have some basic carpentry skills you can build this stuff yourself.

A combination of absorption and diffusion is generally the best solution to getting relatively controlled and even frequency response from your room acoustics. Both absorption and diffusion work best if they operate across the entire frequency range; you want the sound to be either absorbed or reflected as evenly as possible across all frequencies (from low to high). By using a combination of absorption and diffusion you can avoid having to dampen the sound in the room too radically in order to control frequency imbalances or have a room that is too live sounding for comfortable, long-term listening (see diagram 1.4).

3. *Whatever your mixing and mastering environment, stick with it!* Familiarity is ultimately your greatest ally as you develop your mixing and mastering skills. Once you've made your space as acoustically friendly as time and budget

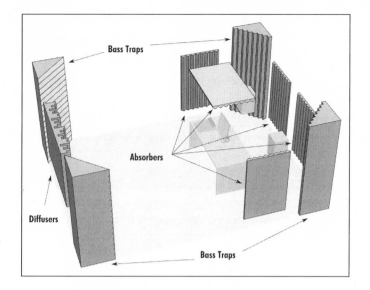

DIAGRAM 1.4

A typical room treatment strategy.

will allow, you need to learn how to interpret what it is that you're hearing and adjust accordingly. This applies to your playback system (especially your speakers) as well as to your acoustic environment. No speakers or environment are perfect, so you will need to become acclimated to your particular situation before you're confident about how your mixes are sounding. This is not to say you shouldn't refine your room acoustics or upgrade your monitors if and when you can, but realize that each time you do that you will need to make some adjustments to how you interpret what you are hearing.

WHAT NOT TO DO

Don't ignore room acoustic issues.
At a minimum, you need to consider the information presented here and apply the principles to your room and your setup. Some expenditure on sound treatment for walls and corners in your room is almost always worth it, and it doesn't have to be a lot to make critical improvements in your listening environment. Following the basic guidelines regarding speaker setup and location of the mix position is critical for getting reliable and consistent results. (I cover speaker placement in chapter 3.)

1.3 The Tools of Mixing and Mastering

This is an introduction to the primary tools used in creating mixes—including an overview that introduces mixers, plug-ins, inserts, send and returns, parallel processing, automation, and recall. There are many ways to accomplish the basic functions of mixing; here I sort them out to provide a broad context for the detailed information that is to follow. Mixers, plug-ins, inserts, and the send and return routing model are all covered in greater depth in my general recording manual, *The Art of Digital Audio Recording*. Parallel processing, automation, and recall are introduced in that book, but they are covered in much greater depth in later chapters of this book, as they are especially relevant to mixing and mastering.

Mixers

You're not going to get much mixing done without a mixer or control surface. Because this book is focused on working "in the box," I am not going to discuss analog mixers, though most things covered in this book have some equivalent in the analog world. For those working in the box you have two basic choices: use the virtual mixer within your DAW, or use a control surface that gives you hardware access to the mixing functions in your DAW (or of course, you can use a combination of the two).

Control surfaces have some advantages—primarily the tactile experience for controlling faders and switches, and the ease of access to multiple functions. They also have some disadvantages—primarily in the space they occupy and in how they may compete for optimum location of your computer keyboard and mouse that will always be needed for some DAW functions. The other main difficulty for many in regard to a control surface is cost. This can be significant, and the more one desires a high-quality tactile experience and broad access to multiple functions, the more expensive the control surface is going to be.

For myself, I have opted to work without a control surface, operating all mixing functions from inside the DAW software. I use Pro Tools, but all the major DAW software packages contain all the necessary functions for high-level mixing, and this book is intended to be relevant for any DAW. I have found that using quick keys along with extensive familiarity with my software interface allows me to work quickly and efficiently. By not having a control surface I retain an excellent working surface for the keyboard, mouse, notes, and so on. There is nothing you would be able to do with a typical control surface that you cannot do within your DAW. That said, there are some things that will be much quicker and easier with a control surface, but many of these functions are associated with recording rather than mixing—such as managing headphone mixes for large recording sessions.

Mixers, whether internal or external, provide access to all mixing and mastering functions, but they start with control over level. The absolute level and the relative volume of each element are the first concerns of both mixing and mastering, and those start at the output fader at the bottom of your mixer. Panning is one of the most crucial elements in the mix process and is also easily accessible on each mixer channel. Of course, there will be much more on setting levels and pan positions, using either the DAWs virtual mixer or a control surface, in later sections of this book (see screenshot 1.1).

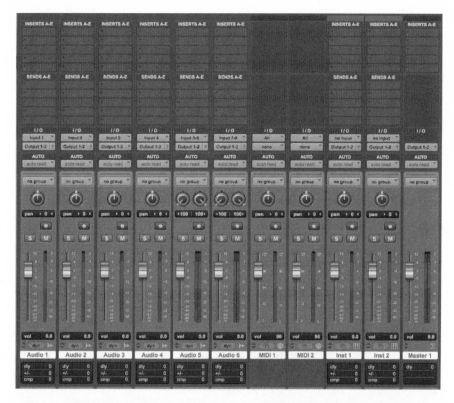

SCREENSHOT 1.1

Several virtual mixers.

14

Plug-ins (Signal Processing)

Signal processing represents the next major stage in mixing and mastering after the setting of levels (and panning, in the case of mixing). Typical signal processing functions include, EQ (equalization), dynamics (compression, limiting, expansion etc.), and FX (reverb, delays etc). In the analog world these tools were either built into mixing consoles or available as hardware processing boxes that could be interfaced with the mixing console In the DAW, all signal processing comes in the form of software that is accessed using the "plug-in" approach to expanding the software's capabilities. These tools for altering sound are critical to mixing and mastering and are covered in detail in subsequent chapters. The basic signal path models for using processing plug-ins (inserts and send and return routing) are covered in the following two sections.

Inserts

The insert routing model is essential to the application of signal processing plug-ins. The easiest way to think of the insert model is to consider the typical analog mixing console. On most consoles there is EQ circuitry on each channel. That EQ is signal processing, but it is included in each mixer channel because it is so essential to so much of the recording and mixing process, and because the most common way we would want to access that particular kind of signal processing is to have it inserted right into the channel signal path. The physical insertion of EQ into the typical hardware mixer channel is equivalent to the signal path taken by a plug-in inserted into a typical software mixer channel. By inserting the EQ into the channel we effectively are making it part of the channel—all audio that flows through the channel runs through the EQ processor (unless it is bypassed). Calling up any plug-in on a mixer channel inserts that plug-in directly into the channel, whether it is an EQ, a compressor, a reverb, or whatever else (see screenshot 1.2).

When we want the processed signal to replace the original signal, and to be applied only to the sound on any particular channel (typical of EQ and compression), we simply insert the processor into the channel (e.g., once the sound has been EQ'd we only hear the EQ'd sound, not the original sound mixed with the EQ'd sound). When we want the processor to be available for multiple channels (typical of reverb and delay), we use the "send and return" routing model, when we want to mix a single sound with its processed sound (e.g., parallel compression), we use the parallel processing routing model; both are covered in the following sections.

Send and Return

In the send and return routing model, we use channel aux (auxiliary) sends to route signal to a processor and then return the effect of that processor indepen-

dent of the original sound. The send and return model allows for much greater flexibility because you can access the processor from any channel, using a buss to send the sound to the processor. An aux return can be used for the signal processing plug-in, allowing access to the effect from internal routing.

Send and Return Model

The basic routing construction for using the send and return model is as follows (and as shown in screenshot 1.3):

1. Create an aux return channel and insert the desired plug-in (typically a reverb or delay processor).
2. Route the output of the aux return to the stereo buss so the effect becomes a part of your mix.
3. Set the input for the aux return to one of the internal busses (typically starting with buss 1 and continuing through the series of busses as needed for additional aux returns).
4. Route any audio channel to the effect by using an aux send that is set to the input buss for the aux return that has the desired effect (in this model case that would be buss 1).
5. Route any audio channels to the same effect by using an aux send set to buss 1.

6. Adjust the relative amount of effect on each channel by varying the send level.

7. Adjust the overall amount of effect on all channels that are sent to the aux return by varying the output fader level.

There are variations on this model depending on the stereo configuration of your audio and your plug-in, and many examples of send and return setups will appear in various specific discussions of mix techniques that follow in later chapters.

Parallel Processing

Parallel processing refers to a technique that is used to give greater flexibility when using common kinds of signal processing such as EQ and compression.

SCREENSHOT 1.3

A send and return routing example, for applying reverb to multiple channels.

SCREENSHOT 1.4

Two identical audio channels in parallel, one with compression. (Note: At the bottom of the Audio 2 channel there are 64 samples of delay compensation so that the two channels will be completely in phase.)

This technique has gained in popularity since DAWs provide the possibility of duplicating audio channels without the channel limitations found in the analog world. In a typical DAW it is simple to duplicate any audio channel and then one can run the two channels in parallel, one with an effect inserted and the other without. Parallel compression is the most common mode of parallel processing, using one compressed channel (sometimes heavily compressed to significantly alter the sound) combined with an uncompressed channel of the same audio (see screenshot 1.4).

Parallel processing may also be used with EQ, especially on complex and important elements such as kick or snare drums and vocals. There will be examples of parallel processing techniques in several of the more detailed discussions of mixing techniques in subsequent chapters.

Automation

Automation refers to the ability to replay changes in mix parameters in real time along the musical time line. Basic automation encompasses simple changes in level. For example, you may want the lead vocal to be louder in the chorus than it is in the verse. Automation allows you to set the desired level for each section and replay the level you have chosen at each point in the song or musical piece. This kind of automation (level control) was generally the only automation available on analog consoles (level and mute, but muting is really just another form of level control). With DAWs it has become possible to automate virtually every mixing parameter. This provides enormous new creative possibilities—and can also consume enormous numbers of mix hours!

Chapter 5 details automation techniques as well as practical suggestions about how to best approach the automation process, where the time is best spent for maximizing results and where you might want to look for other creative solutions rather than too much tinkering with automation.

Recall

Recall refers to the ability to recall (or restore) all of the parameters of any given mix. As with automation, recall was severely limited in the analog world in comparison to recall when working in the box. Elaborate systems were developed to recall mixes done on analog consoles and with hardware outboard gear, often requiring a lot of time for resetting, and with less than completely reliable results. If you are working entirely within your DAW, mix recall is a simple as opening the file. This powerful capability has changed the working process for both mixing and mastering. However, there are potential problems in the digital world, too, revolving around storing and recalling information, so it isn't necessarily the simple matter of double clicking your file icon. In chapter 5, I detail how work flow has changed in the era of complete and easy recall, as well as how to avoid those problematic moments when "complete and easy" recall fails to operate as expected.

1.4 Introduction to the Quick Guide

We want information right when we need it, and there's only so much we can absorb at one time. Just as most of us want to use new gear right away, and won't read anything in the manual past the "quick setup guide" until we need to, most DAW users will or already have plowed into mixing or mastering without "reading the manual"—and, in any event, even the most thorough textbook cannot be complete. Here is a brief introduction to the following two chapters that provide the equivalent of a quick setup guide for mixing and mastering.

Five Best Practices

These best practices focus on the theoretical side of mixing and mastering, offering advice in regard to how to approach your project and some techniques for keeping things in perspective as you work through a project. One of the biggest difficulties with mixing at one's home studio is determining when the mixing or mastering is done. On one level it's never done, but of course, you have to lay it to rest eventually (and sometimes on a deadline, self-imposed or otherwise). Being confident about your mixes and masters may take some time, but there are ways to shorten the time line toward achieving great mixes and final masters.

Four Common Mistakes

These common problem areas address tendencies that can muddle your mixes and masters. More problems occur with low-frequency shaping and balancing, so that's where this chapter starts. The next couple of sections focus on common problems that might stem from an over enthusiasm for certain kinds of signal processing. Many long-term and successful mix and mastering engineers agree that over time they generally have developed a "less is more" attitude to signal processing. I provide many audio examples for each of these sections at the book's website. Finally, I continue to encourage you on your quest for a good monitoring environment, expanding on the information already provided about room acoustics to discuss selecting and positioning your monitors and controlling the sound in your room.

Chapter 2

Quick Guide to Great Mixes and Masters
Five Best Practices

This chapter presents some basic concepts in mixing and mastering that I have found to be very important in getting consistent results that achieve the creative and technical goals you set for yourself. These are all readily attainable. Numbers 1 through 4 are practices that have been around since the beginning of recording and continue to be valuable points of reference for your work, whether or not it is "in the box." Number 5 is a practice that has taken on new meaning and applicability in the digital age—a practice that could only be undertaken in very limited ways in the analog era.

Five Best Practices
1. Have a concept before starting your mix or master.
2. Be aware of how your monitor level affects the mixing and mastering process.
3. Rely on one rather than multiple monitoring options.
4. Understand that mixing and mastering are primarily processes of revision.
5. Live with your mix or master.

2.1 Have a Concept

It is never wise to work in a vacuum. You want to have some sense of the direction of your project before you begin. In the case of mixing and mastering, this means some ideas about how you imagine the final sound of your mix or master. Concepts can be fluid—they can change over the course of the work—and they can even be abandoned for a new concept before the work is complete; but they will still have served their function even as they mutate.

Concepts can take different forms. They may start with an abstract idea like "soft" or "punchy" or "warm" or "aggressive" or "lush" or "dry," but that will need to be translated into concrete practice concerning EQ, compression, effects, and everything else. These abstract ideas do suggest certain practices regarding signal processing and can be good starting points. As I discuss many of the details of both mixing and mastering later in the book, these distinctions will become more clearly defined in practical terms. (What is aggressive compression? How to achieve warmth or presence with EQ as opposed to mud or harshness, etc.)

Genre Practices

Your concept may begin as a reflection of the various qualities of mixes and masters within the particular genre you are working. Certainly folk music has a different aesthetic than metal and each suggests specifics about how mixes and masters are created. Breaking the rules of genre can be powerful, but the accepted practices within a genre are there for a reason: they represent the collective creative aesthetic of many of the best and most successful people working in that genre. You are likely to find greater satisfaction (and success) in exploring ways to adapt your own creative vision within the confines of the general aesthetic of the genre you are working in.

So, folk music needs to be warm, pop needs to be dressed up, rock needs to be raw, metal needs to be aggressive, electronica needs to be propulsive, and rap needs to be in your face. There are many ways to accomplish these conceptual models by the specifics of signal processing, and of course there are literally hundreds of other genres and subgenres that can suggest any number of hybrid approaches to mixing and mastering. Start by doing your best to define the genre of the music you are working on, and then consider what this suggests about your overall approach to mixing and mastering, before you delve into the specifics of any particular mix or master.

What words would you use to describe the way music sounds in the genre you are working in? What do these words suggest about technical approaches? Much of the information in this book is intended to help you to be able to interpret both general creative and specific genre aesthetics for both mixing and mastering.

Natural versus Synthetic

Another way to develop your mix and mastering concept is to consider the continuum of audio processing that runs from natural to synthetic. Some projects—traditional folk and blues, for example—may suggest using only reverb settings

21

found in nature (such as room and hall settings). Other projects—electronica and hip-hop, for example—may suggest the use of synthetic reverbs (such as nonlinear or reverse settings). Whatever the genre, the extent that you plan to use processing that deviates from relatively naturalistic effects—from extreme EQ and compression settings to unnatural acoustic environments—should be a part of your initial concept.

Referencing Other Mixes and Masters

One great way to develop your mixing and mastering concepts is to reference other mixes and masters that you like and that you feel are related to the music you're working with. Selecting a few tracks to listen to before you begin your mix or master can be an excellent way to get yourself pointed in the right direction. Note how the mixes you're listening to positions the various elements in terms of relative volume, panning position and overall frequency balance. For mastering, compare the dynamic range, overall volume, and frequency balance of the tracks from several recordings to see how you would like your master to fit into the spectrum of processing choices that you will be making.

What you must remember when referencing other work is that there are an enormous number of elements that affect your final mix or master and that therefore each piece of music is unique. You cannot totally emulate any other piece of music because the interaction between all the musical elements and the specific positioning and processing choices that you must make will always be different from how they were for the piece you are referencing. "Why doesn't my mix sound like _____ [fill in the blank with your favorite track]? There may be many similarities; if it's a rock track, maybe they're both just one vocal, two guitars, a bass, and drums, but the singers voice has a different timbre, the guitars and amps have a different sound and different degree of distortion, the room the drums were recorded in has a very different sound, and the drummers hit their drums differently. No two mixes or masters sound the same, but listening to other work can help a lot with direction and concept.

Big Picture Concepts and Mixing Metaphors

Mix and master concepts should focus on the big picture—what is the overall quality of the sound I am looking for? After that there may be important specific ideas such as "features the lead vocal" or "features the backing vocals" or "features the interplay between the guitar and the keyboard" or "has slamming drums," but those are limited ideas that need to be achieved within the context of the larger concept. In fact, those four ideas could be incorporated into the same mix—although not everything can be featured. The specific techniques for achieving various aesthetics occupy the bulk of this book, but start with the big picture and your work will be focused and your results more likely to achieve your goals.

One good way to enhance your big picture concept is to apply one or more of the following three mixing metaphors. Besides just considering the overall quality of sound, you can adopt a creative metaphor to help you envision your mix as a single, aesthetic entity.

THE VISUAL MODEL: The Three-Dimensional Mix

One useful metaphor for constructing your mixes is to consider them as a three-dimensional visual field, a kind of three-dimensional object. The three dimensions are height, width, and depth. In mixing, the notion of *height* has two possible meanings. The obvious one is level. You can imagine the relative volume level of each element as equivalent to relative height relationships—the louder the element, the higher it is. And, as already noted, the first job of mixing is setting level for each element.

Height, however, can also be considered in terms of frequency range. We tend to think of the frequency range on a vertical scale—ranging from lows to highs—with the higher frequencies viewed as "higher" in height. A proper height relationship might be considered to be a balance in the frequency ranges from low to high. Listening for balance throughout the frequency range is an important part of both mixing and mastering.

Although you can use a spectrum analyzer to check frequency balance, I only recommend this for gathering a very limited amount of information. An analyzer might reveal problems in areas that your speakers don't reproduce well (very low or very high frequencies), but they might also lead you to make unwise decisions by showing frequency bulges or deficits that are a natural part of the particular program material that you are working on or style of mixing that you wish to create. For most decisions regarding frequency balance, your ear is a much better guide than a spectrum analyzer.

Width in mixing is defined by the panning spectrum from left to right. As I have already pointed out, panning represents one of the most powerful tools in creating effective mixes. It helps to think of panning as width with the goal being to use your entire spectrum from far left to right. Small variations in panning can dramatically alter the sense of space within a mix.

Depth is the subtlest and most potentially artful and creative part of creating a three-dimensional mix. As with height, depth may be thought of in two different ways. Depth can be created just by volume relationships between elements. The development of foreground and background elements is a critical aspect of mixing (see chapter 4 for details) and is one important way to create the sense of depth in your mixes. The other is the delay pool made from all the delays and reverbs that you are using. These delay elements can also have a significant effect on panning and the sense of width in your mixes. It is primarily the degree of ambience included as a part of each sound that controls the sense of depth in a mix.

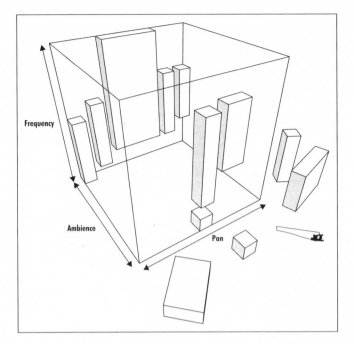

Frequency

Ambience

Pan

DIAGRAM 2.1

Three-dimensional mixing metaphor.

Of course, ambience can be created by mic position as well as by the addition of reverb or delay. You could also think of depth as represented by a movie making metaphor in regard to camera viewpoint; from extreme close up (very close mic), to close up (a small distance from sound source), to medium shot (a mic perhaps a few feet from the sound source or multiple mics that allow the recordist to control the amount of room ambience), to long shot (room mics that pick up considerable room ambience along with the direct sound). So just as camera distance from the object seen in a movie affects our perception and relationship to that object, so does mic distance from a recorded object. This idea was described and developed by the classical pianist and recording pioneer Glenn Gould. (See the next section for a different, extended mixing metaphor using movie making as a model.)

Mixes as three-dimensional entities are really just another way of thinking about all of the practices already covered (see diagram 2.1). It provides a concise way to think about and evaluate your mixes, and gives you a visual metaphor for imagining your mix. While this visual metaphor can be helpful—and we live in a culture that is heavily oriented toward seeing over the hearing—I cannot stress enough that in the end you must use your ears in order to be true to your own aesthetic.

THE CINEMA MODEL: *Your Mix as a Movie*

Another useful metaphor is to think of your mix as a movie—with each element occupying a specific role (see screenshot 2.1). The roles or characters in your film may be the leading roles, supporting roles, bit player roles, and extras

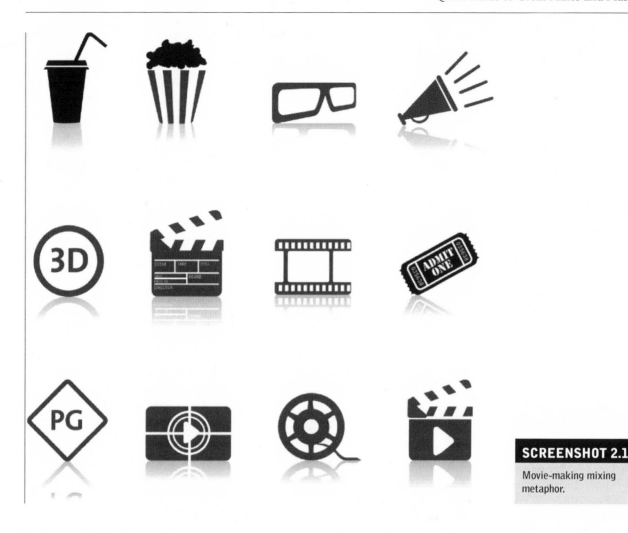

(member of a crowd or battle scene). These four roles represent positions of decreasing importance in your film (or mix), though each is essential to the strength of the final piece.

The leading actor in your mix is typically the lead vocal and/or the lead instruments in solos, themes, riffs between vocal lines, and so on. In a lot of popular music the bass guitar, snare drum, and kick drum also play leading roles. Leading elements are typically placed in the center of the panning spectrum or close to it, compressed to keep them in front of the listener, and often given multiple effects—reverb(s) and/or delay(s)—to make them especially interesting since they demand the listener's primary attention. You can think of the lead character as the one who gets a lot of close-ups so they need to look (sound) just right!

Of course, the supporting characters are also extremely important to a movie so they need attention as well. The supporting roles are often played by character actors who are a bit quirky or unusual in appearance to make them memorable and to give the movie more breadth. The supporting elements in your mix (rhythm guitar or keyboard parts, horn sections, percussion parts, etc.) need to find their special place as well, so they are often panned to one side. You'll want to carefully EQ them so they have their own identity without taking up too much space and stepping on the toes of the leading characters! That may mean rolling off low end to stay out of the way of the bass and the kick drum or making sure that any high-frequency boosting is not at the same frequency that you might be using to add presence to the lead vocal. The supporting elements might also present the opportunity for a special effect (perhaps chorusing or flanging) to make them distinctive.

Bit players in movies are often used for brief walk-on parts, with few spoken lines, to enhance a particular scene. Similarly, there may be elements in your mix that appear only once (like a new guitar part in the bridge) or occasionally (like a tambourine part that only plays in the chorus). You need to find a place for these added bits that allows them to fulfill their role of adding interest and complexity to the mix. This is where creative and careful use of your full panning spectrum often becomes critically important (interestingly, panning is sometimes referred to as "imaging"). If these bits are sitting on top of something else in the panning spectrum they will be hard to hear and they will be obscuring something else as well. Certain kinds of parts, such as a line of feedback guitar or a special effect like a wind chime or a rainstick, might be effective if used with panning automation to make the part move dynamically around the panning spectrum.

Finally, the crowd or battle scenes that use many extras (which are now often created or enhanced with computer-generated imagery) might be compared to the kind of pad or "sweetening" parts that some arrangements use to create a really full sound (a lot of popular music forgoes these kinds of parts, but in certain genres—such as some subgenres of electronica—they are critically important). Pads are typically long sustained notes or chords that fill in the background. They may be prominent enough to be heard clearly or they may be almost subliminal so that most listeners wouldn't even know they were there, but would hear the difference if they were muted. Pads often have some kind of stereo effect (often stereo chorusing) and can usually be split hard left/right without interfering because they tend to be thin sounding and quiet in the mix. Two pads can be blended to sound like one or you may want to split one hard left and the other hard right.

Extras might also be thought of as doubles, triples, or ghosting parts that support lead or supporting characters. Lead or background vocals, rhythm guitars, or other important elements might be doubled or even tripled to add depth to the part. Bruce Springsteen would sometimes add a glockenspiel doubling the rhythm guitar part—mixed way back—to add a subtle touch of brightness. These kinds of "extras" need to be integrated along with the original part early in the mix, as they alter the overall level and sound of the part.

Your mix tells a story, just like a movie, so treat your "characters" with care and help them achieve their proper places in the larger "picture."

THE FASHION MODEL: Mixing as Dress-up and Makeup

A third useful metaphor is to think of your mix as related to getting dressed up and applying makeup (see diagram 2.2). You might think of the recordings as the naked tracks and your job as the person responsible for making those tracks presentable to the world (recognizing that "presentable" can take many different forms in different environments—from nudist colony to grungy punk club, to university coffee shop to black tie affair). First there are the undergarments—the rhythm section. These need to be supportive without being intrusive. They hold up everything and provide the basics to build on. Then comes the outfit—this is all the essential sonic elements that combine to create the heart of the music. These need to fit together, to work together in creating a whole look (sound).

In most popular music the rhythm instruments, solos, background vocals, and lead vocals are built on top of the rhythm section (bass and drums) to create the heart of the music. This reminds us that there really is no way to separate the mixing processing from the composing and arranging elements in music (covered in depth in section 4.1). Just as a clothing ensemble has to work together in design, fit, and color; so a music mix has to work together with the composition and arrangement. Volume and panning are the tools that begin to complete the process begun by composition and arranging.

DIAGRAM 2.2

Dress-up and makeup
mixing metaphor.

Once the outfit has been selected (the initial structure of the mix established), it is time to add accessories. The scarves, hats, and jewelry that might be added to an outfit could be compared to the sonic colors that are sometimes added to a music composition and that have to be aesthetically positioned in a mix to complement the "outfit." Part of the mixer's task is to understand what is fundamental to the composition and what accessories serve the greater composition without demanding too much attention on their own. As we develop the wide variety of mixing approaches, tactics such as introducing the lead vocal into your mix at a relatively early stage in the process come from an understanding that the "outfit" needs to be complete before the accessories are added.

Makeup completes the model's preparation for the runway, and applying makeup is a great metaphor for all the signal processing and sonic enhancement that we do as a part of the mixing process. Makeup can be subtle—it can enhance without the observer even being aware that any makeup has been used. On the other hand, makeup can be over the top, including wildly unnatural colors, false eyelashes, and even sequins and other adornments. It's similar with mixing, and especially with effects such as reverbs and delays. Short reverbs and short delays can be used to enhance sounds without any apparent or obvious effect. Small "room" reverbs (simulations or samples of room ambiences from wood rooms to tile bathrooms) can be added in relatively small amounts to many elements in a mix, giving it a much greater sense of depth and a rich environment without there being any obvious reverb. The listener will experience the mix as completely "dry" and very intimate and "in your face." Yet the same mix with no room reverbs will sound thin and weak by comparison.

Clothing and makeup styles tend to run in fashion cycles and to be somewhat dependent on the particular cultural environment; the same can be said of mixing styles. Different periods have featured different styles (from the opulent seventies stadium rock to the stripped-down punk from late in that same decade). Genres tend to have mixing protocols (from bass heavy reggae to vocal heavy pop), but these can change over time. The current explosion of hybridized musical styles, along with the global access provided by the Internet, has meant that all mixing styles (and endless pastiches of styles) are currently active—in broad swaths or in micro-genre communities of interest.

2.2 Monitor Level

One of the most critical paths to good mixing and mastering involves good monitoring practices, and I address monitor speaker options in my previous book (*The Art of Digital Audio Recording*). In this section I focus on monitor volume and its effect on session flow and musical performance feedback, and on monitor level as it affects mixing and mastering decisions.

Listening at even moderately loud levels may increase your pleasure, but if you listen that way all the time it can create problems with mixing and mastering effectiveness. Two basic facts about loud listening produce negative results. One, the louder you listen, the more quickly you experience ear fatigue. Two, everything sounds better when it's louder, which means your ability to make critical judgments decreases. As we shall see, the key to creative decision making when mixing and mastering lies in the use of a range of listening levels.

Ear Fatigue

While mental fatigue (lack of concentration) is the biggest challenge over the course of a long session, ear fatigue ranks a close second—and ear fatigue contributes to mental fatigue as well. Your ears can take only so much sound over the course of a day. Persistent loud-volume listening will shut down your ear's ability to hear and eventually everything will start to sound muffled. But before things have gotten to that point, your ears will start to lose some of their ability to hear detail. I'm not going to go into issues surrounding actual ear damage, which can be caused by very loud studio monitoring over extended periods of time, but know that sustained moderately loud levels can cause ear fatigue that really prevents you from being an effective listener.

You can have a SPL (sound pressure level) meter in the studio and be monitoring it for levels, but truthfully I think we all know what loud is. It is more fun to listen louder, and I address this next, but effective listening requires low-level listening most of the time. Try to train yourself (and those you're working with) to listen at pretty low levels. Creative use of monitoring level—including loud levels—is important to workflow, but generally the problem is too much loud-level listening.

The key to low-level listening and prevention of ear fatigue is to start the day listening as low as you comfortably can. Your ears are very fresh and you can listen at a pretty low level and still hear all the detail that you need, in most cases. Over the course of the day, there is going to be natural tendency for playback volume to creep up, so by starting low you have the best chance of keeping your ears fresh over the course of a long session.

Everything Sounds Better When It's Louder!

This is generally true (up to a point), and it's part of the constant struggle to be really creative while mixing and mastering. If you want to get more of a kick out of what it is you're mixing or mastering, turn it up! But the problem that arises from too much loud-level listening is not just ear fatigue. At louder levels our ears are less able to discern critical relationships, so trying to make judgments about vocal level in a mix, for example, or relative level between songs in a master, becomes much more difficult.

At louder listening levels the sensitive ear mechanisms can no longer provide balanced feedback on the complete frequency range, and our ears perform a kind of two-band compression on the overall program material. Our sensitivity to lower frequency sounds (below 500 Hz) increases as sounds get louder while the sensitivity to higher frequency sounds (above 500 Hz) decreases. Sensitivity to both lower and higher frequency sounds decreases with lower listening levels. All of this is described by the "equal loudness contour" (see following section for diagrams), which maps the ear's sensitivity to different frequencies at different volume levels. Loud playback has its place, and at the end of the session you might want to do some pretty loud listening just for fun. But ultimately, playback level is a tool and it must be used to further the session's goals. How best to use that tool is described next.

Vary Your Listening Level

It isn't just low-level listening that will provide the best mixing and mastering results. It's important also that you vary your level on a regular basis and that you reference a wide variety of levels over the course of your work. As I noted above, the ear's sensitivity to frequencies changes at different levels. Although it is never "flat" (we hear best in the 2 to 4 kHz range, which provides optimal speech recognition) it is most balanced across the frequency spectrum at moderate listening levels. You can use an SPL meter to measure loudness, if you want. Average levels of about 70 to 80 dB SPL are usually considered a good choice for moderate a listening level, but I think most of us can gauge low, moderate, and loud listening levels without a meter.

Because of the "equal-loudness contour" (originally defined for audio in the 1930s by two scientists and referred to as the Fletcher-Munson curve, but since then it has been refined somewhat), we must recognize that our hearing changes at different listening levels. Fluctuations in sensitivity to different frequencies at different volumes affect both our sense of frequency balance and the volume relationships (as frequency balance is part of what we perceive as volume—e.g., an increase in high frequencies sounds, and in fact is louder). If we understand these qualities we can use this to our advantage. Besides realizing that moderate levels are our best overall reference for frequency and volume relationships, we can also take advantage of the idiosyncrasies of low-level and high-level monitoring (see diagram 2.3).

At low levels, when our ears attenuate the high and low frequencies, we get a really good idea of what is foreground and what is background in our mixes. We can hear if the vocal is really riding above the track as we (might) want it to; we can hear if the bass is apparent even at lower volumes and if the drums are leading the way as we (might) want them to; we can hear if the solo is popping out of the track as we (might) want it to. Generally the elements that we want to be in the front of our mix should sound pretty dramatically so in low-level listening, when all the harmonics and "sweetener" elements naturally recede because of their low volume. Similarly we can gauge if the vocal (or other prominent element) is balanced on a track-by-track basis in our master, because

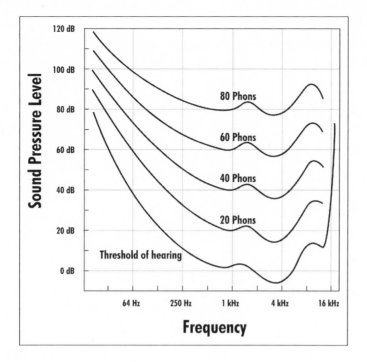

DIAGRAM 2.3

Equal-loudness contour (derived from the Fletcher-Munson curve).

they are more prominent relative to the other elements than during moderate- or high-level listening. Low-level listening omits a lot of detail, and ultimately that won't serve our larger mixing or mastering demands, but it can be a great aid in making judgments regarding certain critical relationships. There is more on these topics in the chapters on the specifics of mixing and mastering.

High-level listening has less obvious advantages than low-level listening and has the additional negative of contributing to ear fatigue. I discuss the value of loud playback in certain recording situations in my previous book, but it really has very little application to mixing or mastering. Moderately loud levels might be helpful for judging overall frequency balance at times; high-level listening can only provide a certain kind of pleasure at the end of a session, when no more critical decision making is going to take place.

2.3 **Monitoring Options**

One of the frequently repeated and accepted best practices of mixing (and to a lesser extent, mastering) is the supposed need to reference your mix on a variety of speaker systems and in a variety of environments. There is value in having various references, but there are also pitfalls. Your mix or master is going to sound different in different environments, and you are going to want it to "translate" as best as possible to living rooms, cars, and earbuds, so shouldn't you reference your work in these environments?

When you first start making serious attempts at mixing or mastering, you may want to reference your work in different environments. Initially you may discover some wildly problematic things that you hadn't been hearing—way too much bass, vocal not loud enough, solos that eclipse the band, and so on. But if this is true, the new environment is probably just shocking you into recognition of the deficiencies in your listening. If you hear an obvious problem—say, the vocal sounds too quiet—in a different environment, you will probably go back to your studio and realize that it was obvious there as well—you just missed it. If you don't hear it when you're back at the studio, which version do you trust? This becomes the key question.

The same principle regarding trust holds true with subtle elements: if it sounds like the rhythm guitar is a bit too loud when you listen in your car, but it sounds right on your studio monitors, which do you trust? Trust your studio monitors and your studio listening environment. Everything sounds different everywhere, and you have to settle on the one thing that you're going to trust to make a final decision. Once you've settled on that, you may not need to listen in other places. While the "shock" of other systems may alert you to problems that you were missing on your studio monitors, they also can be a distraction; and if you "believe" something from an alternative listening environment or speaker system that you don't hear on your trusted studio monitors, it can cause you to make bad decisions. Of course, this emphasizes the need to be using quality studio monitors, to become familiar with them, and to control and balance your studio listening environment to the greatest extent possible.

As will be discussed in the detailed chapters that follow, mastering engineers tend to focus on really accurate monitoring and are less inclined to seek outside validation than are mix engineers.

2.4 Revise, Revise, Revise

The famous expression about virtually every other creative endeavor applies to mixing and mastering as well: "10 percent inspiration, 90 percent perspiration." *Good mixing and mastering requires a devotion to detail—it's the work of many small changes over time.* After you've gone through every element in your mix and set the level and the panning, and you have decided whether to use or how to apply EQ, compression, and effects, you still have barely begun the process of mixing. Similarly with mastering, having set the level and the extent of brick-wall limiting for each track, and having decided whether to use or how to apply EQ, compression, and effects, you have barely begun the process of mastering.

Listen in complete passes from beginning to end, listen section by section, listen to individual bars for detail; listen for level relationships, for frequency balance, for complete use of the panning spectrum, for the depth and sense of space created by ambient effects; listen at a variety of volumes and continue to refine and adjust through it all—and then go back and listen and do it again, and then go back and listen and do it all again. More details on this process will be found in section 5.4 on the time line of automation; also, see the box "What Not to Do" in this chapter for help in figuring out when you're done.

CREATIVE TIP

Take frequent breaks while mixing.

An important part of the revision process is taking breaks to freshen your ears. While there may be some value in alternative listening options, as discussed in this chapter, a more valuable means of refreshing your ear is to take short but frequent breaks while mixing. This can be awkward if you're working at a commercial studio and paying an hourly rate. That's another advantage to mixing in the box in your own room. If I'm working remotely it's particularly easy; I keep track of my actual work time and don't charge for those breaks doing the dishes (or whatever) to refresh my ear. If I'm working with the artist present, I still do most of the mix work before they arrive so that we can focus on the fine details—and so I can use frequent breaks to really prepare for focusing on those details. Recall allows for longer breaks and for alternating work on different songs, as discussed in the following section (2.5).

WHAT NOT TO DO

Don't spread the revision process to a broad network.

You may drive the revision process or it may be the artist, the record company, or some other person who is central to the project. Mixing and mastering tend to be collaborative processes, and I devote whole chapters to both mixing and mastering collaboration. Here, just a brief note of caution: Do not play your unfinished mixes or masters for anyone other than those directly involved in the process and either whose judgment you trust or who has a financial stake and insists on input (and only then, if it can't be avoided). Playing unfinished work for colleagues, friends, or family who don't have experience with the mixing and mastering process is almost always a mistake. You will either get a critique that isn't useful (e.g., "It sounds strange") or, when you play the final version, they will often say "I liked the version you played for me before better" (people usually identify with the first version of anything they hear). Resist the temptation! When your work is done, then play it for everyone—and don't ask what anyone thinks of the mixing or mastering—let the listeners respond to the music!

2.5 Live with Your Mix or Master

Quick, easy, and accurate recall was a luxury that we didn't have working in the analog realm, where the setup was long and complex and the recall process required mixing consoles with extensive recall capabilities and a lot of record-keeping and note taking as well. At the most efficient studios it was possible to recall a mix in about forty-five minutes and the success rate was about 90 percent. That was pretty good, but it required a top-notch facility, which meant you were spending a lot per hour for studio time, and you were probably paying for an hour before you even started working with the recall. It could be quite expensive to make a small change, like raising the level of a guitar solo a small amount (and you were never sure that the recall would come back completely accurately).

The ability to return to mixes and masters hours, days, or even weeks after you have started the process is one of the major advantages of mixing in the box. The computer provides complete and accurate recall of your entire project in the simple act of opening your most recent file. This has dramatically changed the way projects get done—both creatively and practically.

Recall and the Creative Process

I often work on mixes or masters over many days, refining each time and then returning to the project with fresh ears. Having fresh ears is a tremendous advantage, both physically and mentally. Our ears are more sensitive in the early hours of a session and our brains are usually doing a better job of interpreting what the ears hear as well.

If I'm mixing a group of songs, I will often spend the first day setting up a few songs—doing the preliminary work of basic level, panning, and processing on an instrument-by-instrument basis. The next day I might try to bring one of those mixes close to completion in the early going and then spend time setting up some other mixes. The next day I might try to really fine-tune that first mix at the beginning of the session and then take a second song closer to completion, and finally set up the beginning work on another song for the last part of the session. In general, recall allows me to do the work that requires the most critical listening early in the session.

With a mastering job I may take the master to what I think is a completed place, but I will always try to take another pass at the master the next day, with fresh ears, and I almost always will hear little tweaks that I want to make. Because mastering typically involves many fewer elements than mixes, recall was also a standard part of mastering in the analog realm. Recall in the digital realm is faster and more convenient than it was with analog, but ease of recall hasn't had anything like the impact on mastering that it has had on mixing.

Using Recall in Practice

The ability to recall has meant that mixing and mastering can be done remotely, easing the task of scheduling and taking advantage of a larger network of participants if you want to. It has become quite common for mixing and mastering engineers to work on their own, sending mixes or masters via email, ftp sites, other Internet storage (cloud) sites, or on CD-Rs through the mail. Recipients review the work and provide feedback via email or telephone, and the engineer can create and send revisions for review. Working on mixes and masters with people with conflicting schedules and/or in different parts of the world has become routine as a result of these capabilities.

Sending audio as email attachments requires a fairly small file, generally an mp3 or other compressed format, but for critical functions such as mixing and mastering, this is generally not a good idea. I recently sent an artist mp3s (at his insistence) and he was very unhappy with the mixes. It turned out that he was listening to them on his built-in computer speaker! When he finally came over and actually heard what the mixes sounded like, he found that the work was pretty close to what he was hoping for. So, my advice is to never send audio via mp3 unless the only intended format for final production is mp3, or if it's just to review ideas during the recording and editing process and is understood to be a rough mix.

Larger companies will often host ftp sites, and that's a great way to post and retrieve files, but it isn't practical for a small operator to go the ftp route (ftp, or file transfer protocol, uses it own Internet protocol for uploading and downloading files. You need a dedicated application to use ftp—it won't work with your browser—but there are free versions of applications that work well, such as Cyberduck for the Mac and FileZilla for the PC). There are an increasing number of free cloud services that give you Internet storage, but most of them are tied to your libraries and not really set up for large file transfers. There are options for larger amounts of Internet storage that may have free options with smaller capacity and tiered pay options, such as Hightail, Dropbox, and Gobbler, that will give you as much storage as you need. Depending on the level of service you purchase, you can send complete multi-track files that might be many gigabytes to other users, though the upload and download times may run into hours (not bad if you do it overnight).

WHAT NOT TO DO

Don't get caught in the endless mix or master cycle.
Students sometimes ask me "How do you know when a mix is done?" There is no simple answer to this question.

Mixers run the gamut; some accept a mix too easily before sufficient attention has been paid to each individual element and to each musical section. Others work on their mixes endlessly, sometimes losing sight of the original concepts and their creative instincts, generating a monster of a messy mix. The same thing can happen with mastering.

When working with outside clients, the limitations of budget and the demands of release schedules may help make the decision for you. For those working in their own studio on their own or on other independent projects, the inability to complete a mix or master can be a significant obstacle to getting on to new music and new projects.

If you do not have the patience or stamina to stick with the project and give it the attention it needs, you are probably not well suited to the job at hand. For the more common affliction of over-attention to details and the inability to ever come to the conclusion that you're done with your mix or master, here are a couple things to consider. When you find that you're tweaking parameters by very small amounts (changing levels by a couple tenths of a dB, for example), and that's all you've been doing for a while, you are probably done. When you listen to your mix or master with relatively fresh ears and you can't decide whether it needs more work or not, you are probably done.

Also, be aware that what bothers you today will be different from what bothers you tomorrow. When I listen to mixes and masters some months after they've been done (such as when I finally get the actual CD from the artist), I almost always hear small elements of the mix or master that I would like to change, and they are almost always different from the small elements of the mix or master that I worried over in the final stages of the project. Make yourself happy with the way the music sounds—that is difficult enough—and don't seek perfection (it's not possible).

Chapter 3

Quick Guide to Great Mixes and Masters
Four Common Mistakes

In this final chapter of the first part of the book I cover some of the most common problems in creating great mixes and final masters. This is the conclusion of my "quick guide" to mixing and mastering. While some of the elements discussed in this chapter will be covered more thoroughly in the chapters to follow, this information will begin to orient you to common challenges of mixing and mastering, both technical and creative.

Four Common Mistakes
1. Poor shaping and balancing of the low frequencies
2. Overly bright mixes and masters
3. Overly compressed mixes and masters
4. Being led astray by inadequate monitoring

The Website

This chapter presents the first opportunities for you, the reader, to access some audio files at the website created for this book and begin to test and develop your ear along with the conceptual and technical sides covered here in writing. (Note: see page xiii for the web address and code needed to access the audio files.) As discussed in the previous chapter, both mixing and mastering require attention to subtle details of audio manipulation. The ability to hear small changes in sound comes with understanding what it is you're listening for, as well as experience with concentrated listening to be able to actually distinguish between these small variations.

3.1 Poor Control of the Low End

Because mixing and mastering share a final format (usually a stereo file) they also share many of the challenges of creating the best possible version of recorded music. Generally the final version of music contains the full audio spectrum of frequencies from very low to very high, and creating a pleasing balance of these frequencies is a major portion of the job of both the mixing and mastering engineers. Working toward that balance, and recognizing the interrelationships between frequencies, is covered in more detail later; here I want to address what in my experience is the most consistent problem with mixes and masters: poor control of the low frequencies.

Problems in the low end come from two primary sources: (1) overload of bass frequencies in the primary bass instruments (acoustic bass, bass guitar, bass drum etc.); and (2) too many instruments sharing in the same bass frequencies. The best remedy for these problems is in the mix stage, but there can be considerable help in the mastering stage as long as relatively subtle manipulation is all that is needed. First, I'll cover some common approaches to controlling low frequencies in the mix stage; and then, I'll show how these translate to similar problems during the mastering stage. Of course, well-balanced low-frequency monitoring is essential before any accurate mixing or mastering of the low frequencies can take place.

Low-Frequency Overload in the Bass Instruments

It would be difficult to overstate the importance of the low end in contemporary music. The bass and the kick drum provide the heartbeat of most contemporary tracks, in virtually every genre of popular music. These bass instruments need to be full and present, yet the path to that may run contrary to one's first instincts. Adding low-frequency information to the bass instruments often serves to make them muddier and less distinct. In fact, it is trimming low frequencies in bass instruments that often allows them to be most effective in the final mix or master.

Of course, there is no formula as far as boosting or cutting frequencies for any element because it all depends on what the original signal sounds like and what the context is. If the original recording of the bass guitar is very light on low frequencies, it may help to add some. The real key is this: you need to balance the fundamental bass tones with the overtones. Every musical instrument produces higher frequency overtones along with the fundamental musical note. The variations in these overtones are what differentiate the timbre of different instruments—it's why a note of the same pitch played on a piano sounds different when played on a guitar. The fundamental pitch (frequency) is the same, but the balance of overtone frequencies changes the quality of the sound.

With bass tones this becomes especially important because the overtones provide the elements of the sound that are easiest for our ear to pick up (they're closer to the register of speech and our ear is optimized for hearing voices talk-ing). We can hear the fundamental bass frequency (if we have decent enough speaker to reproduce them), and we certainly feel those frequencies as they vibrate our whole bodies when played loudly enough, however, it is the *higher overtones* in the bass signal that really give the definition and presence to the bass sounds.

So, more bass doesn't necessarily mean more apparent low-frequency in-formation. If the lower frequencies are out of balance with the upper overtones, we have to adjust the overall bass sound to compensate. Too much energy in the low frequencies will mean not enough of the overtones, and then the bass sounds muddy and indistinct. Too little energy in the low frequencies means you may hear the bass instrument well but it will sound thin. Where the balance between the two is, and how to achieve it, depends on the nature of the original recording, combined with the other elements in the mix that are sharing fre-quencies with the bass (there are likely to be a lot of those). In the following example, I felt that the bass needed some trimming in the lower frequencies and a small boost at the upper end of the harmonics to achieve the best balance.

Screenshots 3.1 and 3.2 show the EQ on the bass track in the original mix, and then a contrasting EQ, where instead of dipping I have boosted the lower frequencies. Even though the EQ settings are quite different, changes in these lower frequencies can be difficult to hear—and of course the playback in this register is going to vary a lot depending on your monitor system and room, and their bass frequency responses.

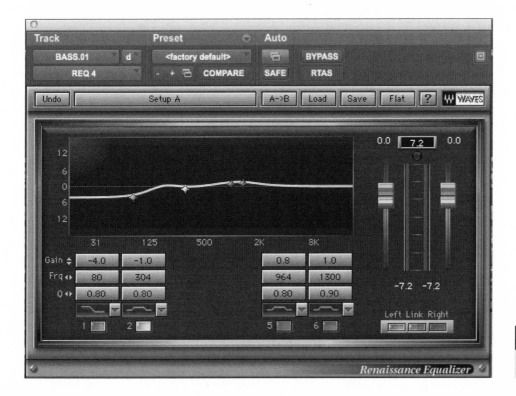

SCREENSHOT 3.1

Bass EQ: original settings.

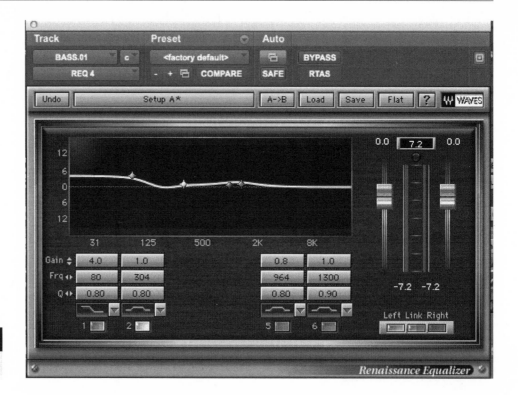

SCREENSHOT 3.2

Bass EQ: added low end.

40

Following is the list of audio clips available for you to listen to at the book's website. These clips will challenge your concept, your ear, and your playback system!

Artist: Dave Murrant CD: *Goodbye Kiss* Track: "Ben Bean"
Audio Clip 3.1 Solo Bass with original EQ
Audio Clip 3.2 Solo Bass with added low end
Audio Clip 3.3 Bass with original EQ in mix context
Audio Clip 3.4 Bass with added low end in mix context

There will be more about shaping the low end of instruments that are most active in the low frequencies in the sections on mixing individual instruments, but this will serve to alert you to these issues and begin to get you oriented toward addressing them in your mixes.

Low-Frequency Overload in the Overall Mix

Most instruments contain some low-frequency information (even cymbals and tambourine), so controlling the overall bass content of your mix is a crucial part of maintaining a focused and distinct bass presence for your bass instruments. In a great deal of contemporary music there are many instruments competing for this space on the frequency spectrum. Guitars, keyboards, horns, and vocals all may contain a considerable amount of low-frequency information, and so do snare drums and tom-toms. Using EQ for effective mixing often means trimming low frequencies from many or even all of the elements in order to keep the

SCREENSHOT 3.3

Rhythm guitar EQ: original setting.

low and low-mid frequencies from becoming overloaded. Of course, losing too much in the low-mids or lows will make your mix sound thin, so as always it's balance on the frequency scale that you should be trying to achieve. That said, the tendency is for mixes to become overloaded in the low frequencies, so trimming lows is often called for.

Screenshot 3.3 is an example using a rhythm guitar track. In this case, I felt that the guitar would fit better with a bit less energy in the low-mids and at the bottom, as well as with a bit less in the upper-mids (presence) frequencies. It's not a lot of dipping, but it definitely creates more space for everything else, especially the vocal and the bass. Here is a screenshot of the EQ that I used:

In the following audio clips (available at the book website), you can hear the subtle change in the guitar. If I were to choose between the two versions in solo, I might choose the un-EQ'd version because it's a bit richer and more present, but in the track I think the EQ'd guitar is serving its function better (propulsion without getting in the way).

Artist: Acoustic Son CD: *Cross the Line* Track: "Google Me"
Audio Clip 3.5 Solo rhythm guitar with original EQ
Audio Clip 3.6 Solo rhythm guitar with no EQ
Audio Clip 3.7 Rhythm guitar with original EQ in the track
Audio Clip 3.8 Rhythm guitar with no EQ in the track

There will be more about choosing between what sounds best in solo and what fits best in the track in the next chapter. There is also information about shaping the low end of almost every instrument in the sections on mixing individual instruments, but the above example should alert you to these issues and begin to get you oriented toward addressing them in your mixes.

WHAT NOT TO DO

Don't draw broader conclusions from any given example.
Every example given throughout this book pertains to the particular clip or situation being discussed. There are no generalizations about applying mixing techniques that can be directly drawn from the specific examples. One time you may decide that cutting certain frequencies is the right thing for a rhythm guitar and the next time you might decide that boosting those same frequencies is best. The tools are there to be used for the decisions you make with your ear. The principles, such as achieving an agreeable balance in frequencies or creating a pleasing sound stage, will drive the decisions regarding processing, but the details of how to achieve those decisions may vary considerably from one element and project to the next.

Low-Frequency Shaping in Mastering

Low-frequency shaping is one of the most challenging and important elements in mastering. It's challenging in part because it requires a playback system that does a good job of representing the low end, but it also requires an ear that is sensitive to small variations in these low frequencies. Low-frequency shaping is especially important because it is often the low frequencies that have the most problems left over from the mixing process. This may be because of inadequate monitoring during mixing or just because there wasn't the proper attention to low frequency shaping in the mix.

You'll notice that in the example of EQ'ing a bass guitar given in the first selection above, the difference in the EQ setting at 80 Hz between the original EQ and the one with added low end is a total of 8 dB (from –4 to +4 dB)—that's a lot! And yet, the difference is relatively subtle, and can even be difficult to hear on a system that doesn't reproduce 80 Hz very well. In mastering, the range of boost or dip in EQ settings will almost always be much smaller and yet the audible difference is likely to be proportionately much greater. That's because the EQ is being applied across the whole audio program.

If you are making an EQ change at 80 Hz, for example, with a typical bandwidth of perhaps .90 octave, that will actually be affecting the frequencies from 30 Hz all the way to 250 Hz. It could even be a broader spectrum of frequencies depending on the extent of boost and cut. And when applied across the audio program that means that every element that contains frequencies between 30 and 250 Hz is going to be affected by that EQ—and almost every element is likely to contain some part of those frequencies, so virtually everything is affected. This is why a 1 dB boost or cut at 80 Hz in a mastering session is likely to be quite audible.

I am using a suite of mastering plug-ins, and the EQ that is provided has a couple of unique features that are particularly suited to mastering. These features also provide some important general information about using EQ in the mastering process. The plug-ins are called "Linear Phase EQ" and they have a particular kind of processing designed to deal with phase problems caused by typical EQs. As I will cover in greater detail in the section on using EQ in mastering in a later chapter, EQ processing always introduces some phase problems.

In general, we accept a certain degree of phase degradation in exchange for the benefits of being able to shape a sound's frequency response. The same is true in mastering, but the effects of phase problems created by EQ are compounded when applied across an entire mix where many elements share frequencies. As a result, software developers have created specialized EQs that minimize the phase shifts created by typical EQs. To do this requires more intensive processing and that results in substantial latency (delay) created by that processing. The linear-phase EQs minimize phasing problems, and today's high-powered computers easily handle the processing issues. The latency is not a problem in mastering because the plug-in is applied to the entire program material; though the audio is delayed by the plug-in, there isn't any other audio that it needs to be synchronized with.

Automatic delay compensation systems found in most high-end DAWs will compensate for the delay caused by plug-in latency, so these plug-ins can also be used on individual tracks in a mix without creating problems. (Although specifically designed for mastering, many people do use these processors on individual tracks; but different EQs have a variety of desirable qualities and are chosen for their sound more than for the technicalities of how they handle phase.)

Another quality of this particular suite of processors is that a separate plug-in is provided that deals only with the bass frequencies. This is a not too subtle reminder that it is common to be very focused on shaping the low frequencies as a part of the mastering process. That's why a dedicated and flexible EQ for working on the low end is a part of this mastering suite of plug-ins.

In the example I've selected, I have done some subtle dipping of low frequencies at three different points: –.5 dB at 86 Hz; –.3 dB at 125 Hz; and –1 dB at 250 Hz. These are all pretty small changes, but the overall effect should be quite obvious if listened to carefully on a good playback system. You will notice that I also have a high-pass filter band at the very low end (the left of the low-frequency EQ which is the plug-in on the left of the screenshot). This is set to 22 Hz and it is using a resonant hi-pass filter setting. The function of the hi-pass filter is to clear out subharmonic frequencies that may have gotten introduced at some point during the recording or mixing. Dealing with subharmonics, in-

SCREENSHOT 3.4

EQ settings for song master (1).

cluding DC offset, will be covered more thoroughly in the section on using EQ in mastering, section 11.2. Screenshot 3.4 shows the mastering EQ on this particular song, followed by the list of audio clips available at this book's website. Here are the audio clips from the website:

> Artist: John Nemeth CD: *Name The Day!* Track: "Tough Girl"
> Audio Clip 3.9 Master with EQ
> Audio Clip 3.10 Master with no EQ

There will be more about shaping the low end in mastering in the later chapters on mastering, but this introduction will serve to alert you to these issues and begin to get you oriented toward addressing them in your masters.

3.2 Overly Bright Mixes and Masters

High frequencies are seductive. For one thing, our ear is biased toward the high-mid frequencies that increase the intelligibility of consonance, and thus our ability to understand speech. High frequencies provide clarity and definition, which are also attractive to our ears. Adding high frequencies also adds volume and louder almost always sounds better—in fact, the "louder is better" problem might be the most seductive aspect of high-frequency boost.

So when are mixes or masters overly bright (too much high-frequency information) and when are they the most clear and present? There is no simple answer to that question, and in fact the answer will vary considerably from person to person. The critical thing is to be carefully considering this question in your own mixes and masters, and making a judgment based on careful listening. *Try not to be seduced by the pleasures of adding high frequencies.*

Subtractive versus Additive EQ

There are two schools of thought in the application of EQ, though they are hardly exclusive. The subtractive school argues that dipping EQ should be the primary means of shaping frequencies. The reasoning is that dipping creates fewer phase-shifting problems (discussed in the previous section on bass frequencies) and therefore provides a clearer sound. You can't increase a frequency that doesn't exist in the original sound, so if you want to bring a frequency out, it will sound more natural to do it by decreasing the other frequencies. On the other hand, the additive school argues that you can never get the same impact from dipping frequencies that you get by boosting them. True, boosting frequencies doesn't sound as "natural," but natural isn't a critical feature of a lot popular music—whereas maximizing impact often is.

So, as you might suspect, both techniques are valuable and it is likely that you will want to use both in your work. Partly it depends on your own preferences for sound quality, partly it depends on the genre of music you're working in, and partly it depends on the tools you have to work with. While neither technique will prevent you from having overly bright mixes or masters, subtractive EQ is less likely to create the problem. However, if too much subtractive EQ is used to create a greater balance of high frequencies, a mix may still sound thin and/or harsh. For many of us, common applications of EQ use both an additive and a subtractive approach at the same time.

I don't think it would be helpful for me to provide a clip of an overly bright mix to try to prove my point. It would be easy to create such a mix by heavily boosting the high frequencies or drastically dipping the mids and the lows. Instead, I'm going to start with an example of high-frequency boost and low-mid dipping that I think serves the music without becoming overly bright, thin, and harsh. Again, final judgments are going to vary from one individual to the next; the key is to be considering where you fall along the spectrum of high-frequency content (see screenshot 3.5).

Keeping in mind the previous warning about making broader judgments from the specific examples given here, I would not be surprised to find myself using something like the following EQ settings on a lead vocal. This high-frequency boost might provide greater clarity, and the dip in the lows might prevent mushiness. This is the EQ I used on the vocal clip that follows (but this could be exactly the wrong EQ for some other vocal recording).

In the following clips (available on the website), you can hear this EQ applied to the vocal and then the vocal without the EQ. The comparison is somewhat deceptive because the EQ also provides a volume boost. I could have tried to compensate by raising the level of the non-EQ'd vocal, but there's no way to exactly match the two (after all, they sound different because of differing frequency response). The EQ'd vocal does lose a little warmth—or you could say it's less muddy sounding. It is also brighter and clearer—or you could say it's thinner and harsher. Using EQ is always involves a value judgment and there is no "right" or "wrong" EQ, although when used in extreme it can be pretty obvious that an EQ is going to sound wrong to almost everyone.

45

SCREENSHOT 3.5

Possible EQ setting for a vocal.

Artist: Rachel Margaret CD: *Note to Myself* Track: "Right Between the Eyes"

Audio Clip 3.11 Vocal with EQ

Audio Clip 3.12 Vocal with no EQ

Making EQ Judgments About "Brightness"

So how does one make the judgment about whether an element has the right amount of high-frequency information—not bright enough, just right, too bright? While such a judgment is highly subjective, one of the best ways to gauge your work on the relative brightness scale is to compare it to other music that you particularly like. It is generally easy to import music from just about any source into your DAW, so you can bring one or more tracks that you like right into your working session and use those to compare with your work. This can be very helpful but it also can be very frustrating.

The frustrations come if you try to get your mix or master to sound the same (or even similar) to the track that you've imported. "Why doesn't my mix sound like their mix?" is usually an impossible question to answer in generalized terms. There are so many factors that go into a recording—the sound of each individual instrument of course, but beyond that, the specifics of how many instruments are playing, the panning, the use of effects, and so on that all play a key role in the final sound of the mix. What's more, the specifics of the arrangement—of what each instrument is playing at any given moment—has an enormous effect on the sound of the track. So no two tracks are ever going to sound "the same"; in fact, it is unlikely that they will even sound similar to each other in specific terms.

What you can gain from comparing your mixes or masters to others are some generalized perspective (to benefit the most from this you might want to read the first section of chapter 4, "Building a Mix," that covers tips on how to listen for mixing). If you A/B your mix with one of your favorite mixes, some things might jump out at you, like "my mix [or their mix] is a lot brighter" and this can help you discover your own sense for what is not bright enough, just right, or too bright. The reality is that music varies enormously in this regard, so the key here is what music you choose to compare to—this is how you make your own aesthetic judgment about how bright music should be. That judgment gives you a benchmark to then use in your own work. I will return to this comparison technique at various points in the book; it works well for making judgments about many things, including other frequency issues (how much low end), how loud should the lead vocal be (or the guitar solo or whatever), degree of image spread (panning), and so on.

High-Frequency Shaping in Mastering

Much of what has gone before in this section is applicable to the mastering process as well. The primary difference is that EQ'ing of masters is generally much more subtle than the kind of EQ'ing that might be applied in mixing. Nonetheless, the seductive quality of high-frequency boost can lead to unwanted results in mastering just as easily as in mixing. I searched some of my master files to find an example of significant high-frequency boost in a mastering session, and the following is what I found (see screenshot 3.6). You'll see below that no frequency band is boosted by more than 1 dB—but because there is boost in three different high-frequency ranges, the total effect is a fairly substantial boost in

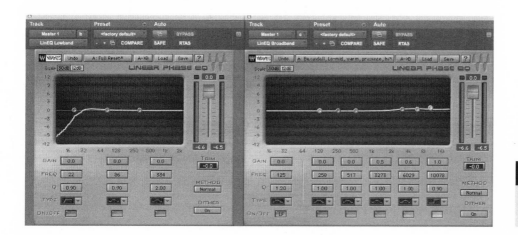

SCREENSHOT 3.6

EQ settings for song master (2).

the high end. Remember that in mastering this may be done as much (or more) to match this track to the other tracks, as it is just a question of trying to get this one track to sound as good as possible ("good" continuing to be a highly subjective judgment). The tension that sometimes exists between "sounds best" and "fits best" extends to mastering as well as mixing.

On the website, there are two clips from the master, one with the EQ and one without. It is especially important to notice how EQ in mastering affects virtually every instrument in the track. In this case, the vocals, the guitar, the snare drum, and the cymbals are all clearly altered by this EQ. You need to be careful; if just one instrument is made to sound too loud or overly bright (by your own standards), you need to rethink the EQ on your master.

Artist: Claudette King CD: *We're Onto Something* Track: "Too Little Too Late"
Audio Clip 3.13 Master with EQ
Audio Clip 3.14 Master with no EQ

3.3 Overly Compressed Mixes and Masters

The third topic in our quick guide to common mixing and mastering problems concerns dynamics processing, and specifically the issues around compressing and limiting audio in mixes and masters. As with EQ, this is a highly subjective area where creative and aesthetic choices need to be made. Compression has been called the "sound of rock and roll," so it is clearly an important processing tool in mixing. On the other hand, there has been a lot written about over-compression and it how it might diminish the experience of a lot of contemporary popular music, with detrimental effects on music's popularity. Here I will pinpoint the most common areas of concern, with more detail provided in later chapters.

Individual Instrument Compression in Mixing

Compression is an important tool that can aid in creating great mixes where all the parts fit comfortably together. By limiting the dynamic range, especially of critical elements like the vocals and the bass, we are able to maintain the presence of those elements without resorting to boosting their overall levels in order to keep them prominent. We don't want the vocal or the bass to come and go, leaving gaps in their critical role of propelling the music. Generally, when used to gently control dynamics, compression is relatively transparent; we aren't aware of it altering the sound except as a subtle control over the dynamic range. I will be covering more on this important function in the chapter on building a mix, but here I want to focus on compression when used to produce a more pronounced and obvious effect. The most common use of compression in this way is on the drums.

Drum compression can define the sound of a popular music mix and it can also be a source of over-compression. Some amount of drum compression is used on most popular music mixes (including samples that have had compression used when they were first mixed). Drum compression helps maintain the presence of the drums, as just described regarding vocals and bass, but it is also used in a more extreme fashion to dramatically alter the sound of the drums. This can be appropriate to a particular genre and generally pleasing (as well as powerful and dramatic) or it can seem overblown and serve to undermine a natural musicality to mixes.

Individual drum tracks are often compressed, especially the kick and snare, but often the tom-toms, hi-hat, and overhead tracks as well. If there are room mics used for the drums, they are sometimes heavily compressed. Then the whole set might be sent through a compressor for overall compression (or parallel compression, as explained in chapter 4). Because the overall mix of all of the instruments might be compressed and limited as well (see the next section on buss compression), the drums might go through as many as three distinct stages of compression. This might be fine, and sound great, but it might also be a source of over-compression, making the drums bombastic in a way that might initially provoke the "wow" factor but can wear the listener down over time (there is more on the effects of over-compression throughout this book).

On the website is a clip of the drums from a song, first with compression and then without. I have tried to approximately balance the levels, though it's not possible to do that thoroughly—the compression alters the dynamic range so the overall levels will never be equivalent. Whether or not you like the end result, it is significant to note the extreme difference in sound between these two clips—compression has dramatically changed the sound of the instrument. I don't think this takes compression too far for this particular song, and there are plenty of examples in contemporary music where there is substantially more drum compression than I have used here, but for some this may qualify as over-compressed. In any event, this is a long way from the kind of relatively transparent compression that we often use on vocals, bass tracks, and other mix elements.

Drummer: Kevin Hayes
Artist: Acoustic Son CD: *Cross the Line* Track: "Back from the Edge"
Audio Clip 3.15 Drums with compression
Audio Clip 3.16 Drums with no compression

It is not hard to imagine how drum compression, taken to an extreme, along with compression on almost every other instrument in a mix, might produce an overly compressed sound. Controlling dynamics can serve to make a mix much more listenable—allowing the featured elements to remain featured and the whole mix to gel—but it can also squeeze the life out of the music. Massive compression provides initial impact, but creates music that assaults the ear, leaving no breadth of dynamic range to provide musical contrasts. As always, use these techniques to match your own taste.

50

WHAT NOT TO DO

Don't adopt an anti-compression attitude.
I have found a tendency among some purists to adopt a "no compression" attitude to recording, mixing, and mastering. I appreciate the motivation, and I would certainly encourage you to limit your use of compression depending on the style of music you are working in and the sound that you want to achieve. That said, taking compression off the table as an aid in creating recordings prevents you from allowing your audience to appreciate the music that you have recorded to the fullest. Recordings will be listened to in a variety of situations, and many of them present challenges from ambient sounds—like in the car or noise coming from an adjacent room. By creating a more consistent presence, compression improves the listening experience. Accept the fact that recordings are not, and can never be, the same as live music, so do not try to pretend that you can reproduce the live music experience exactly as it was played live; use compression to make recordings be better recordings.

Buss Compression in Mixing or Mastering?

The practice of using a stereo compressor across the mix buss, effectively compressing the entire mix, is very common in popular music production. Once again, this presents an opportunity to either improve your mix or squash the life out of it. Stereo buss compression can help to subtly blend all the elements and provide increased punch to the overall sound as well. Too much compression on the stereo buss, however, will flatten the dynamics, and while seeming to add wallop to the track, leave the listener unsatisfied by sapping the musical vitality. Finding that balance is a key element in the final stages of the mixing process.

If you do decide to use buss compression, there are some things to keep in mind that might help you avoid over-compression. First, I should note that there is some disagreement about whether buss compression should even be applied as a part of the mix process or whether it should be reserved for mastering. As a mixer you can simply forgo buss compression and leave it to the discretion of the mastering engineer. Personally, because of the significant effect it has on the mix, I prefer mixing with buss compression and leaving the final brickwall limiting to mastering (more on that in the next section).

That said, it should be remembered that, whether a part of the mixing or mastering, buss compression shares a basic quality with mastering, which is that it is applied over the entire audio program. As we saw with EQ, the effect of processing on the full program tends to require much more subtle applications than when dealing with individual elements. Generally, buss compression should be at a fairly low ratio (probably 4:1 or less) and maximum compression should probably not go beyond 3 to 6 dB of reduction at the peaks.

Another key to effective use of buss compression is to wait until fairly late in the mix process to engage the compressor. This means really trying to get your mix sounding right without buss compression and then allowing it to subtly blend and add punch to a mix that is already very close to what you want. If you start with the buss compressor early in the process, you begin to unconsciously depend on it to balance elements and ultimately you are much more likely to over-compress as a part of building the mix. Once you discover that you're hitting the compressor harder than you realized, it's usually too late to back off without drastically altering your mix—causing you to have to either go with the compression or start again from close to the beginning.

Although any plug-in compressor might work well for the mix buss, there are some that are specifically designed for that function and they will often yield the best results. The most famous buss compressor was developed by Solid State Logic (SSL) and built into their analog consoles (see screenshot 3.7). It provides relatively aggressive compression that adds a discernible punch to the typical popular music track. There are several companies (including SSL) making authorized software versions that emulate the original analog unit, and adopt a graphic of the original interface.

Once again, what constitutes too much compression requires a subjective judgment. Perhaps the starting point has to be a realization that there can be too much. Just as with high-frequency EQ, buss compression can be seductive—more punch, more punch—until what passes for punch has pummeled the track into submission. The audio clips on the website give an example of moderate buss compression on a straight-ahead rock track. It's difficult to match the levels because the dynamics are altered, but what I've tried to do is maintain the level of the vocal on both clips.

You'll notice that the compression brings up the band and helps it envelop the vocal. Without the compression the track lacks the same punch and the vocal feels more removed from the instruments. Yet all of this is a relatively subtle difference, without any of the obvious pumping and other artifacts that can occur with heavy compression.

> Artist: Laurie Morvan Band CD: *Fire It Up!* Track: "Testify"
> Audio Clip 3.17 Track with buss compression
> Audio Clip 3.18 Track with no buss compression

Brickwall Limiting in Mastering

Brickwall limiting will get further treatment at several points in the more detailed discussions of mastering later in this book, but no startup guide to mixing

52

and mastering would be complete without a discussion of this very powerful processing tool.

Brickwall limiting raises the overall level of your audio file while at the same time creating an absolute ceiling (a brick wall) to prevent overload (distortion) (see screenshot 3.8). In order to do this, a brickwall limiter uses "look ahead" processing so that it can make the best decisions about how to process the incoming audio. The look-ahead function adds considerable latency (delay) in order to

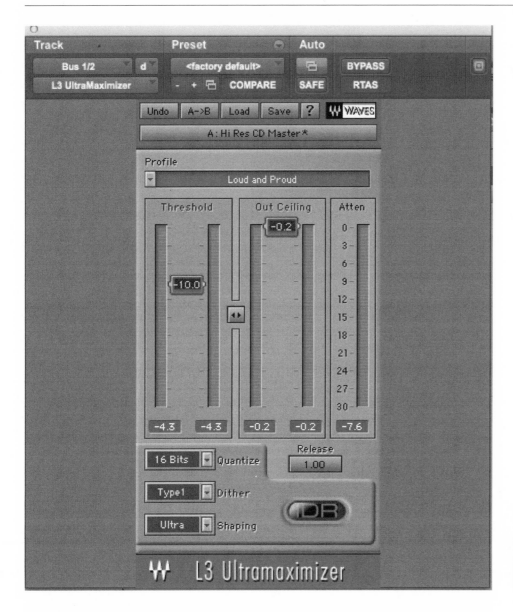

process most effectively so it requires delay compensation except when used over the entire program material (which is the most common application).

Although the maximum level for digital audio is digital zero, the output of a brickwall limiter is typically set to slightly below digital zero (e.g., –.2 dB) to avoid processing problems for playback technology such as CD players (extended passages that reach digital zero can cause some CD players to "hiccup"). As the threshold of the brickwall limiter is lowered, the volume of the entire program is raised, with any audio that exceeds the threshold limited to the maximum output. Thus, if the threshold is set to –10 dB and the output to –.2 dB, any audio that is louder than –10 dB will be limited to –.2 dB output and any audio below the –10 dB threshold will be raised up 10 dB.

In screenshot 3.9, you can see the effect of a brickwall limiter. The top waveform is the original audio. The middle waveform has been process with a

SCREENSHOT 3.9

Waveforms showing the effects of brickwall limiting.

brickwall limiter with the threshold set to –10 dB and the maximum output to –.2 dB below digital zero. The bottom waveform has been processed with the threshold set to –15 dB and the output to –.2 dB. In the middle waveform a few parts of the file exceeded the threshold and were limited to the maximum output of –.2 dB—all the remaining audio was raised 10 dB but otherwise unchanged. In the bottom waveform quite a bit of the file exceeded the threshold and was limited at –.2 dB (creating a kind of "buzz cut/flat top" effect at either end of the waveform) and the remaining audio was raised 15 dB but otherwise unchanged.

As with buss compression, there is a question as to when this processor should be applied. As mentioned above, I use buss compression as part of the mixing process, but I reserve brickwall limiting for mastering. I do this so that the limiting may be used as part of the final level-setting process during mastering. It also becomes the final processing element in the creation of a master, typically dithering from 24 bits to a 16-bit file (more on all of this in the chapters on mastering). However, because it has such a potentially profound effect on the final sound of the audio, I always put a brickwall limiter on the stereo buss when mixing.

Toward the end of the mixing process I activate the brickwall limiter and set it within the range that I expect the final master will be limited, so that I can finish my mix, hearing a closer approximation of how the final master is likely to sound. I also deliver all mixes to the artist or other involved parties (record company, etc.) with the brickwall limiter so that what they hear sounds closer to what the final version after mastering is going to sound like. I remove the brickwall limiter prior to creating the final mix file that is used for mastering.

How Much Brickwall Limiting Is Too Much?

Is the continuing trend of more and more brickwall limiting in order to increase the apparent volume of music having a profoundly adverse affect on the listener's ability to appreciate music? This question is at the center of a raging debate about the "loudness war." It really isn't a debate so much as it is differing aesthetics about how much brickwall limiting to use in a final master, and frustration with the increasing tendency for masters to have what many believe to be excessive brickwall limiting.

There are some who would argue that any brickwall limiting is too much, and for some kinds of music, in some situations, that may be the answer. The reality for most of us is that if we don't use any, or even just use light brickwall limiting on our masters, they are going to sound much quieter than almost any other contemporary master recording. This could be fine if the only difference were that the listener would have to adjust the volume on his or her playback system to make up for any difference in volume; however, with mp3 players and carousel CD players, it is often not practical or likely that the listener will adjust the volume from one track to the next and therefore your lightly limited master is going to sound a lot quieter than all the other recordings. That is probably going to mean that it will have less appeal and be more likely to be ignored or dismissed.

On the other hand, many are arguing that excessive use of brickwall limiting is one of the central reasons for the decline in popular music sales; it makes music less emotional and therefore less appealing (even though it increases the sense of initial impact). What is excessive? Again, this is highly subjective, although many are arguing that most commercial music that is being released today has excessive brickwall limiting. You can read and hear as much about this subject as you like by searching "the loudness war" on the Internet, and I will have more to say on this topic in later chapters.

Can the entire decline of the music industry be laid at the feet of the loudness war? I doubt it, but I have no doubt that the excessive brickwall limiting that is rampant in popular music mastering now significantly reduces the pleasure of listening to recordings. It may create greater initial impact on first listening, but *the severe loss in dynamic range* caused by excessive brickwall limiting fatigues the listener and reduces the desire to continue listening.

There is a free metering tool—the TT Dynamic Range Meter—than indicates how much limiting you are doing with a brickwall limiter. It is color coded in a way that suggests when you are using too much brickwall limiting (see screenshot 3.10).

3.4 Trusting Inadequate Monitoring

In the previous chapter I wrote about the need to reference mixes and masters on different kinds of monitors (from headphones to speakers of different types),

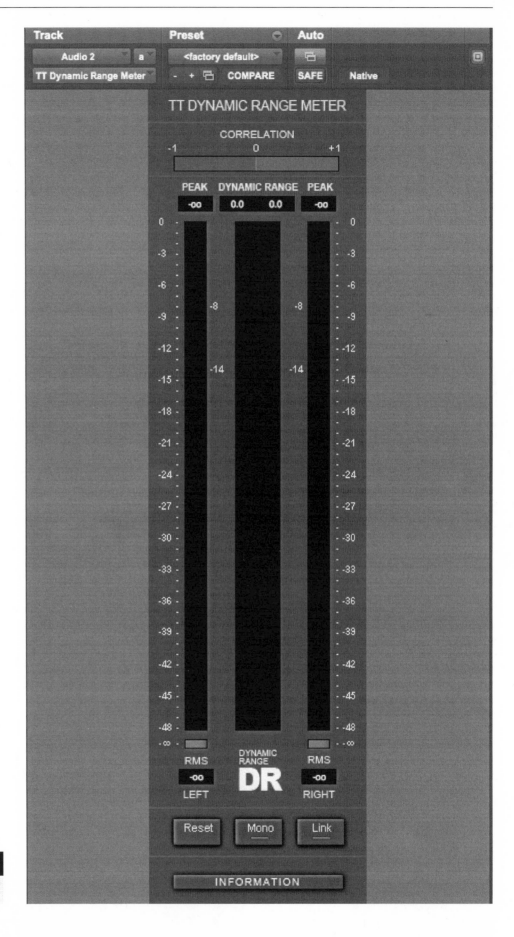

SCREENSHOT 3.10

TT Dynamic Range Meter.

but I also emphasized the idea that ultimately you must have one speaker system that is your final reference. Here I want to briefly summarize the monitoring pitfalls that can subvert your best attempts to have that final reference for making good mixes and masters. I will also suggest ways you might avoid these problems and improve your listening environment. If you are putting your trust in an inadequate monitoring environment, you will never achieve consistent results with your mixes or your masters, and you may be unable to figure out why that is.

Your Speakers

The long and short of speaker selection is: *use studio monitors!* There is an essential difference between studio monitors and typical home stereo/hi-fi speakers. Studio monitors are attempting to give you reasonably flat frequency response, whereas typical home stereo speakers (including most expensive models) are often designed to hype the music by boosting high and low frequencies. Yes, it's true that studio monitors aren't always that "flat," and it's also true that you will need to get used to whatever speakers you choose, but you will be at a significant disadvantage if you use commercial speakers that are not designed as studio monitors.

Speaker design has come a long way, and it is no longer necessary to have large speakers to have accurate low-frequency reproduction suitable for mixing. Using a subwoofer is therefore optional, but it makes a good addition to many speaker systems and is especially important for mastering, unless your monitors are capable of reproducing very low frequencies. Because mastering is the last step in the process, it is the last opportunity to make sure that there isn't problems with very low frequencies that aren't even reproduced on many systems. You never know when your music will be played on a system with a subwoofer, so at some point it's a good idea to see how it responds in that situation.

Speaker Placement

Placing speakers in your room and in relation to the listening position are both important elements in establishing the best monitoring environment. The basic rule on placement in the room is to keep the speakers as far from walls as possible, and wherever the nearest walls are, to use some baffling to reduce reflections from the walls back to the listening position. Typically you will place your speakers parallel to the longer wall in your room, but keeping some distance from the back wall (see diagram 3.1). If your room is small or narrow, you may be better off positioning the speakers parallel to the shorter wall and baffling the side walls half way between the listening position and your speakers (to avoid the primary reflection from the speaker, off the wall, to your ear); see diagram 3.2. You will want to baffle the ceiling between the listening position and your speakers as well.

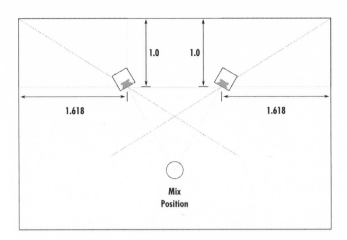

DIAGRAM 3.1

Nearfield speaker placement against the long wall.

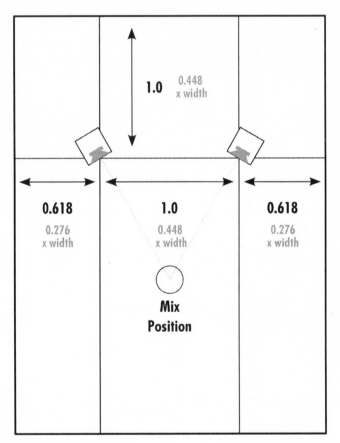

DIAGRAM 3.2

Nearfield speaker placement against the short wall.

There are formulas for exact studio speaker placement and a "golden triangle" for optimal placement in a perfectly proportioned room, but it isn't necessary to have perfect speaker placement or a perfect room in order to get reliable results. Probably the worst possible speaker placement is in a corner (with the corner of the room between the two speakers).

The rule for speaker placement relative to the listening position is simple—the speakers and listener should form an equilateral triangle, which means that the distance between the speakers is equal to the distance from each speaker to the listener (see diagram 3.3). You can aim each speaker directly at you, or at your ear closest to that speaker, or even a bit farther off of each ear, as long as it's consistent. Generally you want the tweeter to be right at ear level. If you set your speakers sideways, or if the tweeter is offset from the woofer, you will generally want the tweeter placed outside of the woofer.

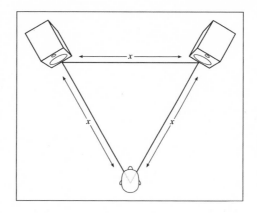

DIAGRAM 3.3

Nearfield speaker placement.

59

Your monitor speakers need to be decoupled from whatever surface they are sitting on. A piece of open-cell neoprene rubber works fine for that, though there slightly angled foam pads for speakers that can be a helpful (and inexpensive) addition to your monitoring setup (from Auralex). More substantial (and more expensive) pads can do more to stabilize your speakers, increasing the coherency of the low end (from PrimaAcoustic and others). Sand-filled speaker stands and wall speaker mounts are good options if your setup can accommodate those.

If your speakers are sitting directly on a hard surface they will radiate low frequencies into the surface, causing the lows to lose both gain and definition.

Your Room

The acoustic properties of your room are critically important to the accuracy of your monitoring, and thus to your ability to mix or master with confidence. There are entire books about room construction and acoustical design for studios, but there are a few guidelines that can help everyone achieve a reasonable acoustic environment to work in.

Almost every room will benefit from a certain amount of acoustical treatment, and there are inexpensive options for wall and ceiling materials that help control the sound of your room. See chapter 1 for an introduction to room acoustics, room treatment, and solutions to typical problems for rooms not designed and built as recording studios.

WHAT NOT TO DO

Don't ignore any of the critical monitoring elements.
Poor monitoring, whether caused by bad speakers, faulty speaker placement, or bad room acoustics, represents what I call "the fatal flaw syndrome." Without reasonably good monitoring ("good" meaning reasonably flat through the frequency range), it is not possible to be an effective mixer or mastering engineer. The good news is that it is not that hard to achieve a workable situation. Pay attention to these three factors: speakers,

speaker placement, and room acoustics. Do what you can to optimize each for your room, and even if working within a very limited budget, you will probably be in good shape to concentrate on what the music actually sounds like. Over time, as you get used to your speakers and environment, you will be able to produce consistent, reliable results.

II

MIXING

This part of the book dealing with mixing covers a large range of material from conceptual elements, to ear-training for mixing, to the application of processers of all types, to automation and recall, to various approaches to mixing individual instruments and instrument types. It also covers the collaborative process and the details of delivering final mixes. What it doesn't do is guarantee you great mixes—that's up to you. There's no substitute for practice, and trial and error is part of virtually every difficult endeavor. However, it is fairly easy to be riddled with doubt about one's mixes, so here is one story to help put things in perspective.

First a disclaimer: I don't remember when I read this interview or what magazine it was in. It was a long time ago, and I can't find it on the Internet. My memory of the details may not be accurate. But it doesn't matter if it's not factually correct; the message is 100 percent on target!

In an interview, Frank Zappa was relating a particular recurring nightmare. He would be dreaming that he was just completing a mix and he was listening to the playback. The mix sounded absolutely perfect! Everything was balanced exactly how he wanted it, and all the panning, EQ'ing, and effects were beautifully matched to the musical and emotional content. Nothing was the least bit out of place and each element sounded just as he hoped it would. Suddenly he would wake up and realize that he was having a nightmare—because this was a dream that could NEVER COME TRUE!

Chapter 4

Building a Mix
The Concepts and Tools in Detail

This chapter on building a mix details the conceptual and technical process that forms the bulk of the work on a final mix—the thinking about and the doing. There is considerable detail here, but because the technical discussions are organized by process rather than by instrument, this remains an overview of the tools used in mixing. Chapter 6 will take these tools and techniques into the specific realm for each family of instruments. Listening skills are essential to mixing skills, so all the elements in this chapter are designed to help increase your listening sensitivity.

Level and panning are the fundamental mix elements and are covered first. Building the mixer's toolbox is an endless process of acquiring and learning how to use new tools in the service of these two fundamentals. The primary tools of mixing—EQ, dynamics processing, and use of effects—are covered here along with some of the specialty tools in the digital domain, as well as the use of stereo buss processing. Finally, some advanced mixing concepts and techniques are discussed.

4.1 Starting Concepts and Setting Level

The starting point for any mix is the development of a concept, and that is covered as one of the essentials in chapter 2's Quick Guide to best practices. The concept forms the basis from which all the details emerge. *The main task of mixing is setting the level relationships between all the elements.* Before starting with setting levels, though, I cover the practical basics regarding file organization, which is essential to staying organized throughout the complicated process of mixing. I then cover the two broad concepts that help develop the listening skills and context needed for making musically sensitive decisions regarding level relationships. The first concept is the basic relationship between mixing and musical arrangements; the second concept is the idea of foreground and background as essential elements in both mixing and musical arranging. Lastly, I cover the need to establish a healthy gain structure in the early stages of your mix.

Organizing Your Mix File

At the beginning of good, fundamental in-the-box mixing techniques are the technicalities of file organization. Over the course of a recording it is very likely that your file will become somewhat bloated with parts and tracks that you will end up not using in the final mix. The order of your tracks on your "virtual" mixer may no longer make much sense, as you will have moved things around to facilitate the recording, overdubbing, and editing processes. The time to clean up and organize that file is now—before you get into the serious business of mixing. If you didn't do the recording and are getting a file for mixing, you will want to review each track carefully to understand what is on it and then label the track in a way that is easy for you to identify.

Here's a laundry list of clean-up items (first the abbreviated list and then the same list with full explanations):

1. Save the file under a new title (e.g., <Song Title> Mix 1).
2. Disable, hide, delete, or otherwise get rid of any tracks that you're not using.
3. Clear your file of all audio files and audio regions that you are not using.
4. Arrange your tracks in an order that makes sense to you.
5. Group your tracks in order to control related tracks as one.
6. Arrange your auxiliary (aux) inputs in a way that makes sense to you.

Now let's consider each of these in turn.

1. *Save the file under a new title.* You do this so that you can start to log the progression of mix files and you can access information from previous files, if needed. This also allows you to take the following steps without permanently losing access to any tracks or files that you eliminated from this mix file in one of the following steps.
2. *Disable, hide, delete or otherwise get rid of any tracks that you're not using.* You do this so that your monitor-screen "real estate" allows the clearest view of the elements in your mix. Just muting and hiding tracks gets them out of the way, but your computer is

still using CPU power to keep them immediately available. So if you can't disable them, or if you're pretty sure that you won't want to access them, you should delete them from your file. If your DAW allows you to important individual tracks from other files (in Pro Tools, called "import session data") you can always regain access to deleted tracks by importing them from an earlier version of the song file. If your DAW will both hide and disable unused tracks, this is usually the best strategy for tracks that you think you may end up wanting to bring back into your mix.

Disabling the tracks means the file won't use CPU power to keep them immediately accessible, yet they are still easily accessed by re-enabling them. The disadvantage to disabling the tracks is that your file will keep all the audio associated with those tracks accessible and that can bloat your file (see no. 3, next).

3. *Clear your file of all audio files and audio regions that you are not using.* Different DAWs use different names for audio files and the regions or clips that are created in the editing process. DAW files don't actually contain audio files, but they must contain a record of all the audio files that have ever been used by that file. This record is what allows them to access the audio (or portion of the audio) from its place on the hard drive and play it on the time line (and allow it to be further edited, processed, mixed, etc.). With large projects, the number of audio files and regions that have been created can easily run into the thousands, and this becomes a substantial file-management burden.

Once you have gotten rid of all the tracks that you don't need for your mix, find the function in your DAW that allows you to clear the unused audio files and regions from the file (clearing them means eliminating them from your file but not removing them from your hard drive). In the case of large files, this can make an enormous difference in speed and ease of operation, as well as access to CPU power to run plug-ins, manage mix automation, and so on. If you end up needing a track that you have deleted, when you import that track it will import the audio and region management data needed to access the audio associated with that track.

4. *Arrange your tracks in an order that makes sense to you.* You want to be able to find tracks easily and quickly. For me, in a typical band type file, this means something like the following:

> *Drums – Bass – Rhythm instruments (e.g., guitars and/or keyboards) – Solo tracks (e.g., guitar solo or sax solo) – Lead vocal – Background vocals*

65

I may arrange a more involved recording something like this:

Drums – Percussion – Bass – Rhythm instruments (e.g., guitars and/or keyboards) – Horn section – String quartet – Solo tracks (e.g., guitar solo or sax solo) – Lead vocal – Background vocals

Good track organization can really be critical with big sessions where the track count can run to 50 or more tracks. Here's how the track count might get so high in a session that includes the elements listed above (67 total tracks outlined here).

Drums: 14 tracks (including kick drum with mic inside the drum, kick drum outside, snare drum top, snare drum bottom, hi-hat, 4 individual tom-tom tracks, overheads left and right, ride cymbal, and room mics left and right).

Percussion: 6 tracks (2 channels for conga drums, one each for tambourine and woodblock and a stereo track for misc. small hand percussion); bass mic, bass direct; rhythm guitar 1, rhythm guitar 2, rhythm guitar 3.

Piano, organ, clavinet: 8 tracks (piano in stereo, B3 organ with stereo tweeter and stereo woofer recording of the Leslie speaker, clavinet in stereo).

Horn section: 10 tracks (5 piece horn section consisting of two trumpets, tenor sax, alto sax, and trombone each tracked individually and then doubled).

String quartet: 6 tracks (two stereo recordings for doubling including 1 spot mic for the cello on each complete quartet take).

Guitar solo: (1 close 1 far mic).

Sax solo (1 bell mic one keys mic).

Lead vocal; lead vocal double; harmony and background vocals (can easily run to 12 or more tracks including three-part harmonies, doubles, triples, or quadruples with each part organized from low to high in terms of pitch).

5. *Group your tracks in order to control related tracks as one.* Typical groups include things like drums and background vocals, but you will also want subgroups such as overhead mics, or low, mid-, and high-background vocal parts. Creating and managing groups is an essential part of effective mixing. Screenshot 4.1 shows 14 tracks of drums grouped together, with subgroups for the kick, snare, toms, overhead, and room mics.

SCREENSHOT 4.1

Drums with group settings.

6. *Arrange your auxiliary inputs in a way that makes sense to you.* You may have two different kinds of aux inputs. As you build your mix, if you follow the guidelines over the course of this book, you will likely generate a large number of aux inputs that are used as effects returns (and as the insert point for the effect plug-in as well; see section 4.5 on effects processing). Some people like to place all their effects returns together; this has the advantage of keeping all the audio tracks located in a more compact space so that moving from element to element is easier.

Some people like to place the effect return right after the element that it is associated with (e.g., drum rooms and reverbs after the drum tracks, guitar rooms and delays after the guitar tracks). This has the advantage of easy access to the effect while you're working on a particular track. I fall into the second camp, but use whichever you prefer—just keep them organized.

7. *Arrange your auxiliary subgroups in a way that makes sense to you.* The other kind of aux input that you might be using is subgroups. These differ from the groups described above in that they require an aux input. Create subs by assigning the outputs of all the tracks you wish to subgroup together to a stereo buss and then create a stereo aux input track that has the same stereo buss inputs as the individual track outputs, and set the outputs of your sub to your primary stereo output. This allows control of all the tracks with the subgroup output fader, but that really doesn't provide any greater functionality than just grouping the tracks together without a dedicated aux input subgroup.

However, subgroups allow you to place processors across a group of tracks by using the inserts of the aux input subgroup (e.g., a single compressor across the entire group of drum tracks). Some people like to place all their subs together and some like to place them right after the elements that they control. Again, I fall into the second camp, but use whichever you prefer—just keep them organized. See screenshots 4.2 to 4.4.

SCREENSHOT 4.2

Aux inputs organized together.

SCREENSHOT 4.3

Aux inputs organized after the related audio track(s).

SCREENSHOT 4.4

Aux submaster for 14 tracks of drums.

Mixing and Musical Arranging

Developing a good "ear" for mixing requires a certain kind of objective listening, along with a musical and creative orientation toward the goal of a final mix. By "objective listening" I mean the ability to hear the sonic qualities of the music as at least somewhat independent from the musical qualities. Listening for overall frequency balance, for the imaging across the panning spectrum, for the dynamic contour, for the spatial environment—all these involve a certain separation from the quality of the performances or the musical content. I had a conversation with one musician who said, "I could never mix because I get too caught up in the music." As mixers, we must be able to divorce ourselves from the performances and musical content and "hear" the mixes as sonic occurrences—as *sound*—and pursue the practical and creative objectives and directions that result from objective listening. This requires practice!

As this book progresses through the primary kinds of mixing techniques, you will have the opportunity to listen (on the web) to examples of variations in sound created by the wide range of mixing techniques. As you focus your attention on the specifics of sound, you will be developing your ear to listen objectively and to apply the tools of mixing in ways that shape the sound to your creative concept. You will also be learning techniques and approaches to listening to your own mixes as sonic events.

That said, we can never fully separate mixing techniques from musical content. In fact, poor musical arranging can make it almost impossible to create satisfying mixes, while great musical arrangements can almost mix themselves. We need to be sensitive to musical qualities as well as sonic qualities. The subtleties of these relationships might best be understood by considering musical arranging as both horizontal and vertical events.

Vertical Arranging

Vertical arranging refers to the musical content, thought of as a vertical combination of events—that is, all the sonic events happening at the same time (stacked on top of each other, so to speak). Musical events have frequency content; though each event may have both a fundamental frequency—its pitch or note—and a combination of frequency overtones that create its timbre (tonal quality). The fundamental frequency may give the sound a well-defined pitch (middle C, for example) and that may be combined with overtones that differentiate sounds (middle C on a piano versus middle C on a guitar, for example). The combination of frequencies may be less well defined and have no clear pitch (a snare drum, for example).

Musical events that share a lot of similar frequency content will compete for those frequencies if played at the same time. As mixers, it is often our goal to give each musical event a clear presence in the mix—we want to hear each instrument clearly and distinctly. If two instruments are competing for frequencies, it becomes more difficult to create a place for both of them. So, a musical arrangement that clumps a lot of similar-sounding instruments into the same frequency range is going to be difficult to mix. Conversely, a musical arrangement that combines very different-sounding instruments in noncompeting frequency ranges is going to be rather easy to mix. Simple examples follow:

> *Song #1* (difficult to mix): a lead vocal, a piano part that contains the notes of the melody and other notes in close proximity to the lead

vocal, two electric guitar parts that also contain the notes of the melody and other notes in close proximity to the lead vocal.

Song #2 (much easier to mix): a lead vocal, a piano part that contains the notes well above the range of the lead vocal, two electric guitar parts with one containing notes above the range of the lead vocal and the other containing notes that are all below the notes in the melody.

It is probably not ever possible to create a satisfying mix of Song #1 if you hope to achieve the traditional goal of clarity in your mix, and all the elements in Song #2 will sound reasonably distinct no matter what you do (within reason, of course; one can screw up anything—or give it one's own "muddifying" effect, if that is your goal).

So to some fairly substantial degree, mixing depends on musical arranging. As mixers, we are generally tasked to do the best we can with what we are given, but if you are involved in the arranging of the music you're going to be mixing, you can take note of the mixer's dilemma regarding frequency and use that as a partial guide to your arranging techniques. Even if you're not involved in the arranging, you may wish to alter the arrangement of the music you're mixing by eliminating certain parts—but this involves some very delicate interaction with the original arranger(s) and is covered thoroughly in the section on mix intervention (chapter 7).

WHAT NOT TO DO

Don't include the "songwriter part" in your final arrangement. *This is a bit off topic, but it may relate to your work as a mixer and it will come up again in the section on mixing intervention and collaboration. The musical accompaniment that a songwriter uses as the basis for writing the song is usually not a part that should end up in the final arrangement of that song. The "songwriter part" is typically a guitar or keyboard part that outlines the rhythmic and harmonic structure of the song—the musical backbone. As such it often contains thick chords (including the notes in the melody and notes in the bass register) and active rhythms.*

A good ensemble arrangement usually takes all the elements of the "songwriter part" and divides them up among many instruments. Thus, the drums outline the rhythm, the bass takes the low frequencies, and the guitars and keyboards fill in rhythmic and harmonic structure, often staying out of the immediate register of the melody and using single-note parts or partial chords of two or three notes. If you lay the original songwriter part in with these elements, you are duplicating, thickening, and competing for rhythmic and harmonic territory.

Horizontal Arranging

Horizontal arranging refers to the progression of musical events along the time line. A typical horizontal arrangement for a song might read something like this:

Intro/verse/chorus/verse/chorus/bridge/chorus/vamp/fade

Part of your job as a mixer will be to sustain interest over the progression of the song. You will also want to be aware of where the highpoints are, in both dynamic terms (volume) and emotional terms (musical/lyrical intensity), and reinforce these elements with the mix. The techniques for how best to enhance the strengths of the horizontal arrangement will vary, but they should be developed as a part of your initial concept.

The challenge may be to avoid having the climax of the song overwhelm other elements. You may need to reduce the volume of certain instruments and vocals during peak sections (often, bridges or vamps) to avoid this. You want those sections to stand out, but you don't want them to be too much louder than other sections. *Finding that balance is essential to good mixing.* Conversely, introductions or breakdowns may be significantly quieter than the rest of the song and may need a boost in volume to sound relatively balanced.

Another important aspect of horizontal arranging is the progression of individual music elements (drums, bass, guitar parts, keyboard parts, vocal parts, etc.). What are "through" elements (always there) and where are the new elements that distinguish one part from the next? For example, a new guitar part may come in on the choruses only. A typical mix strategy will be to get the sound and relationship of through elements established (e.g., drums, bass, primary rhythm instrument(s), lead vocal) and then begin adding the new elements (e.g., solos, second rhythm instrument, melodic line, background vocal(s), etc.).

I always get the lead vocal into the mix early in the process, as everything ultimately is there to support and balance the lead vocal. Understanding the role of each instrument and introducing it into the mix accordingly help you to understand the organizational structure of the song and to find the best ways to take advantage of the introduction of new elements.

Foreground and Background / Setting Level

One essential part of your concept that needs to emerge from having explored the vertical and horizontal arranging of the piece you are working on is a sense for which elements will be featured in the foreground of your mix and which will remain a part of the background. This is the starting point for setting the final level for all the elements in your mix. *The need to have both foreground and background elements is a fundamental (and often overlooked) starting point for every great mix* (except for solo instrument recordings).

71

Recognizing the need for foreground and background, and starting with a concept for how you will accomplish that in your mix, is essential. Panning and processing will change your level relationships, and you will be revising levels over and over again, so you don't need to try to really fine-tune level placement at the beginning of a mix. However, setting basic level relationships and establishing a sense of foreground and background at the beginning of the mix process should be done within a larger creative concept.

In the following clips (on the website) there are two mixes of the same material. In the first clip (4.1), I have tried to force all the elements into the foreground. The mix lacks perspective and the listener's attention isn't focused, as it should be. In the second mix, I have created foreground and background elements, providing perspective and focus.

Artist: The Blues Broads CD: *The Blues Broads Live* Track: "Mighty Love"

Audio Clip 4.1 A mix with drums (kick, snare, hi-hat), bass, rhythm guitar, lead vocal, and harmony part, with all the elements competing to be in the foreground

Audio Clip 4.2 The same piece of music with the mix providing foreground and background by placing the hi-hat, rhythm guitar, and harmony parts into the background

Gain Structure

As you are setting initial levels, pay attention to overall gain structure to avoid problems later in the mix process. As outlined in the previous section on setting levels (foreground and background), you need to start somewhere, though it is assumed that level setting is going to be a process of frequent revision. The first requirement for monitoring gain structure is a stereo master channel or track that controls the sum of all the elements in your file. The master channel meter shows you the overall level and the master fader controls the overall output. (The master channel is sometimes referred to as the "master fader" because that's what it was on an analog console—there wasn't a whole channel for the main output, just a fader. It may also be referred to as the "2 buss" or the "main output").

Although you can control the overall level in a variety of ways—most easily with the master output fader—it is still a good idea to watch your level and try to keep your mix from running too hot or too weak when the master fader is at unity gain (0 dB). As you raise individual fader levels, keep an eye on the master channel meter to see how your overall level is doing. If you start with the drums you'll probably want them to peak at around −10 dB in order to allow headroom for the bass, lead vocal, and other prominent elements. Ideally, your overall mix will peak in the −6 to −3 dB range. By maintaining a healthy overall gain structure you ensure that your individual fader outputs and sends will be operating in the range that gives you the most fine-tuning control.

4.2 Panning

Panning is the most neglected or underutilized element in many mixes. The term comes from the word *panorama*, which means an unobstructed and wide view, and that definition provides some clues to understanding and using the panning function. Panning provides the best strategy for avoiding "obstruction" between elements in your mix. By giving an element a position on the panning spectrum that is occupied by the fewest elements with competing frequencies, the mixer is able to free that element to be heard distinctly. A wide audio "view" is also primarily a function of creative use of the full panning spectrum (usually referred to as the "stereo image"). *A solid panning strategy is an essential part of every mix, and the full panning spectrum is a playground that provides tremendous opportunities for creative approaches and applications.*

Use the Entire Stereo Image

Rule number one in regard to planning is to use the entire stereo image from hard left to hard right. What this means in practical terms will vary greatly depending on the project and your creative aesthetic, but it generally means that you need to consider the entire range of the stereo field. Panning stereo recordings is covered in a later section, but panning mono (single channel) tracks provides pinpoint control over panning placement and the capability of placing an element anywhere on the panning spectrum from hard left to hard right.

In popular music mixes, it is common for the most prominent elements to be center panned. The lead vocal, bass, snare drum, and kick drum are often placed center. Center panning in a stereo system is actually a "phantom center" because equal level in the left and right speakers will fool our ears into hearing that element as coming from right between the two speakers (the difference when something comes from a center speaker in a surround environment is quite remarkable—it makes you realize that "phantom" center is an appropriate way to describe how we experience center panning in a stereo environment; there's more on this in appendix A on surround mixing and mastering). From the phantom center, mono elements can be placed anywhere from very soft left or right through to hard left or right.

CREATIVE TIP

Use the full panning spectrum.
The farther an element is toward the edge of the panning spectrum the more apparent it is going to be: closer to the center will cause the sound to blend more. On the other hand, elements at the far edge of the spectrum may sound dislocated and removed if there aren't very many elements filling in the image from the center.

Circumstances and aesthetics will determine how you ultimately use the entire stereo image, but the process begins with recognizing that the panning palette encompasses the entire spectrum from hard left to hard right. I find mixers in the earlier stages of developing their craft tend to be wary of using hard left or right for individual elements. Don't be!—take advantage of the entire spectrum.

Start with a Panning Strategy

A panning strategy needs to incorporate all the audio elements that you are planning for a final mix (panning of effects can be determined as they are added, and this will be covered in the section on effects). Panning is about relationships, so your panning strategy will come from considering how you want all the elements to sit in relation to each other.

The relationship of elements in regard to frequency is one of the keys to creating a successful panning strategy. Elements that share a frequency range (playing notes in the same or a similar register) will do best if panned as far away from each other as possible, whereas elements in very different registers (a fat midrange guitar part and a guitar part using high inversions and partial chords might fit well pretty close to each other on the panning spectrum).

A key element in any panning strategy is to maintain a good balance between left and right. This means that you will generally want to balance an important element on the left with a similarly important element on the right (e.g., rhythm guitar on the left, piano on the right, or hi-hat on the left, tambourine on the right). This isn't always possible, so you will want to adjust the extent of the panning depending on the ability to balance the element with something on the other side. In a simple arrangement with only one rhythm instrument, you might not pan the rhythm guitar as far left as you would if you had another instrument (another rhythm guitar or a keyboard, for example) to balance it with on the other side. At the end of this section are some sample track lists with possible panning strategies.

One of the important aspects of panning and the need for a panning strategy at the beginning of your mix is that there is a power curve to panning controls. This means that sounds increase in volume as they move farther left or right (the difference between center position and far left or right is between 3 and 6 dB depending on the system). Consult your DAW manual if you want to know what scale is used for your system, but using your ear is best for setting volume regardless of specs. If you change the panning of an element during mixing, its volume will be both apparently and actually different— "apparently" because its new relationship to the panning of other elements will affect the perception of its level, and "actually" because the power curve of panning will have altered its actual gain output.

WHAT NOT TO DO

Don't let panning be an afterthought.
A panning strategy needs to be developed at the very beginning of the mix process. You can always adjust levels to accommodate changes in panning over the course of your mix, but because panning affects volume as well as position, too many changes will start to erode all the level setting you may have done prior to resolving most of the panning issues.

Panning Stereo Tracks

Stereo tracks are generally not two distinct elements, though they occupy two distinct tracks. Typically, stereo tracks represent the stereo qualities of a single element such as a piano or drum set overhead mics. Just because something was recorded (or sampled) in stereo that doesn't mean you have to use its full stereo capability in your mix. When you create a stereo track it defaults to placing the two panning controls set to hard left and hard right. Sometimes you will want to leave them set this way, but often you will want to adjust the stereo balance within a stereo recording.

For example, even though the piano is recorded in stereo (using two microphones), there may be a lot of elements in your mix and the piano will be heard better if it occupies a smaller piece of the stereo image and doesn't compete across the entire stereo spectrum. You may want to set the one panning control soft right and the other medium right, keeping the piano on the right side but allowing it to be spread a bit across the spectrum on the right. Or instead, you might want to set both panning controls to hard left and let the piano have its own place at the far left end of the spectrum. The two tracks are still providing complementary information to fill out the piano sound, even if they are panned to the same place, making them sound like a mono recording.

Too many elements spread out in wide stereo will often make a mix sound indistinct and congested. I find that I rarely use stereo recordings split completely hard left and hard right unless there aren't too many elements involved or if the tracks are part of a multi-mic setup like the drum overheads. The following audio clips illustrate this positioning.

> Artist: Sista Monica CD: *Sweet Inspirations* Track: "You Gotta Move"
>
> Audio Clip 4.3 A mix with drums (kick, snare, hi-hat), bass, rhythm guitar, and piano with the stereo piano recording split hard left and right
>
> Audio Clip 4.4 The same piece of music with the piano soft spread soft right, opposite the rhythm guitar

Auto-Panning

Auto-panning is the creative use of dynamic (moving) panning effects, and it has been greatly enhanced by the capabilities of the DAW. Having elements change position in the panning spectrum as the music plays can be distracting and disorienting, but it can also add a playful aspect or enhance the rhythmic presence of an element. Typical options range from the rapid movement of a single sonic occurrence from one side to the other (e.g., a long sustained note that is bending up or down in pitch while moving from one side of the panning spectrum to the other), to a slow and steady movement from left to right and back again that is in time with the rhythm of the music (e.g., making the cycle in half notes, or quarter notes, or eighth notes), to a rapid oscillating of an element over small part of the panning spectrum (e.g., a sustained synthesizer pad rapidly moving from back and forth from soft left to medium left). I revisit this topic under "Advanced Automation Techniques" in chapter 5 and provide detailed instructions and screenshots for these panning effects.

Examples of Session Panning Strategies

The detailing of tracks for a typical session that I used for organizing your tracks provides a good context for describing a possible panning strategy. Here is a brief outline for a strategy and the thinking behind it.

A typical small band file
Tracks

Drums – Bass – Rhythm instruments (e.g., guitars and/or keyboards) – Solo tracks (e.g., guitar solo or sax solo) – Lead vocal – Background vocals

Panning Strategy
Drums: Kick and snare center, the rest of the kit panned in a way that reflects the physical setup of the kit (e.g., hi-hat panned left, toms moving from left to right and overheads split either hard or soft left/right depending on the number of competing elements and your aesthetic regarding the spread of the drums over the stereo image.

Bass: Center

Rhythm instruments: Rhythm instruments often provide the best opportunity for utilizing the entire stereo field. We might split two rhythm guitars hard left and hard right and place the keyboard soft right (collapsing it if it's recorded in stereo). We might run the organ split hard left and right (especially if it utilizes a Leslie speaker or Leslie speaker effect) and run the rhythm guitar soft right. We might run one rhythm guitar hard left, the other guitar (less rhythmically critical, perhaps something like long, blending chords played in a high register) soft right, and the piano hard right. Number of elements, their rhythmic and harmonic role, and presence and complexity of other elements such as background vocals will all go into determining a panning strategy for the rhythm instruments.

Solo tracks: Center, unless there is trading or combined elements in a solo passage that may do better panned soft left and right, opposite each other.

Lead vocal: Center

Background vocals: Often splitting these soft left and right will create a nice bed for the lead vocal to sit in; however, if there are a lot of backing vocal parts and you want them featured, you may want to spread them across the full stereo image (typically with the lower parts more centered and the higher parts closer to or at the edge). Focusing your backing vocals on one side or another might also help to leave space if there are several rhythm instruments forming critical rhythm content and propulsion to the track.

A typical large band file
Tracks
Drums – Percussion – Bass – Rhythm instruments (e.g., guitars and/or keyboards) – Horn section – String quartet – Solo tracks (e.g., guitar solo or sax solo) – Lead vocal – Background vocals

Panning strategy
Start with the strategy listed for the smaller band above. Then adapt for the addition of the percussion, horn section, and string quartet.

Percussion: There is a huge range of possibilities when it comes to percussion and strategies will vary depending on the number and type of percussion elements. Tambourines and shakers need to be positioned relative to each other and the hi-hat and cymbals from the drum set (often set apart—e.g., tambourine opposite the hi-hat because they occupy the same high frequency territory). Other hand percussion (cowbell, claves, woodblock, guiro, etc.) may fall anywhere in the spectrum but rarely will benefit from center panning unless they are intended to dominate the mix. Other drums (bongos, congas, timbales, djembe, etc.) may be split left and right in stereo though there's rarely enough room on the panning spectrum to justify that. I will often pan the lower conga drum (tumba) just off center (right or left) and the higher drums (conga and/or quinta) a bit farther toward the edge of the same side (left or right). Some percussionists will record some elements (especially certain instruments such as wind chimes or rainstick) so that the sound moves from one side to the other as it is played; typically you will want to maintain that movement in your mix by having that element on a stereo track that is panned hard left and hard right.

Horn section: Again, strategies will vary depending on the size of the horn section. You may group the horns on one side or the other, with the lower instruments (Trombone, tuba, baritone and tenor sax) more toward the center and the higher instruments (trumpet, flugelhorn, alto and soprano sax) shifted a bit farther to the edge. It's pretty common to double the horn section (record all the parts with all the horns twice) in which case you may want to place one left and one right. Whether you still spread the individual instruments on the left or right will depend on the needs of other elements in your mix and the extent to which you want to feature the horns. You could also place one of the section soft left or right and the other slightly farther in the same direction to get a thick, but relatively focused section that doesn't occupy too much of the stereo image.

String quartet: A string quartet, or any string section, can be dealt with in a way similar to what I have described for the horn section above, and in popular music applications if is fairly common to double the string section as well. When there are strings and horns they usually serve different functions (e.g., one will be more rhythmic and one more sustained) and that allows them to occupy some of the same space in the stereo image without competing with each other too much.

Mono Mixes and Panning

It used to be that we had to be concerned with mono compatibility when mixing since some significant playback formats were mono only (AM radio and televisions in particular), but that has not been the case for some time now. Virtually every playback system is stereo (or surround), though speaker placement and actual stereo balance between the two speakers may be far from ideal.

When mono compatibility was much more of an issue, we would be cautious about placing elements far to one side or the other; the panning power curve means that those sounds that are hard left or right would lose volume (3 dB or more) when dumped to mono. Because mono playback circumstances are rare now, and because of the tremendous creative advantages to using the full panning spectrum, I think the contemporary mixer can safely disregard mono compatibility when setting panning positions for a mix.

It's similar for concerns about one-sided playback, such as shared earbud listening or really bad speaker placement. Yes, these things are going to happen, but I think that limiting your panning to accommodate mono playback is not worth the creative sacrifice. However, referencing mono playback of your mix can be a valuable tool for applying EQ—see below on EQ'ing tactics—and other functions such as phase relationships.

4.3 Processing: EQ

EQ is the most powerful and frequently used processor for shaping audio in the mix. For the technical details of how EQs work, see my previous book *The Art of Digital Audio Recording*. Here, I focus on the application of EQ in the mix environment, beginning with some basic techniques and important considerations. I then describe approaches to working with the primary EQ parameters, and I cover the most frequently used tactic for applying EQ. Finally, I survey the various kinds of EQs and how they might fit into your arsenal of mixing EQ processors.

The Smile EQ

The kinds of EQ settings that produce the smile EQ are so named because, when viewed on a graphic EQ as shown in screenshot 4.5, the EQ curve looks like a smile. The principal behind the smile EQ is the fundamental quality of our ear's capabilities as described by the equal-loudness contour (early versions were called the Fletcher-Munson curve). Simply put, the ear has a bias for the midrange frequencies, so the lower the listening level, the less high and low frequencies are heard. The effect of this on monitoring levels for mixing was described in chapter 2 on why mixers need to vary their listening level.

The smile EQ works to correct the natural frequency bias of our hearing by increasing the lows and highs, but there is another factor as to why variations on this basic approach are common in the application of EQ. Musical sounds are, to a large extent, defined by their timbre (the quality of the sound), and the timbre

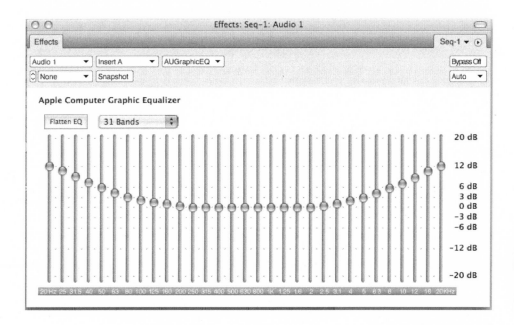

SCREENSHOT 4.5

The smile EQ on a graphic equalizer.

is primarily determined by the nature of what is called the *overtone series*. This overtone series is what explains the difference in sound between a piano that plays the note middle C and a guitar that plays the same note. The note is defined by its fundamental pitch (or frequency) and the fundamental frequency of these two notes is the same (middle C). Why, then, does the guitar sound so different from the piano? The answer is in the timbre (the quality of the sound), which is a result of the way the instrument is played, as well as the physical qualities of the instrument. Thus, the overtones of a middle C created by the piano string struck by a piano hammer and resonating within the chamber of a piano are much different from those created by a guitar string struck with a plastic pick (or finger, etc.) and resonating inside the body of the guitar (or in the speaker of a guitar amplifier). The difference creates the timbres that make it easy for us to distinguish between a piano and guitar, even when they play the same note.

The overtone series is made up of a series of higher tones (called *harmonics*) above the fundamental or root tone that gives the note its name (and its primary pitch). These harmonics vary in their frequency relationship to the fundamental tone, their volume, and their waveform patterns; and these variations give the sound its character. Therefore, *boosting the higher frequencies emphasizes the qualities of sound unique to that particular instrument*. Similarly, boosting the lower frequency content of the sound enhances frequencies that counter the deficiencies in our ears capabilities. Variations in frequency location and breadth, along with the degree of boosting, define many approaches to applying EQ—as described below—but high and low frequency boost—a "smile curve"—is a common way to apply EQ.

Boost and Dip EQ

Many of the benefits and challenges of both boosting and dipping EQ were discussed earlier in the Quick Guide, in chapter 3. The introduction of phasing problems and the deceptive quality caused by the increase in volume that accompanies boosting of frequencies make the application of EQ less than straightforward. As discussed in section 3.2, the "dip only" approach to EQ avoids some of these problems but also fails to produce some of the desirable results created by boosting EQ. Specifics on how to approach the application of EQ follow in the next sections on various EQ'ing strategies and in chapter 6 on mixing individual instruments.

Sounds Best versus Fits Best

There is often a tension between two different aesthetics when EQ'ing for your final mix. The first is the desire to make each element sound its best—that is, to sound in whatever way you think is optimal for that particular element when you are listening to it in solo. The other is whatever is going to make that element fit best when combined with all the other elements in your mix. Of course, you still want that element to sound good, but the demands of fitting with other elements may mean that, in the mix, the instrument should not be EQ'd the same as it would be when listening in solo. The key here is the difference between working on the element in solo and working on it in combination with all the other elements in the mix (and sometimes in stages along the way—in combination with certain other elements but not all of them).

Because there is always some overlap in frequencies between elements in a mix (except for solo recordings, of course), that means that these elements are competing for your attention (your ear) at those shared frequencies. This competition can be handled partly by panning strategies as described above, but EQ can be a critical tool in balancing (equalizing!) the frequencies in a way that provides the optimal fit for all the elements in a mix.

Taken in solo, you might well EQ something in a way that is pleasing, but that creates problems when it is placed in combination with other elements. This is particularly true with low-frequency information. The warmth and body that is pleasing when listening to an instrument in solo may well become problematic when combined with many other instruments that also have warmth and body occupying the same frequency range. So you may need to trim those frequencies, even though it makes the individual instrument sound relatively thin when you're listening in solo. It doesn't sound its best by itself, but it fits best into the mix environment with all the other instruments.

An example that illustrates the tension between sounds best and that fits best is the use of acoustic guitar in a full band setting. The difference may be quite dramatic if the acoustic guitar is played across all six strings (a common kind of strumming technique, though one you might want to reconsider in a band setting, as discussed in the previous section regarding the songwriter part and vertical arranging). On its own (or in solo), you will want the acoustic guitar to sound full-frequency—richly resonant from the lows of the bottom strings to the highs of the top strings. However, in a band context it is very likely that a richly resonant acoustic guitar will take up way too much space, and thereby competing with almost every other instrument, from the bass guitar, to other rhythm instruments, to vocals.

Often a very thin acoustic sound—achieved with considerable low and midrange roll-off along with some high-mids and high-frequency boosting—will fit best with the other instruments. The thin acoustic won't sound very good in solo, but in the band context it will fulfill its role of providing some acoustic timbre with the emphasis on its percussive drive. On the website I have posted these clips to illustrate how differently one might EQ an acoustic guitar to fit best versus sound best.

Artist: Acoustic Son CD: *Cross the Line* Track: "Better Days"
Audio Clip 4.5 Acoustic guitar EQ'd to sound best
Audio Clip 4.6 Sounds best acoustic in the mix

Audio Clip 4.7 Acoustic guitar EQ'd to fit best

Audio Clip 4.8 Fits best acoustic in the mix

Note: The tension between "sounds best" and "fits best" applies to many decisions in mixing and mastering beyond questions regarding EQ decisions.

WHAT NOT TO DO

Don't EQ exclusively in solo or in context.
Using EQ in mixing requires finding a balance between sounds best and fits best for each individual element. To accomplish this requires considering the element both in solo (where it's easiest to determine what sounds best) and in the context of all the other elements (where it's easiest to determine what fits best). Because you are adding elements as you build your mix, you must continue to review EQ'ing decisions as the mix evolves, constantly trying to balance all elements for level, panning and the sonic characteristics created altered by signal processing.

CREATIVE TIP

"Sounds best" versus "fits best" is a recurrent issue.
The potential conflict between what sounds best and what fits best is not limited to EQ'ing decisions. Virtually every decision you make regarding signal processing—from compression through EQ to reverbs and delays—may be affected by questioning how what sounds best in solo relates to what fits best in the track.

EQ'ing Tactics

I discussed EQ'ing strategies above, here I turn to EQ'ing tactics— meaning the applied techniques used to make EQ decisions. How do you decide which EQ plug-in to use (assuming you have more than one)? How many frequencies to adjust? Whether to boost or dip frequencies? Which frequencies to either boost or dip? How much to boost or dip them? Whether to use bell-shaped EQ curves or shelving? How steep of a bell or shelf to use? There are a lot of decisions to be made, but there isn't a formula for how to make them.

When referencing the strategies mentioned above, how do you achieve the optimal frequency balance for each element or the best compromise between sounds best and fits best? There is one primary tactic in the service of this process, and that is using extreme settings to uncover the ways boosting or dipping certain frequencies affects the material that you're working on.

CREATIVE TIP

Use your ears!

Before jumping into the practical tactics of applying EQ, and while these strategies are still fresh, it is good to remember the overriding bottom line when EQ'ing any element: use your ear! You set EQ based on the way things sound and in service of your aesthetic vision. Developing your ear for EQ'ing takes time and experience; there is no substitute for the hours of trial and error using EQs on program material of all types, combined with critical listening of music that you love or admire that is clearly related to the music you're working on.

Remember that there are no hard-and-fast rules (or presets!). And even where there are generally accepted practices, some of the most interesting (and effective) mixes come from breaking the rules in service of a creative vision. See the final section on EQ where radical EQ'ing is discussed—nothing should be considered out of bounds!

WHAT NOT TO DO

Don't rely on a spectrum analyzer.

As indicated in the creative tip above, when it comes to EQ (when it comes to mixing in general!) your ears are your best guides. I mentioned in chapter 2 that a spectrum analyzer could be useful to uncover strange anomalies that might be out of the range of your speakers (or your hearing), such as infrasound (very low frequencies below the hearing threshold) or ultrasound (very high frequencies above the hearing threshold), which may have strayed into your mix. It's also a good tool for beginners to catch very out-of-balance mix elements (caused by inexperience or poor monitoring). It's worth checking your mix on a spectrum analyzer, but other than as a way to catch the oddities, it's dangerous to use for anything more than very rough guide to frequency balance. You need to learn to trust your ear, through experience.

CREATIVE TIP

Double your fun.

EQ'ing sometimes demands close work on many frequencies. This may especially be true on drum tracks and loops. It can be helpful to copy your track and use two tracks to EQ the same thing twice. You might use one track to work on the high frequencies and another on the low. Kick drums and snare drums might benefit from this approach, especially if you feel like they need a lot of EQ shaping. Loops that include full-frequency

> material, like drum loops or full band loops, might also be easier to manipulate to your liking by combining EQ efforts. You might also employ the parallel compression tactic (see the section on dynamics for details on this, page 94) by heavily EQ'ing the duplicated track and mixing that with its un-EQ'd counterpart.

Choosing Frequencies

The key to selecting frequencies that are going to achieve the best results for enhancing or fitting an element in your mix is to use exaggerated settings and listen to the way the material responds. One of my favorite EQ plug-ins (MDW, from the master EQ designer George Massenburg) supplies a shortcut to this technique called ISO Peak (see screenshot 4.6). For each EQ band there is a button that shifts that band to a setting with a very high boost (+12 dB) and narrows the bandwidth to very narrow setting (Q = 8 is the default, but the user can change this to 4, 12, or 16). You can then sweep through frequencies (by sliding the mouse over the frequency select control) and listen to an exaggerated version of the effect on the various frequencies. This often immediately reveals the points at which the effects of the EQ are particular sweet or sympathetic and the points at which they are particularly unpleasant or problematic. Of course, you will still need to decide how much to boost or dip and what kind of bandwidth setting to use, but this technique to select the center frequency to work from gets you off to a good start.

Choosing Bandwidth

Broad or narrow bandwidth? Bell curve or shelving? Making these decisions can be confusing, but at least to start with, you can use the default settings on your EQ and this will often produce good results (some EQs only have default settings, without user access to bandwidth control and that isn't necessarily a problem). EQs often default the highest and lowest bands to shelving curves with a moderate rise and mid-bands to bell curves with a moderate width. Generally you will want some compelling reason to vary from these settings (e.g., you may not want the low-frequency boost to extend into the infrasonic or subharmonic (lower than 20 Hz) range, so you'd opt for a bell curve rather than the default shelving setting). *As a rule of thumb, broader bandwidths and shelving*

SCREENSHOT 4.6

The MDW EQ with one band set in the ISO peak mode.

EQs are gentler and more musical than narrow bandwidth settings (see the later section on other forms of EQ for a discussion of EQ with very narrow bandwidth settings, commonly called notch filters).

Choosing EQs

Which EQ plug-in to select for the goal you may have with a particular element in the mix requires some amount of trial and error. There are EQs based on all different kinds of hardware construction, including vacuum tube, transformer, and/or integrated circuit (IC) technology. The sound of any software EQ is a combination of the goal of the designer and the execution of that goal through the construction and algorithms of the computer code. Some EQs supply limited control in the interface; often modeling hardware EQ interfaces from some vintage and/or famous EQ. In all likelihood those earlier EQs limited the parameter controls because they were designed before strategies had been developed to provide all the possible EQ parameters and/or for financial reasons. These may sound great and be very useful, but I generally prefer EQs that give full access to gain, frequency, and bandwidth control; these may still model earlier hardware designs and strategies sonically, without the parameter limitations.

Some main strategies for EQ design are tubes, transformers and/or ICs, and linear phase. I describe each here, along with some comments on their qualities in practice and a screenshot of one popular example. (Some developers have plug-ins that emulate tube, transformer, or IC designs simply by selecting different presets.)

Tube emulation designs. These EQ plug-ins attempt to emulate vacuum tube-based hardware EQs, either vintage (e.g., the various Pultec EQs) or contemporary (e.g., the various Manley EQs); see screenshot 4.7. Tube EQs have a reputation for a "warm" sound produced by the introduction of even-order harmonic distortion. Even- and odd-order harmonics are related to the overtone series that gives instruments their particular timbre (discussed earlier). Even-order harmonics produce smooth, musical characteristics as opposed to odd-order harmonics, which tend to sound harsh. Both hardware and software tube

85

SCREENSHOT 4.7

Vacuum tube emulation EQ plug-in.

or tube emulation EQs can vary considerably in their characteristics, but they tend to introduce some degree of even-order harmonic distortion that produces a "warming" effect by thickening the overtones of the original signal.

WHAT NOT TO DO

Don't assume that even-order harmonic distortion is always good or that odd-order harmonic distortion is always bad. *There are many factors that define the effects of harmonic distortion, including the level of the signal being processed and the extent of processing gain being used. While the judgment that even-order harmonics equal "warm" and odd-order harmonics equal "harsh" may be the norm, it is also possible for overdriven even-order harmonics to sound "mushy" or indistinct and subtle odd-order harmonics to add "presence" or definition.*

Transformer or IC-based designs. Solid state EQs replaced tube EQs primarily because of the reduction in cost, but as the designs were perfected they also generated their own versions of even- or even- and odd-order harmonics, and some became highly valued for the tonal characteristics (especially the transformer-based designs of the early Rupert Neve EQs); see screenshot 4.8. Integrated circuits replaced transformer-based designs because of cost savings. Early IC designs tended to introduce odd-order harmonic distortion that gave them their bad reputation for sounding harsh, but later designs have become highly valued (e.g., the Solid State Logic - SSL - EQs). See screenshot 4.9. The reality is that tubes, transformers, and ICs can be designed to create either even- or odd-order harmonics, and they may be either more aggressive with the addition of tonal qualities or more transparent (tonally neutral), so the current state

SCREENSHOT 4.8

Transformer emulation EQ plug-in (use neve).

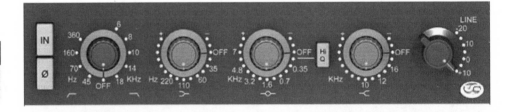

SCREENSHOT 4.9

Integrated circuit (IC) emulation EQ plug-in (use SSL).

of both hardware and software EQs should be judged on their tonal qualities rather than the origin of their design.

Linear-phase designs. Linear-phase EQs represent a new breed of processors that have emerged in the context of software EQ development. These processors use techniques to deal with the issues of phase that emerge in the application of EQ. Anytime we process a selective part of the frequency range of a sound (EQ'ing the highs, or lows, or whatever), the delay required to process those frequencies changes the phase relationship of the sound (phase being the relative arrival time of sounds or frequencies at their destination—generally your ears!). These changes in phase relationship may produce unwanted artifacts (such as harshness) in your sound.

Linear-phase EQs work to solve this problem by delaying the unprocessed frequencies (and/or the frequencies processed separately but incurring different delay times) and then delivering the full sound in the same phase relationship as it came into the processor, but with the inclusion of the various frequency processing that has been added. See screenshot 4.10. As a result, these EQs tend to exhibit pretty long latency times (delays), though these can be solved using the delay compensation that is built into most DAWs now. Linear-phase EQs also tend to be CPU hogs, which can be an issue depending on the size of your file and your computer configuration.

It may seem that linear-phase EQs would always be the most desirable kind of EQ to use, and they do tend to have a particularly smooth and pleasing sound, but they have their own set of compromises to consider. They handle phase issues especially well, but they are still subject to distortion and other artifacts typical of all EQs to varying degrees. They may be particularly useful

SCREENSHOT 4.10

Linear-phase EQ plug-in.

on individual tracks in multi-miked situations (such as drums or acoustic piano), though other elements of the sound of any particular EQ may prove equally or more important to you and cause you to choose something other than a linear-phase style EQ—as always, the ear needs to be the final judge.

On the website, an EQ "shootout" provides clips of the same settings on each type of EQ applied to the same program material:

Artist: Cascada de Florees CD: *Radio Flor* Track: "Collar de Perlas"

Audio Clip 4.9 A brief clip with the following EQ setting using a tube emulation EQ software plug-in: bell curve set to 3 kHz, +5 gain, and .8 bandwidth.

Audio Clip 4.10 The same piece of music with the same EQ settings but with transformer emulation EQ.

Audio Clip 4.11 The same piece of music with the same EQ settings but with an IC emulation EQ.

Audio Clip 4.12 The same piece of music with the same EQ settings but with a linear phase EQ.

Other Forms of EQ

There are other kinds of specialty EQs, such as notch filters and band-pass filters, that are offered as stand-alone hardware units, but software programming is able to include many different kind of functions in one plug-in in a way that was too cumbersome to be practical for hardware design. As a result, these capabilities are now frequently a part of one full-feature software EQ plug-in. Notch filtering is the use of very steep bandwidth dipping, generally to eliminate problems such as narrow bands of noise that have inadvertently been recorded with your audio (such as 60 cycle hum). Band-pass filters (high pass or low pass) attenuate some frequencies and allow others (high or low) to "pass" unaffected (as covered thoroughly in my previous book, *The Art of Digital Audio Recording).*

Other processors that perform functions related to what is done with a traditional EQ include de-essers and multi-band compressors. While these processors really are more akin to EQs than they are to what we traditionally think of as dynamics processors, because they use dynamics type control (and even dynamics-type nomenclature, like the multi-band compressor), I will covering them in the section on dynamics processors.

Radical EQ

While the majority of the time we are using EQ to enhance sound while balancing our desire for it to sound as good as possible, and to also fit into the sonic environment, there are times when radical EQ can be used as part of a creative approach to a mix. The most commonly heard use of radical EQ is the "tele-

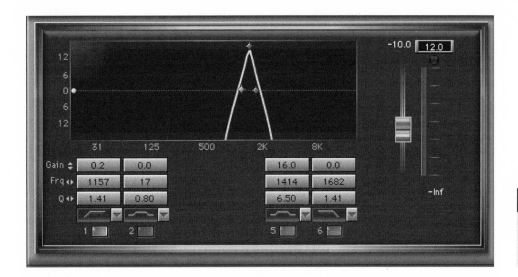

SCREENSHOT 4.11

A typical EQ setting to produce the "telephone effect" on a vocal.

89

phone" effect, in which a voice is made to sound like it's coming through a telephone handset speaker (or any similarly lo-fi playback system). This is often used for one section of a song or one particular line, and it can be a very effective way to grab the listener's attention (see screenshot 4.11).

I was surprised the first time I explored this effect by how radical an EQ setting was required to produce the telephone effect—severe high- and low-pass filtering and a considerable amount of midrange boost is needed (and considerable reduction in output as well to compensate for the gain in the midrange).

Other uses of radical EQ might involve severe high or low band-pass filtering in order to transform a sound by eliminating major portions of its frequency content. An organ or synthesizer part that includes bass notes might be EQ'd so that the low frequencies are almost eliminated and only the high, right-hand figures can be heard—or vice versa, to retain only the bass parts. A snare drum that sounds particularly "thuddy" with little "snare" or "snap" to the sound might be heavily EQ'd in the high frequencies and dipped in the mids and lows to make it sound more like a traditional R&B snare drum. Yes, EQ can produce very harsh effects and certainly mixes can be ruined with too much EQ, but there is a place for even the most radical EQ settings.

CREATIVE TIP

EQ'ing a mono mix
Referencing your mix in mono is something we used to have to do to ensure mono compatibility when AM radio and most televisions always played in mono. As discussed above under panning strategies, I don't believe you should pan "safely" in order to ensure reasonable results in mono—there just aren't sufficient examples of mono playback environments to require that. However, panning is a primary tactic for getting

elements to fit together that have frequency conflicts, and as a result you might do less EQ'ing of those elements thanks to the benefits of panning. At the same time, your mix might be further enhanced if you do EQ for frequency conflicts before relying solely on the benefits of panning.

So, try dumping your mix to mono and listen to the interaction of elements. Because elements are still interacting, even when panned apart from each other, getting each element to sound more distinct by EQ'ing it in mono may really benefit your mix when it reverts to stereo. Take care when using this tactic not to EQ too much—the goal isn't a mono mix, which might require more radical EQ to sound its best—but some subtle increase in distinction in elements might be more easily achieved with a bit of mono mixing.

4.4 Processing: Dynamics

Dynamics processors are the most difficult of the common processors to understand because their effects are often very subtle, but they have widespread application in almost every typical mix. For the technical details of how dynamics processors work and the various kinds of dynamics processors, see my previous book *The Art of Digital Audio Recording*. Here, I focus on the application of dynamics processing in the mix environment.

Common techniques such as compression, limiting, and brickwall limiting on individual tracks, subgroups, and the master buss, as well as parallel compression, are explored. I also consider side-chaining (de-essers and other) and multi-band compressors in a separate section, "Dynamic EQ's," as they are really a hybrid processor that uses dynamics processing to produce EQ effect. Expanders have a much more limited role in mixing (and audio, in general), but I briefly consider how they may be useful in certain circumstances.

Dynamics Types

I will briefly review types of dynamics processors (covered extensively in my previous book) for reference in the following discussion regarding dynamics tactics.

Compressors/Limiters and Expanders/Gates

Compressors limit the dynamic range of program material by reducing the volume of the louder sounds. What is reduced is determined by the user-controlled threshold setting such that any sound that goes over the threshold is compressed and those under the threshold pass through unchanged. The degree the louder sounds are compressed is controlled by the ratio—the higher the ratio, the greater the compression. Limiting is simply compression with a high ratio (typically 20:1 or higher).

Expanders are the opposite of compressors—they expand the dynamic range of program material by decreasing the volume of the quieter sounds. What is reduced is determined by the user-controlled threshold setting, such that any sound that fails to goes over the threshold is reduced in volume and those above the threshold pass through unchanged. The degree the quieter sounds are reduced is controlled by the ratio—the higher the ratio, the greater the expansion. Gating is simply compression with a high ratio (typically 20:1 or higher). What follows focuses on compressors/limiters because of their much more widespread use in mixing.

Tube and Optical Compressors verses VCA and FET Compressors

There are a variety of technologies used to detect level and thereby trigger compression or expansion based on the threshold setting. Tube and optical detectors are both older technologies (e.g., the Fairchild 660 and the UA LA-2A), though modern versions are also manufactured (e.g., Manley Variable Mu and the Tube Tech CL-1B). VCA (Voltage Control Amplifier) and FET (Field Effect Transistor) detection designs use newer technologies (e.g., dbx 160 and the Empirical Labs Distressor). Software compressors emulate the characteristics of one or more of these kinds of detection circuits.

While various technologies create different characteristics in regards to attack, release, and ratio functions, software design can model any characteristics and create any kind of hybrid compressor function. As a rule, the tube and opto type compressors have slower attack-time capabilities and a softer knee. The slower attack makes the compressors suitable when there is no need to clamp down quickly on transients. The softer knee (variable ratio) means that the louder sounds above the threshold will be compressed more than the quieter ones that are also above the threshold.

The VCA and FET compressors are capable of very fast attack times and greater control over ratio characteristics so they are more flexible in use. Each compressor design is capable of more or less transparency—that is the extent to which they do not color the sound—but the VCA and FET designs are capable of producing less coloration while the tube and opto designs can provide the classic "valve distortion" (a thickening or "warmth" created primarily by even-order harmonic distortion), which is highly valued in some circumstances but may not be desired in others (it may read as muddiness or blurring of the sound). (There's more on this in the sections on dynamics strategies and in chapter 6 on processing individual elements in your mix.)

RMS versus Peak Level Reading

Compressors can also vary in how they read audio level. RMS level detection (Root of the Mean value Squared) looks at average level over time, whereas peak level detection reacts to the momentary audio peaks in level. Some compressors offer a choice between the two and some offer control over the "window" size of the RMS readings. That is, as the RMS detection looks at a smaller and smaller window of sound for its average, it becomes more and more like a peak detecting compressor. In general, RMS detection is better at general "leveling" compressor function and is going to produce gentler results while peak compressors do better at taming sounds with a lot of quick dynamic changes (like snare drum tracks).

Variations in attack time function similarly to peak versus RMS detection, with slower attack times producing more gentle, leveling type results and fast attack times better at taming sharp dynamic transitions (and consequently dulling the sound in some circumstances).

Brickwall Limiters

Brickwall limiters are similar to traditional limiters in that they reduce the dynamic range of program material, but they employ a ratio of infinity:1. That means that program material is never allowed to exceed the threshold (this is the "brick wall"). They employ "look-ahead" technology to do this, meaning they analyze the signal and then process it, causing significant delay in the processing and requiring delay compensation if used any place other than the final stage (stereo buss) of the mix.

Brickwall limiters represent a kind of hyper-compression that has found significant application in both mixing and mastering, with some questionable results. The most frequent application of brickwall limiting is on the overall program material—the stereo buss. Many argue that the brickwall limiting is significantly overused and a detriment to both the sound of the music and the experience of the consumer (search "loudness wars" on the Internet for more information/opinions). Because of its prevalence and importance, I have covered this critical issue in chapter 3 and also discussed the way it has changed the relationship between mixing and mastering in appendix B.

Brickwall limiters are sometimes used on individual tracks or on subgroups to provide maximum leveling. Tracks (such as lead vocals or raps) and subgroups (such as drums) are sometimes both compressed and brickwall limited to make them as present as possible. At what point the "presence" afforded by brickwall limiting becomes overbearing or unmusical is an aesthetic decision—it has its place, but should be applied with a clear understanding of its effect.

Dynamics Strategies

Dynamics processors have two typical functions in mixing: (1) they may control fluctuations in volume by either reducing the dynamic range (compression/limiting) or increasing the dynamic range (expansion/gating) while remaining relatively transparent in regards to the overall timbre of the audio; or (2) they may significantly alter the timbre and be used as an audible effect that also influences the dynamic range of the audio. I have already covered the dangers of using too much compression in chapter 3, so here I focus on the more advantageous ways compression gets used in mixing.

Dynamics for Volume Control

Controlling the volume through the use of compression is standard practice on many elements in a typical popular music mix in all genres. There are often a large number of instruments and voices in many popular music tracks making it especially challenging to keep elements such as lead vocals, bass, and drums present throughout the mix. A reduction in the dynamic range through the use of compression allows the mixer to avoid having to turn up these elements relative to others in order to maintain their presence in the mix. Typical examples include lead vocals where the quiet words might get lost or the loud words stick out too far above the band. With compression, the vocal will remain more audible at all times and maintain a consistent and comfortable level in relationship to the band. Similarly, with the bass; we generally want the bass to be present at all times, without the loss of support that might happen if the level dips too far or the conflict with other elements if the level jumps too high.

Strategies for compression usually start with a single compressor set to a moderate ratio (between 2:1 and 5:1) and with the threshold set so that the loudest sounds achieve about 6 dB of compression (gain reduction). The type of compressor to be used and the setting of other parameters (attack, release, knee, etc.) will depend on the nature of the program material and the desired effect (more on this in chapter 6's review of processing different elements in your mix).

More pronounced compression might best be achieved by using two compressors in tandem. A typical strategy might be to compress peaks first and then level the output using a compressor that is reading the average level (RMS), or the opposite if more dramatic leveling is desired. Similarly, you may want to compress peaks during recording for both initial dynamics control and some overload protection, and then use an RMS style compressor during mixing. It is not uncommon to use as much as 15 dB (or more!) of total compression on a lead vocal, and this is best achieved in two stages rather than by pushing the threshold to such a dramatic extent with a single processor.

It has become increasingly common for extreme compression to be achieved through the use of traditional limiters and brickwall limiters. High-ratio compression produces more distortion and unnatural artifacts, but it is remarkable the extent to which contemporary processors can achieve extreme dynamics control and maintain reasonable transparency of sound. Extreme compression certainly places audio "in your face." This might be seen as a positive (lots of impact) or a negative (no relief). Whatever your aesthetic judgment, this kind of process suggests the next topic—dynamics for effect.

But first, listen to the following audio clips to compare the use of compression.

Artist: Mike Schermer CD: *Be Somebody* Track: "Corazon"
Audio Clip 4.13 A brief clip with no compression on the lead vocal.
Audio Clip 4.14 The same clip with moderate compression on the lead vocal.
Audio Clip 4.15 The same clip with extreme compression on the lead vocal.

Dynamics for Effect

Relatively extreme dynamics settings go beyond traditional volume control to produce very audible changes in the timbre of sound. The most common and obvious of these is the effect of a lot of compression on drums, and I will cover the specifics of that in chapter 6 on mixing drums.

To understand how compression and limiting can create very audible effects, you might consider a rubber ball. If you compress a rubber ball, you are concentrating the energy of that ball into a small space. A highly compressed rubber ball will bounce with much greater energy than a ball with the same mass but greater volume. Similarly, compression of the dynamic range of a sound has concentrated the sonic energy. This explains the kind of explosive drum sounds that are produced with large amounts of compression.

Even small degrees of compression concentrate the energy in ways that give audio more immediate impact—a more "in your face" quality. Combined with the advantages of a more consistent presence in the crowded environment typical of so many popular music mixes, compression becomes both very appealing and a virtual necessity. The unfortunate result has been too many cases of over-compression, where expressive musical dynamics lose out to the desire for the immediate impact created by excessive compression.

Parallel Compression

A popular strategy for gaining some of the advantages of aggressive compression without the excessive loss of musical dynamics is parallel compression. Compressing in parallel means using two "parallel" tracks of the exact same audio in order to compress one of the tracks and not the other. You can then balance the compressed signal with the uncompressed signal to create a blend. Or, if your compressor plug-in has a wet/dry control as is increasingly common with new compressor plug-ins, you can balance the uncompressed signal (dry) with the compressed signal (wet) in order to implement parallel compression.

Parallel compression allows you to use extreme compression settings but to avoid the very unnatural effect of those extremes because you blend them with the uncompressed (or even lightly compressed) signal to gain the advantages of extreme compression without the obvious side effects. If you use a very low threshold, so that you might be hitting 20 dB of compression or even more, you can use a low ratio (2:1 or less) and still have a highly compressed signal that, when mixed with the original signal, can greatly increase the presence, or "in your face" quality, of a track.

Typically you would want a fast attack and slow release to create even compression and to avoid some of the unnatural pumping caused by the return of level after compression. Higher ratios (with low thresholds) will produce even more dramatic effects along with the heavy pumping caused by the return of the uncompressed level. It will also start to produce distortion (which may or may not be desirable). Parallel compression used in this way gives a great degree of fine control over the effects of compression.

If you EQ the signal going into the compressor channel, you can use the compressed signal to emphasize certain frequencies. For example, if you feel the original sound is a little thin, a little sibilant, and/or overly bright, you can low-pass the signal feeding the compressor and can get a warm and rich sound without much high-frequency information, but with the increased presence provided by the compression. You can combine as much of that with the original signal as you want, and then feed that back into the original sound—adding body, warmth, and presence to the original signal.

Because of the latency (delay) caused by plug-ins, it's important that you either employ delay compensation or, if that isn't available to you, use all the same plug-ins on both tracks, bypassing the compressor on the uncompressed track, in order to keep the two tracks phase aligned (plug-ins generate the same latency in bypass mode as they do when they are in operation).

The Individual versus Cumulative Effect of Dynamics in Mixing

Good mixing requires that attention be paid to both the individual and the cumulative effects of dynamics processing. It is here that compression for level control and compression for effect may overlap as subtle compression on many individual elements, on subgroups, and on the stereo buss can combine to produce a very audible overall effect; see diagram 4.1. Even on mixes where there isn't any element getting a heavy dose of compression for effect, the cumulative effect might well be very audible; see diagram 4.2.

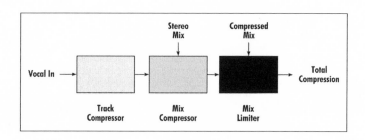

DIAGRAM 4.1

The chain of processors in a typical mix that combine to create the cumulative effect of compression and limiting.

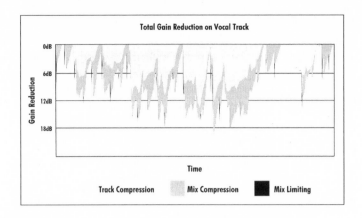

DIAGRAM 4.2

The cumulative gain reduction of compressing and limiting in mixing.

Check out this audio clip and see the section later on stereo buss processing.

Artist: Claudette King CD: *We're Onto Something* Track: "Can I Walk You to Your Car?"

Audio Clip 4.16 A brief clip of a final mix.

Audio Clip 4.17 The same clip with all the compression removed.

CREATIVE TIP

Finding your aesthetic perspective

From an aesthetic point of view, the cumulative effect of compression might be considered the element that binds all the pieces together, that makes the track "gel" and "sound like a record," as opposed to a less "finished" demo. It does this at the expense of a certain rawness, a "natural" quality, and a broader musical expressiveness that are a result of musical dynamics. The trade-off between impact and expression when using compression reflects the aesthetic balance that recordists wrestle with in creative mixing.

Like many recordists, I mix in a variety of genres, and I find that some artists respond very negatively to the cumulative effects of compression and some very positively. Typically this is genre-based—roots musicians and chamber musicians may dislike the cumulative effects of compression while contemporary pop, rock, and hip-hop musicians may love it. On the other hand, you may discover the opposite to be true. It would be very rare for me to mix anything without any compression—I think it's an almost essential element in transforming a live music environment into a recorded environment—but the extent of compression represents a critical aesthetic choice.

Dynamic EQs

De-essers and multi-band compressors—sometimes referred to as "dynamic EQs"—are devices that use compression technology to produce EQ-type effects.

This is also called "frequency conscious compression," and that is a good description of how they work. They read frequency bands and use those frequencies to trigger gain reduction. De-essers are the most common dynamic EQ processor, but multi-band compressors have become more widely available as plug-in software, and they can be a powerful alternative to traditional EQ.

De-essers

A de-esser typically just reads very high frequencies, as these are the most prominent in sibilance, and it uses these to compress "esses" and other highly sibilant sounds. Because sibilance contains so much more high-frequency information than any other sound produced by the voice, when it is exaggerated by using a side chain EQ it is relatively easy to trigger compression only on sibilant sounds. *Side chain* refers to a signal path that is used to trigger an effect (in this case, compression) while the original signal is what gets processed and output by the compressor.

Many compressors have the capability to work as de-essers by providing side-chain access, and some provide side-chain EQ as well. Dedicated de-essers tend to provide ease of operation and they may offer more flexibility, such as the ability to split the program material so the compression will only affect the higher frequencies.

Of course, de-essers work on "ess" sounds but other common sounds are equally likely to be affected, such as "shh" and "th," as well as some hard consonants depending on the particular recording. Generally if you feel that the vocal needs de-essing you will welcome the operation on all sounds with a lot of high frequencies, but that isn't always the case. An alternative, though more cumbersome, means of dealing with excessive sibilance is to turn down the offending sounds using automation. Because we can use graphic automation control to select very small pieces of audio very accurately, it is possible to accomplish the same basic results as de-essing with much greater control over each incident, although a much greater amount of time is needed to complete the task. See section 5.7 for more details and a screenshot of manual de-essing.

De-essing can also be used for taming the incidence of excessive high frequencies on instruments other than vocals and on entire mixes. Horn tracks such as sax or trumpet may be candidates for de-essing, and you could use it to reduce the attack on a kick drum track. To be effective, de-essing full mixes usually requires a dedicated de-esser that can split the mix so that the de-esser has an easier time operating only on the upper frequencies.

Multi-band Compressors

A multi-band compressor is a processor that has never found a proper name. It is more accurately described as a "dynamic EQ," as it changes the frequency balance of the sound source—similarly to the effect of a multi-band EQ. The difference is that the multi-band compressor alters each frequency by compressing

97

(dipping) or expanding (boosting) frequencies based on their relationship to a user-defined threshold, whereas EQs act on each frequency band consistently over the entire program material. Because multi-band compressors typically compress, expand, and/or limit, they are sometime labeled as a "multi-band parametric processor," but that could easily be a long name for an EQ and it is the compression/expansion model that is central to the operation of the processor, despite the fact that the effect is more akin to an EQ.

Whatever you call them, more to the point is what they might be used for. The ability to EQ based on dynamics allows you to make frequency adjustments in cases where the frequencies are being altered in a way that corresponds to dynamic changes. This is not unusual. Singers' voices tend to increase in high-frequency content as they get louder, as do many instruments where the sound is created by breath (such as brass and woodwinds). In many cases this is not a problem—it may even be a desirable quality—but sometimes you may want to change the frequency content only during louder (or softer) passages.

If you feel that the singer's voice becomes overly harsh at louder volumes but sounds well balanced the rest of the time, you may want to do some dynamic EQ'ing. By compressing the high frequencies above a certain threshold you can soften the high end of the voice when it's loud without making it sound duller when it is not so loud. You would set the frequency and the threshold accordingly—reducing frequencies in the 2 to 4 kHz range above a threshold that reflects the onset of the hard-sounding vocal production (see screenshot 4.12).

Conversely you might feel that a bass part has a nice rich sound when it's played more quietly but that when it's loud it becomes a bit thin. You don't want to add low-frequency EQ because it will make the quiet passages sound too

SCREENSHOT 4.12

A multi-band dynamic processor set to compress (dip) frequencies in the 2–4 kHz range that go over the threshold.

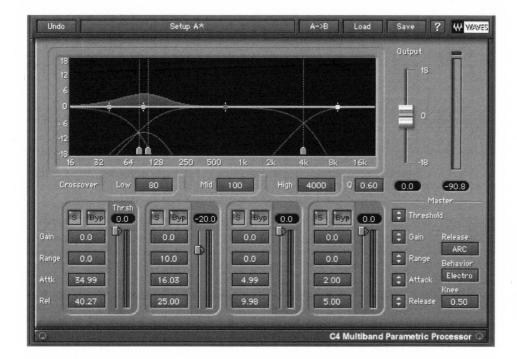

SCREENSHOT 4.13

A multi-band dynamic processor set to expand (boost) frequencies in the 80–100 Hz range that go over the threshold.

boomy, so you use dynamic expansion to add bottom to the louder passages—elements over the threshold are expanded (have increased gain) in the low frequencies (perhaps 60 to 80 Hz) while quieter passages (below the threshold) pass through unchanged (see screenshot 4.13).

This kind of frequency conscious compression is also candidate for use in parallel compression, when the desire to blend in compression with the uncompressed signal is accompanied by a desire to shift the frequency content of the original sound. For example, adding the vocal with the high frequencies compressed on the loud passages can be used more subtly if blended with the unprocessed vocal.

Using multi-band dynamic processing on the stereo buss is an option to solve certain problems as well, but typically this would be done in mastering, when there wasn't the option of returning to the mix stage. If you feel that the multi-band processor is needed on the stereo buss while mixing, you are probably better off trying to isolate the issue in a way that takes you back to the individual elements in the mix and address the problem there. (Read more on multi-band dynamics processing in mastering in chapter 11.)

WHAT NOT TO DO

Don't go looking for ways to use multi-band compression and expansion.
Multi-band dynamic EQ may sound appealing, and it certainly has its application, but it really is a specialty tool, used best in moderation and

only when the situation really demands it. Generally, traditional EQ will sound more natural. When you do hear something that suggests the use of the multi-band processor, spend some time fine-tuning the parameters— finding the right threshold and getting the frequency bandwidth set optimally will be crucial to achieving the desired results without creating unnatural sounding artifacts. Some multi-band processors allow you to set a maximum degree of compression (positive range) or expansion (negative range) so that you can lower the threshold and still avoid applying extreme levels of processing.

4.5 Processing: Effects

Signal processing effects can encompass a huge array of tools, but in this section I limit the discussion to the traditional effects of reverb and delay (still a very large category of processors). These are all time-based effects, which means they reproduce the effect of acoustic environments where sound is delayed as it travels in space and the delays are heard as an additional part of the sound. The cumulative effect of reverbs and delays produce a "delay pool"—the "environment" created by the mixer. Other kinds of processors that might fall into the "effects" category are covered in the section that follows. Again, the technical elements will be briefly reviewed first, but the focus here is on application. For more details on the basics of effects, see my previous book *The Art of Digital Audio Recording*.

From exceeding "dry" to exceedingly "wet," great mixes employ effects to create a soundstage that defines a musical world.

Reverbs and Delays

While reverbs and delays are the general categories that make up the world of traditional effects, the terminology is a bit confusing. *Reverbs* refers to reverberation, and that is the natural ambience that is created by the reflection of sound off surfaces in any environment. Those reflections create delayed versions of the original sound that combine to produce the kind of "cloud" of delays that we call reverb. *Delays*, on the other hand, refers to distinct individual repetitions of the original sound that are delayed by the natural environment and then reproduced. So, both reverbs and delays are created by delays! While reverbs for the most part attempt to simulate (or now they often sample) the effects of an actual environment, delays are "unnatural" repetitions of sound in that there is never a perfect delayed version of a sound in nature (a large rock quarry might come closest), yet they still give the ear the sense of an acoustic environment—the sense of space.

Reverbs

Reverb plug-in presets generally fall into the categories that define different kind of acoustic environments—concert halls, churches, auditoriums, theaters, nightclubs, rooms, bathrooms, closets, and so on (see screenshot 4.14). Reverb plug-ins also simulate or sample reverbs from earlier analog technologies, such as chambers, plates, and springs, as well as from digital reverbs that are (or were) available as stand-alone effects processors. Other reverb-type environments that aren't necessarily a part of the natural world, such as nonlinear reverbs or flanged reverbs, may also be available. Within each larger category there may be many specific kinds of spaces, such as large, medium, or small versions of each category of environment, as well as more specific spaces, such as kitchens, bedrooms, or bathrooms.

SCREENSHOT 4.14

Typical groups of reverb presets.

101

      There are two primary types of reverb plug-ins: digital reverbs and convolution reverbs. Digital reverbs use algorithms to create the reverb effect and convolution reverbs use impulse responses (samples) from recordings. Both can be highly realistic and both offer "unnatural" reverb-type effects as well (sampling reverbs can sample effects from algorithmic reverb processors to provide reverbs that don't exist in natural acoustic environments). The quality of the algorithms or the impulse response samples determines the quality of the reverb. There is a huge selection of reverb plug-ins to choose from, and having a couple of different options can give you a lot of flexibility and variety. One favorite sampling reverb and one algorithmic reverb may provide all you need for even the most complex mixes.

      There are three input/output configurations for implementing reverbs: mono in/mono out, mono in/stereo out, and stereo in/stereo out. Exploring these configurations, along with the more detailed possibilities with reverb panning, is an important part of the mix process.

      Mono in/mono out reverbs are handy when you want to place the reverb return directly behind the direct signal in the panning scheme (e.g., guitar panned 37 percent left and mono reverb return panned 37 percent left). You can also use these mono reverb returns to push the ambience farther to the edges of the panning spectrum (e.g., guitar panned 75 percent left and mono reverb return panned 100 percent left).

      The *mono in/stereo out* reverb configuration is the most common one used for applying reverb. This reflects the most typical listening experience in which a sound is coming from a single (mono) source (a voice, a guitar, a trumpet, etc.), but the sound interacts with the room and arrives at our two ears with slightly different ambient qualities (stereo). Reverbs in the mono in/stereo out configuration use a variety of tactics to alter the mono input to create a stereo reverb output that approximates the kind of variations our ears would likely hear in any given environment.

Reverb configurations that have stereo inputs use varying strategies for feeding those inputs to the reverberation algorithms and generating stereo returns. Many reverbs sum the inputs to mono at some stage in the processing, so that the return remains equal in both channels no matter what panning strategy is used to feed signal into the input. True stereo reverbs maintain the stereo position of the signal's input in the reverb's output. That means that if you feed a signal only to the left input of the reverb, then the reverb for that signal will be returned only on the left channel.

Stereo in/stereo out reverbs, or true stereo reverbs, can be very useful in mixes with multiple channels of one type of element. For example, if you have six tracks of background singers, you can feed them all to a stereo submix by using a stereo send to a stereo aux track, and then feed the stereo submix to a true stereo reverb. This will put the same reverb on all of the singers' voices while maintaining the panning position of each voice within the reverb return, helping to create a distinct position for each voice while blending them in the same reverb.

CREATIVE TIP

Avoid too many stereo output reverbs with hard panned returns.
Try to avoid too many instances of the most common configuration—mono in/stereo out, with the stereo outputs (returns) split hard left and right. This spreads the reverb return across the whole panning spectrum, and more than a couple reverbs in this configuration can blur a mix rather quickly. Rather than having the returns fully panned, you can use this configuration to spread the reverb a bit over the spectrum (e.g., source guitar track panned 60 percent left and the two reverb returns panned 40 percent left and 80 percent left). You might spread the return even farther but still avoid using the entire spectrum (e.g., source guitar track panned 35 percent left and the two reverb returns panned 70 percent left and 20 percent right).

Delays

Delays fall into three general categories: short, medium, and long delays. Medium and long delays simulate the effect of sound bouncing off of a far wall—

the kind of single repeat you might hear in a rock quarry. There may be multiple repeats if there is a wall behind you as well as in front of you, sending the sound back and forth between the two walls. The farther away the wall, the longer the delay. Although we may hear a very distinct "repeat echo" in natural environments, the delayed sound is never a "perfect" reproduction of the original, as is the case with an unaffected digital delay.

Originally, medium and long delays were created using a dedicated tape recorder—feeding the signal in and allowing the delay between the record head and the playback head to create a delay that could be fine-tuned by adjusting the tape speed. Delay plug-ins may have settings to simulate the effects of tape delay (loss of high-end especially) and other variations on a strict digital reproduction of the original sound.

Short delays really belong in a separate category from medium delays, long delays, and reverbs. Short delays thicken and enhance sounds in ways that become a part of the original sound, as opposed to any kind of discernable ambience as might be created by an acoustic environment. Doubling, chorusing, phasing, and flanging are all short delay effects that simulate or create various kinds of "thickening" of audio (as what happens with a choir of singers).

Delays can have the same three configurations as reverbs: mono in/mono out, mono in/stereo out, and stereo in/stereo out. Medium and long delays are most typically mono in/mono out, though there are plenty of stereo delays that play with different delay and panning effects. Short delays are very often stereo returns, especially modulating effects that take advantage of the panned stereo outputs to emphasize the movement created by modulation. I include more on this under specific application of delays below.

Effect Tactics

Following are some basic technical approaches to working with effects that give you proper control and flexibility, as well as allowing you to make critical judgments about the "effect of the effect." Following this is a section on creative strategies with effects. (More detailed information on use of effects on an instrument-by-instrument basis can be found in chapter 6.)

Send and Return Model

The most common routing tactic for implementing a reverb or delay plug-in is the send and return model—covered in much more detail in my previous book, *The Art of Digital Audio Recording*. Using auxiliary (aux) sends and aux returns provides maximum flexibility when dealing with effects. Even when you're only using the effect for one track (which is frequently the case for many mixers), the control over level and panning in the send and return model has great advantages over inserting the effect directly on the track and using the wet/dry control to set the level of effect. The exception is with short delays such as chorusing or flanging, which are often best inserted directly onto the track, creating an integrated sound rather than a distinct ambience.

Solo Isolate

In most cases, when you solo any individual element or group, you want to hear the effect as well as the source signal. In order to do that, without having to place the return channel in solo as well, you need to isolate the soloing function of the return channel from the muting that normally occurs on all unsoloed tracks. Put another way, the typical solo function (solo in place, or SIP) actually operates by muting all other tracks, but when you put a track in solo, you usually don't want the reverb or delay that you're using on that track to be muted—you want to hear the soloed sound along with its effect.

By isolating (or defeating) the normal muting action on all aux returns used for effects, you hear the effect along with the soloed track (without having to also place the aux return in solo). Of course, you can mute the aux return if you don't want to hear the effect. Even if you're sending multiple tracks to the same effect, when you put one of those tracks into solo you will only hear the effect on that individual track—the other tracks and their sends are muted by the soloing action.

Stop and Listen

Effects can be used very subtly, in which case they can be difficult to hear; or they may be used very aggressively, in which case it is easy to identify the addition of the effect to the sound. In any case, it can be difficult to hear the exact nature or extent of the effect when the sound is playing, even when soloed, because the effect (reverb or delay) is often obscured by each subsequent sound. To better hear what your reverb or delay actually sounds like, it is best to solo the effected track and then stop playback so that that you only hear the trailing effect. If the effect is a medium delay or short reverb, it can still be hard to hear, but once you get used to listening for the delayed signal, you will start to be able to judge the nature, quality, and extent of the effect by stopping the track and listening to the isolated effect. Short delays serve a different function (as discussed earlier) and will only be heard as a part of the original sound, not as an added ambience. The following audio clips illustrate the trailing ambience.

Artist: Sista Monica CD: *Can't Keep a Good Woman Down* Track: "Cookin' With Grease"

Audio Clip 4.18 A short clip with a long delay (500 ms) and 30 percent feedback, stopped to hear the trailing ambience.

Audio Clip 4.19 The same clip with a medium (slap) delay (125 ms) and no feedback, stopped to hear the trailing ambience.

Audio Clip 4.20 The same clip with a long reverb (2.2 seconds), stopped to hear the trailing ambience.

Audio Clip 4.21 The same clip with a short reverb (.8 seconds), stopped to hear the trailing ambience.

Effect Strategies

Here I discuss the creative use of reverbs and delays in general terms, discussing the various pros and cons of different types of these effects in the creative decision-making process. The focus here is on reverbs, or medium and long delays, as I cover short delays later in the chapter. There is also more detail on the creative use of reverbs and delays in chapter 6 on mixing individual elements.

Reverbs versus Delays

Whether to use reverbs or delays (or both) to add ambience to a sound is the starting decision for building an acoustic environment for your mix. Reverbs are more realistic and richer in enhancing timbres, but they also take up more space in the frequency range and can cause muddiness and blurring. You might think of medium and long delays as a kind of shorthand for communicating ambience to the listener: medium delays read as small ambiences and long delays read as large ones. However, delays are pretty stark; they don't even exist in a pure form in nature, and they can be distracting because they might call attention to themselves (what's that echo I'm hearing?).

We sometimes want to make elements in our mix "larger than life" or "more real than real," so we may combine reverbs and delays to create complex ambiences. Medium and long delays are typically used on sounds that have some kind of reverb effect as well—rarely are they used without any additional ambience. The reverb tends to soften the sound and also soften the stark quality of delays. Balancing the multiple effects is one of the most creative parts of mixing. The overall combination of reverbs and delays you use throughout a mix—the "delay pool"—creates the acoustic environment. For more detailed information on combining effects, see chapter 6 on mixing vocals (where the use of multiple effects is particularly common). There are also references to clips on the website so you can hear various effects combinations in action.

Tweaking Reverb Parameters

Reverb programs vary greatly in terms of the quantity of effects parameters available to the user. I have spent hours tweaking reverbs, and I have come to the conclusion that, for the most part, those hours are not very productive. Reverbs are tremendously complex, but large variations in parameters tend to produce unnatural effects (we usually want to our reverbs to sound relatively natural), and small variations in parameters are very difficult to hear once the reverb is blended into the entire mix. For this reason I recommend limited parameter tweaking (except when you are trying to create a truly unusual, and probably unrealistic, ambience effect). If you aren't happy with the reverb preset that you've chosen, try a different preset.

That said, there are a few reverb parameters that you definitely want to be familiar with and that can be an important part of tweaking the preset that you like into the exact ambience that you want. Once you've selected a basic reverb type that seems to fit your aesthetic goal, you might want to consider small alterations in the reverb time or length (sometimes referred to as "size"). This parameter controls the time that the "cloud" of delays lasts and that is determined by the size and degree of reflectivity of the surfaces of the acoustic environment being simulated or sampled. The longer the reverb time, the larger the environment and/or the greater the reflectivity of the surfaces.

I say that you might consider a small alteration because large alterations in the reverb time will likely defeat the purpose of the preset you've selected. If you take a large hall reverb that begins at 2.4 seconds and reduce it to 1 second, you probably should have started with a small hall. Reverb is made up of a set or early reflections, followed by a reverb tail. The number of repeats in the reverb tail is defined as the reverbs "density." Large adjustments to overall reverb time will put the early reflections and density out of sync with any natural acoustic environment. Although you may be able to tweak early reflections or the reverb tail (including density) separately, these are likely not the best use of your tweaking time—pick a new preset.

Some mixers like to "time" the length of the reverb to the tempo and I encourage this, although I have not found the time readout to be very helpful in "timing" your reverb. The time parameter is not a clear indication of timing (as it is with decays, which will be discussed next). This is because reverbs generally have a tail that decays into silence. The accepted standard is to calculate the reverb time by how long it takes for the reverb signal to drop 60 dB from the initial level of the reverb; but your perception of where the decay ends will change considerably depending how loud you're listening (listening louder will make the reverb sound like it's longer) and how dense the sonic environments is—dense environments will make the reverbs tail become inaudible faster. My advice on trying to time reverbs is to use your ear: make small adjustments in the overall length until you feel like the reverb is "breathing" with the track—that it is supporting the tempo of the pulse.

Besides overall time, pre-delay is the other parameter that you should be familiar with and you might want to consider tweaking. The pre-delay sets the amount of time (delay) before the onset of the reverb. This mimics the real-world quality of reverb because the initial (direct) sound must get to the closest reflective surfaces and return to the listener before any reverb is heard. Larger rooms or halls will have a longer pre-delay, and the pre-delay is one element that cues your brain regarding the size of the environment that you're in (or that you're hearing). You can trick the listener by placing a relatively long pre-delay

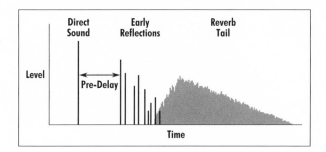

DIAGRAM 4.3

Reverberation impulse response.

(20 to 40 ms) on a short reverb, creating the illusion of a larger space without the long reverb tail; see diagram 4.3.

Reverberation is exceedingly complex, and some reverbs may offer a large number of additional parameters, including diffusion, decay, damping, envelope, and EQ options. In practice, most recordists pick reverbs based on the space or quality of the sound that is desired. From the preset, it may be desirable to adjust the time or size parameter and perhaps the pre-delay. Beyond that, while it can be interesting to hear the very subtle differences in small parameter changes, it can also consume a lot of time and may have negligible results. In chapter 6, I explore various reverb options in regards to specific instruments.

CREATIVE TIP

Short versus long reverbs
Choosing reverbs often starts with a basic decision between a short reverb and a long reverb. Short reverbs are typically about 1 second or shorter, and long reverbs are about 1.5 seconds or longer (in between is . . . in between). Most types of reverbs can be either short or long, whether they represent the acoustics of rooms, halls, churches, plates, or whatever. Reverbs create the sense of space in your mixes, so they are critically important, but they can cloud the sound and turn your mix into mush if you get carried away with them. Some good principles to keep in mind (and to violate when your aesthetic sees the opportunity) are:

1. *Don't use a long reverb when a short reverb will do—short reverbs give the sense of space without the long reverb tails that can clutter the soundscape.*
2. *Foreground elements might benefit from a longer reverb, but background elements will usually do better with short reverbs if any—though background parts that are mostly sustained notes might do well with a long reverb, giving them more of an atmospheric quality.*
3. *A short reverb combined with a small amount of a long reverb can give the sense of a very rich and spacious environment without the need for excessive long reverb.*

CREATIVE TIP

Warm versus bright reverbs
Another basic quality of reverbs is the extent to which they are either warm or bright. Short and long reverbs can be anywhere on this scale. Warm reverbs might include wood-paneled rooms, churches, and concert halls. In between warm and bright might be regular rooms, chambers, and auditoriums. Bright reverbs might include tiled rooms, plate, and spring reverb simulations. You might want the reverb to provide balance to the original sound, such as warm reverbs on bright female vocals, medium reverbs on electric guitars, and bright reverbs on warm male vocals. You may instead reinforce the fundamental quality of the sound by placing bright reverbs on female vocals, and so on.

Medium and Long Delays

There are two fundamental kinds of delay effects, and they are very different in the way they are used. Medium and long delays provide the kind of shortcut to ambience discussed above, and they are often used in combination with reverbs to create more complex environments. The most critical setting in using medium and long delays is the delay time. Delays are almost always much more effective if they are timed to the music. Because medium and long delays are creating their own rhythm, they can either reinforce the existing rhythm by being "in time" with the music, or they can disrupt the rhythm if they are out of time. While it is possible that you might want to use a delay to disrupt the pulse of the music, it would be an unusual choice.

Many delay plug-ins include settings that allow you to select your delay length based on musical time (note types) rather than clock time (milliseconds). In order to function properly, the file must be set to the correct tempo for the song—in BPMs (beats per minute). This is easy if the song was created to a click track or to loops that generate a consistent tempo—the plug-in will take the tempo set for the file and use that to provide delay options based on note types (quarter note, eighth note, etc.). If the music was not created to a click track, you will need to determine the tempo.

Most DAWs offer a "tap tempo" function that allows you to tap one of your keyboard keys in time to the music and the DAW provides a read-out of the tempo being tapped. Because tempo may fluctuate, you will need to take the tempo at various points and use some kind of average. In general you will want to set your tempo on the faster end of the tempo fluctuations because delays that are a little short of the exact tempo at any given moment will be less disruptive than delays that lag behind the beat. So see how to set the options for delay time, take a look at screenshot 4.15.

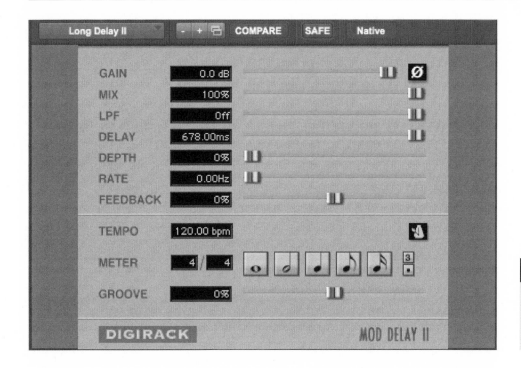

SCREENSHOT 4.15

A delay plug-in with both time and musical note options for setting the delay time.

The use of multiple repeats offers delays greater depth and suggests the kind of rock-quarry effect of sound bouncing back and forth between walls. The effect was originally simulated by feeding sound back into a tape recorder used to produce tape delay, so in the digital world the parameter that controls multiple repeats is usually called "feedback." Feedback can add depth and drama, but it can also blur the mix with trailing audio, so it should be used with care. Two or three repeats before the delayed audio is so low as to have no effect is usually sufficient unless a more obvious kind of effect is desired.

Besides delay time and feedback amount, delay plug-ins may have any number of additional parameter controls (see screenshots 4.16 and 4.17). Common options include multiple delays, high-frequency roll-off (simulates the dulling effect of repeated tape echo), other analog effects (harmonic distortion, which is also simulating tape echo), and ping-ponging (delays bouncing from left to right and back again, creating dramatic panning effects). They may also include parameter settings needed to create the short delay effects (modulation depth and rate) discussed below.

Short Delays

Short delays, typically between 1 and 50 milliseconds (ms), don't simulate the kind of environmental space that we associate with medium delays, long delays, and reverbs. Instead, short delays add a kind of thickening or doubling quality to sound. The easiest way to understand the larger universe of short-delay effects is to consider the most common one, and that is chorusing. Chorusing uses short delays to simulate the effect of choral singing. In choirs, the singers are never perfectly aligned with each other; neither are they perfectly in tune with each

110

SCREENSHOT 4.16

A more elaborate plug-in with parameters for short, medium, and long delay effects.

SCREENSHOT 4.17

Another elaborate delay plug-in with many parameter choices.

other. The variations in timing and pitch create the very pleasing choral effect (pleasing as long as the variations are reasonably close to each other). The digital simulation of the choral affect typically involves using one or more short delays in the 20 to 40 ms range that are also slightly shifted in pitch. This subtle pitch shifting is referred to as *modulation*.

To create modulation, a low-frequency oscillator (LFO) is used to oscillate (shift) the pitch of the incoming audio. The waveform of the LFO nudges the pitch in a regular pattern back and forth from sharp to flat. The depth setting controls the extent to which to which the pitch is shifted and the rate controls the speed that the pitch is shifted. Chorusing typically has a fairly slow rate, and some plug-ins allow you to time the rate to the music—a quarter note or eighth note rate would work well for a chorusing effect.

Phasing and flanging are similar to chorusing, but typically use shorter delay times. Definitions vary (there is no standard), but *phasing* is usually considered to use delay times in the 3 to 6 ms range and *flanging* in the 1 to 3 ms range. Both use modulation, often deeper and faster than with a typical chorusing effect, and sometimes with feedback to produce even less naturalistic sounds.

Many unusual sounds can be created using these kinds of delay plus modulation effects. Settings can vary widely in regard to delay times, modulation depth and speed, type of waveform used for the LFO, and feedback, producing a wide variety of effects. Other controls, such as phase reversal, EQ, filters, and multiple delay lines, can increase the variety of these modulating effects.

Doubling uses one or more short delays without any modulation but with a subtle and consistent pitch shift. This can thicken a sound without the regular cycling that is created by modulation. Doubling has a less obvious effect than modulating effects like chorusing, but it still has a strictly regular and therefore somewhat artificial quality that is different from physical doubling (doubling done by physically playing or singing the same part two or more times). Doubling was made possible by development of the digital harmonizer effects box that introduced pitch shifting without changing the speed of the original audio, and now many plug-ins provide the capabilities of the original harmonizer.

A typical doubling effect might include two short delays (unequal settings between 10 and 30 ms—12 and 24 ms, for example) and each delay is pitch-shifted between 5 and 9 cents—one slightly sharp of the original note and one slightly flat (there are 100 cents in a semi-tone). You can run this return in stereo, panning the two delays hard left and right, or you can collapse the returns to soft left and right for a more subtle effect. To compare the effects of these adjustments, listen to the following audio clips.

> Artist: Sista Monica CD: *Can't Keep a Good Woman Down* Track: ▶
> "Cookin' With Grease"
> Audio Clip 4.22 A short clip with no short delay effect.
> Audio Clip 4.23 The same clip a typical chorusing effect.
> Audio Clip 4.24 The same clip with a typical flanging effect.
> Audio Clip 4.25 The same clip with a typical doubling effect.

CREATIVE TIP

Checking effects

Check all your effects in many modes. Stop the track with the element in solo to hear the isolated effect. If multiple delay and reverb effects are used on one track, stop the track in solo and listen to each isolate effect and then to each combination of effects together (e.g., the long reverb and the medium delay, the long reverb and the short reverb, the short reverb and the medium delay, and then all three effects—long and short reverb and medium delay). Then listen to each effect independently and in all the various combinations with the track playing with the rest of the music. Finally, listen to all the effects on all the tracks by stopping the track and listening to your full delay pool. This can be done very quickly once you get the hang of it, and you will develop an ear for hearing the subtle ways that effects combine to create the most effective ambience for your mix.

Delay and Reverb "Tricks"

Besides all the standard applications of delays and reverbs, there are more unusual applications of these effects that can be used in mixing. Many of these "tricks" are the kinds of effects that you might use in an isolated instance during a mix, requiring specialized automation techniques (covered in chapter 6). Following is a list of reverb and delay approaches and effects that you might want to explore. You'll need to check the parameter controls and/or presets on the plug-ins you have available for some of these to see if you have access to the effect described, although many of the effects here are accessible from any DAW or can be created on your own, as noted.

Reverb and delay "tricks"

- Put your effects send into the pre-fader position rather than the much more typical post-fader position. This allows you to use a "reverb only" or "delay only" effect by turning the direct sound fader down all the way. Available on any DAW.
- Try using a reverse reverb for a solo or vocal entrance as a dramatic sweeping effect. This is done by placing a reverb on the direct sound and then recording that reverb onto its own channel. Isolate the reverb on the word or sound you want use to precede that word or sound and then use the "reverse" processing effect available in most DAWS (reverses any sound—can be a cool effect on sounds and words as well as reverbs) and place the reversed reverb in front of the sound that was originally used to create the reverb.
- Try the chorused or flanged reverb setting on your reverb plug-in—or if that isn't available you can place a chorus or flange effect on the insert of your reverb return. Modulating reverbs can provide subtle or dramatic soundscapes that will seem otherworldly.
- Try long pre-delay times on short reverbs using a timed delay so it reinforces the rhythm of the music. This creates a cloud of delayed sound that follows abnormally far behind the direct signal. This can be very effective if used in conjunction with a traditional reverb that masks the entrance of the delayed reverb.

Used subtly this creates a large sense of space without having to use a lot of reverb; used in a more pronounced way this creates an eerie effect.

- Using a delay effect in an obvious way is common, such as the repetition of one word or line of a vocal for emphasis and to fill a space. This may be a single repeat or multiple delays (feedback). This is best created by automating the effect send, described in chapter 5.

- Some delay plug-ins provides multiple taps, meaning many separate delays that can be individually set for delay length, feedback, and panning. These can provide extreme thickening of sounds using short delays or strange clusters of repeats using medium and long delays.

- Some delays provide ping-ponging effects that bounce the delayed signal(s) back and forth in the panning spectrum. Typically you will want these ping-ponging delay effects to be timed to the music, and many plug-ins provide this as a parameter (selecting quarter notes or eighth notes or combinations of note lengths etc.). These can create very dramatic effects for the headphone/earpod listener.

- Delay-based plug-in often have a long list of presets, some of which are obvious, like Slap delay or Light chorus, but many can be merely suggestive of an effect or the simulation of an older piece of analog gear (like various guitar stomp boxes) or completely incomprehensible. The variations are endless, and while they can be fun to listen to, more often than not they are only useful in the occasional situation where a truly strange effect is desired. Here's some actual preset names taken from a variety of delay-based effects: Oil tanker, Circular, Flutter, Wow, Dirt, Sweeper, Fried metal, Underwater, Seasick, See live alien!, Raspberry sparkle, Mushroom therapy, HallucinoSpread, Mootron, Metal Ringer, Wobbly dirt.

Effects Panning

Panning of effects can be an important part of using them most effectively. When effects are inserted directly onto a track, the panning options may be limited—a mono effect inserted on a mono track will automatically be panned with the track. However, many effects, when inserted directly onto a track, will transform a mono track into a track with stereo output (e.g., a stereo chorus effect inserted on a mono guitar track). The default will put the output hard-panned left and right, but this may not be best for your mix.

Remember, just because you have a stereo output doesn't mean that the two channels should be hard panned. For example, if you put a stereo chorus on

113

a rhythm guitar track that was panned 85 percent to the right, you will probably want to pan the stereo output pretty hard right. You might pan the two channels 75 percent right and 100 percent right to keep the guitar pretty far on the right, while allowing the stereo quality of the chorus effect to still have some movement.

The send and return model offers more flexibility for panning effects. If you send a mono track to a mono effect, you have the option of panning that effect differently from the direct signal. For example, if you put a room reverb on a rhythm guitar that is panned 85 percent to the right, you might want to put the reverb return 100 percent to the right. It will still sound like it is coming from the guitar, but it will subtly nudge the overall guitar sound slightly more to the right, keeping it out of the way of other elements in your panning spectrum.

Stereo reverb and delay returns offer even more opportunity for creative use of effect panning. For example, if you have two rhythm guitars panned hard left and right, both feeding independent stereo reverbs, you might consider panning the left guitar's stereo reverb return with one side hard left and the other center and the right guitar's stereo reverb return with one side hard right and other center (see screenshot 4.18). This maintains their relative panning position but spreads the ambiance across the whole spectrum.

WHAT NOT TO DO

Don't collapse a stereo reverb into mono.
The stereo quality of both natural and simulated reverb is created by phase relationships. In the natural world that's because the same signal source is altered slightly and arriving with slightly different timing to your two ears; simulated and sampled reverbs share this quality. When heard separately (by your two ears), these phase anomalies create a pleasing stereo spread, but when collapsed into mono you get a considerable degree of phase cancellation from the slight variations in phase. If you want a mono or near mono reverb—often desirable for a mono track in a mix with a lot of elements—choose a mono in/mono out reverb; don't collapse a stereo reverb return.

4.6 Processing: What Else Is in the Box?

Beyond the standard class of effects—EQ, dynamics, reverb, and delay—lay a world of other processors, many unique to the digital world of DAWs. I discuss some of these by category, but it's not possible to include the whole world of new processors, in part because that world is growing almost daily. Here I consider distortion devices (including analog simulation), pitch and time "fixers," pitch and time enhancers, and spatial processors.

SCREENSHOT 4.18

Two rhythm guitars, hard-panned left/right with their ambiences spread across the panning spectrum.

Distortion Devices

Distortion—typically considered the enemy of recording—turns out to be highly desirable when it means particular types of distortion in particular situations. Two widely used processors involve two common kinds of distortion—the first is processors that simulate the harmonic distortion created by analog recording technology and the second is the distortion created by guitar amplifiers and overdriven speakers.

Analog Simulation

For a time, analog simulation plug-ins were the hottest area of signal processing development. There are now so many different versions of this technology as to be a world unto themselves. Analog simulation plug-ins run the gamut from single processing effects with no or very limited processor control, to complex plug-ins with many parameter and preset options, to processors that simulate very specific analog gear (such as various tape recorders using various tape formulations and running at various speeds). It is sometimes debated as to whether these processors are a perfect reproduction of the effect of their analog antecedent (they aren't), but that really isn't the point; the question is (as it always is), What does it sound like? And do you like it?

Many standard plug-in processors (EQs, dynamics, reverbs, and delays) now have an "analog" parameter switch (usually just an on/off function), especially ones that emulate analog hardware processors. I've found these options to be generally very subtle and I tend to use them. The dedicated analog simulators tend to be more aggressive, although almost all of them have parameter controls that allow you to adjust the degree of processing so they can be used lightly or heavily (see screenshot 4.19).

Whether or not you use one of these simulators, and which one and to what extent, depends on the sound of each individual instrument and your goals for your overall mix. In general these processors apply a kind of "warming" or "thick-

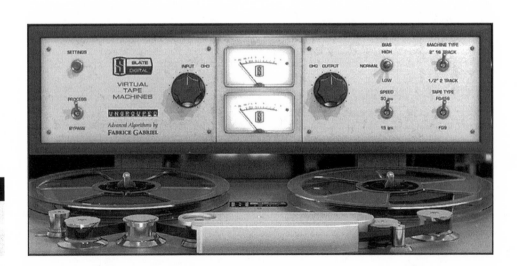

SCREENSHOT 4:19

An analog simulation plug-in (one of the tape recorder ones).

ening" that can be pleasing but can also be muddying. I have found that I often (but not always) like some of this effect on the overall mix (more on this in the next section, on the stereo buss). Too much of this processing on individual tracks is usually counterproductive—a little like putting the same EQ boost on everything.

WHAT NOT TO DO

Don't use analog simulation on everything all the time.
You might argue that "I like the sound of recordings made on analog tape machines" so it makes sense to put analog tape simulation on every track and on the stereo buss. There are two arguments against this practice. The first is that digital simulation of analog processing is not exactly the same as the effect of analog tape, so if your goal is to accurately reproduce the sound of analog tape you need to record on analog tape.

The second is that we used to spend considerable effort trying to mitigate the negative effects of analog tape (wow and flutter, noise floor, degree of distortion, etc.), so it is regressive to be introducing the elements that gave us problems when we had no choice. I love the analog simulation plug-ins, but I use them on a case-by-case basis, which generally results in less than 25 percent of the possible points of application. I love the pristine quality of digital as well!

Amp and Speaker Distortion

Another class of distortion-producing processors emulates the effect of over-driving guitar amplifiers and speakers. These plug-ins have been consistently improved in their capability to create realistic amp effects, and it has become fairly common to record electric guitar direct (with no amp) and to use an amp plug-in to create the guitar sound (see screenshot 4.20). The plug-ins usually allow various combinations of amps and speakers modeled on old and new hardware models, including both tube and solid-state designs. Amp modeling plug-ins have also found to be useful on elements other than guitar, including vocals, harmonica, keyboards (both analog and digital), and virtually any sound where distortion might be desirable.

Lo-Fi Aesthetic

There is a whole subgenre of pop known as lo-fi, and it crosses many genre boundaries. The lo-fi aesthetic embraces the use of older and cheaper instruments and technologies to capture sound—cheap guitars, amps, keyboards, microphones, and so on. Achieving lo-fi effects in mixing might include intentional lowering of fidelity through techniques such as bit reduction, sample rate reduction, and

SCREENSHOT 4:20

A guitar amp simulation plug-in.

saturation. Lo-fi effects and approaches may also be used for effects on particular elements in any genre of music, without necessarily ascribing to the broader lo-fi aesthetic.

Pitch and Time "Fixers"

While it may well be debated as to whether pitch or time fixing is a part of the mixing process, virtually every mixer does a certain amount of it over the course of a typical mix. This is an area that needs to be explored with the artist and/or producer either before or during the mixing process. Some tracks have been heavily vetted for any pitch and time issues, and you may feel that there's absolutely no reason for any more. Some artists and/or producers may say that regardless of what you hear, they don't want any additional pitch or time fixing. Mostly I find that, when I inquire about this, the response is "go ahead and fix anything that sounds to you like it needs it," and that's what I do—up to a point.

Pitch and time fixing can add significant hours to a mix, and if you feel that it's needed, then budget concerns need to be a separate conversation. In any event, always keep the unfixed elements easily available (on alternate virtual tracks, playlists, takes or comps). If you are mixing your own work, I encourage you to do all the pitch and time fixing that you feel is needed before you start mixing. Fixing is a distraction from mixing.

Pitch Fixing

There are many pitch-fixing plug-in programs, though right now Auto-Tune and Melodyne are the most commonly used (using Auto-Tune as an effect is covered in the next section). There are generally two ways to use these processors—

in real time or off-line. Real-time processing adjusts pitch as the track plays, with the processor choosing the closest note to the one sung or played, though you can constrain the program to certain notes or scales so that only compatible notes will be chosen. The real-time option is certainly the simplest, and it can produce desirable results quite quickly and easily, but it can also be problematic—making incorrect note choices or glitching on difficult-to-read notes or passages. You can either correct the problem spots using the off-line technique described below so that they are not a problem in the real-time mode, or you can automate the bypass function and skip over the problems. There are a variety of settings that allow you to control the rate and depth of pitch correction, and these can be useful in setting the relative subtlety of the effect.

Off-line pitch correction allows you interact with the graphic interface that shows a read-out of the pitch information from the original audio. You can draw in the desired pitch relationships or use a variety of pre-programmed techniques for moving the original pitch (see screenshot 4.21). Off-line pitch correction allows for much more dramatic or much more subtle control over changes in pitch.

I prefer not to have to do any pitch correction while mixing, but if the desire is for real-time pitch correction, then it may fall to the mixer to implement (and troubleshoot, if need be). It is possible for the producer, artist, or engineer to run the audio through the processor and record the output for use in the mix, and this is preferable for the mixer if you can make it happen. If I have been encouraged to fix pitch, I will fix anything that sounds particular problematic to

SCREENSHOT 4:21

Graphic pitch fixing.

me, but try to keep that to a minimum. I refrain from more detail on pitch fixing here, since it would take a lengthy discussion to do justice to the subtleties of off-line pitch fixing, and I don't consider it to be in the mixer's domain. (On the other hand, I cover it briefly here because it is sometimes left to the mixer regardless.)

Rhythm Fixing

Much of what I just said about pitch fixing applies to rhythm fixing as well, although there is no dedicated plug-in that does rhythm fixing in real time, as there is for pitch (at least not yet). There are numerous programs that assist with off-line rhythm fixing, which I will not detail here. Suffice it to say that, while rhythm fixing is not a mix function, it is not uncommon for it to become part of the job of the mixer. As with pitch fixing, this is something you would want to consult with the artist and/or producer, but if you're working on your own, I encourage you to do any desired rhythm fixing prior to the mix stage. I try to limit rhythm fixing to the occasional moving of a note or phrase where there is an obvious and unintentional lack of rhythmic agreement.

Fixing rhythm can take the form of *quantizing*, which was developed with the use of MIDI recording where musical data is easily manipulated because it is only data, without the complexities of actual audio recordings. Quantizing places individual elements on a user-defined grid (typically small division of the beat such as a sixteenth note), but it also allows variations in placement including shifting elements very slightly earlier or later than the grid placement and using a "strength" parameter to move elements closer to the exact grid placement but not perfectly aligned to a metronomic beat structure. The strength parameter maintains the place of the beats relative accuracy (elements originally closer to their exact beat location remain closer and those further away keep the same relative relationship). Digital audio can now be quantized just as MIDI recordings were and there's software that helps you "slice" up your audio in a way to best allow for the use of quantizing (see screenshot 4.22).

Harmonic and Rhythmic "Enhancers"

As with "fixers," "enhancers" are not really in the domain of mixing, but they can end up there nonetheless. Using pitch shifting to create new harmonies is

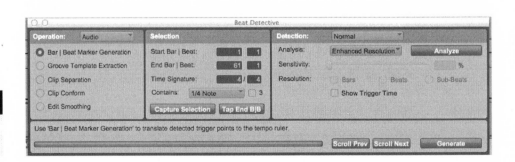

SCREENSHOT 4:22

A plug-in that assists with fixing rhythmic placement.

part of arranging, but it is sometimes introduced in the mix stage. There are programs that create complex harmonies, following the rules of key and scale, but I would never consider using these except in collaboration with the artist or producer. If you are introducing these on your own project I encourage you to do so before the mix stage.

The most common harmonic "enhancer" being used in popular music is the Auto-Tune effect. This involves pushing the pitch-fixing capabilities of the Auto-Tune plug-in into the realm of unnatural vocal effects—notes that sound part human and part electronic and that are not something a vocalist could produce on his or her own. Related effects have been used for some time, starting with the Vocorder and including excessive use of modulating delays such as flangers. Pushing sounds into the realm of the unnatural is not for everyone, but in the right circumstance it can be fun and effective. This so-called abuse of technology is really nothing more than creative interaction. One of the great sources of musical innovation is the exploration of unintended uses for any new capability.

There are not many rhythmic "enhancers" available as a real-time mixing tool, unless you include the various delay effects already discussed. It isn't possible to reposition elements in real time in any way that significantly alters their rhythmic position on the time line. You can apply dynamic alterations to elements that affect their rhythmic feel. This happens with compression and expansion, but it can also be done with automation, in either a regular pattern or random. These capabilities are explored in chapter 5 on advance automation techniques.

Spatial Processors

There is a category of plug-ins that might be grouped under the title "spatial processors" because they alter the perception of space in some way other than the typical reverb or delay effects already discussed. These might simulate a real-world phenomenon such as the Doppler effect, or they might strive to create new spatial relationships, such as stretching the panning spectrum beyond the perceived limit of hard left or right. My experience with these processors is that they have pretty limited applications in most mix environments.

The Doppler effect might be a cool special effect (or be useful for fx processing of real-life Doppler moments like the classic fire engine siren passing by), but it isn't going to be useful very often. Processors that claim to push sound beyond hard left or right are playing with phase relationships and with "tricking" the mind/ear into hearing beyond the normal spectrum. They can produce interesting and somewhat otherworldly effects, but by their very nature they sound unstable and may do as much to create a lack of focus as a broadened horizon. I see this as an area that may well provide some powerful and useful new effects in the future, but I'm not hearing much of interest to the mixer right now.

4.7 The Stereo Buss

The master fader channel, which controls the full mix (the stereo buss), is where the end-stage processing occurs on every mix. It is also represents the interface between mixing and mastering, because adjustments to the stereo program material are considered the mastering domain, but it also occupies the end stage of the mixing process. For a complete discussion of the two most common kinds of stereo buss dynamics processing—compression and brickwall limiting—see the Quick Guide, in chapter 3.

Beyond compression and brickwall limiting, I have found the most useful stereo buss processors to be the analog simulation plug-ins. As previously discussed, too much analog simulation on individual tracks can lead to a lack of definition—a kind of analog mud. However, on the stereo buss, the analog simulation can provide just the right amount of warmth, in the low-mids especially. I find that mixes that are already very warm and thick often do not seem to benefit from analog "distortion," but many mixes come to life with some tube- or tape-type distortion added at the stereo buss.

Other standard processors such as EQ and reverb may also have a place on your stereo buss. Using EQ on the master fader channel again steps right into the mastering domain, but the mix engineer's goal is to make the best-sounding mix possible. If you feel that buss EQ is enhancing your mix (in a way beyond what you can do with EQ on individual tracks), then it is perfectly legitimate to use. Individual EQ provides much finer control, but something like a very delicate smile EQ on the stereo buss may be the perfect finishing touch to your mix (or it might make it thinner and/or boomier and be working against your concept). Remember—ideally, the mastering engineer uses EQ only to balance songs with each other, not to make a mix sound "better." "Better" is the goal of the mix engineer, so everything should be in play.

Reverb or delay on the stereo buss is usually going to just muddy up your mix except on solo recordings, or possibly on recordings with very few elements. However, your concept just might include the unusual, and reverb on the stereo buss might be just the right thing. I remember one mix where I put the whole mix through a flanger; for that particular band and that particular song, it was the perfect effect. Breaking a few of the rules may produce the best results, but this is almost only possible when the most frequent best practices (or "rules") are generally and applied and well understood.

Chapter 5

Automation and Recall
Fine-Tuning

Automation and recall capabilities have been greatly expanded within the DAW environment. *Automation* refers to the ability to alter parameter settings in real time as a mix plays. *Recall* refers to the ability to remember all the settings in a mix. The ease with which a computer can handle data management has resulted in the ability to automate virtually every parameter in a mix. Automation and recall as technical processes and as primary sources of creative expression are both covered in this chapter. First the theories and practices behind both online and off-line automation are detailed, then the more practical application of those techniques is covered.

The extent of automation capability can be either a blessing (greatly increased creative options) or a curse (we can get lost in the endless number of possibilities). The ease, speed, and accuracy of the automation functions are only a blessing. Several timelines of the automation process for different kinds of mixes, from simple to complex, are described here to provide a complete picture of how automation is best used in various mixing situations. More advanced automation techniques for special effects, or to solve particular problems stemming from issues created by the initial recording, are also covered. Finally, the joys of the recall capabilities that come from working "in the box" are discussed: how complete, reliable, and very quick total recall has changed the mixing process.

CREATIVE TIP

Postpone automation as long as possible.
For all the joys and benefits of automation discussed in this chapter, using automation can distract you from more fundamental mix issues. By this I mean that once you start digging into small details like one vocal line (or word!) louder or quieter than another, you may stop listening for more basic, overall relationships. (Is the overall vocal loud enough? Are the guitars panned to best advantage?) Therefore, it is generally best to try to get your mix as far along as possible before starting to fine-tune relationships with automation. When you feel as if you just can't adjust any element any further without getting into automation so that you can control sections separately, then it's time to get the automation going.

That said, sometimes some automation moves need to be done early on because of some basic relationships (e.g., the chorus rhythm guitar needs to be quite a bit louder than the same rhythm track in the verse). In those cases, you might separate the parts into two tracks (e.g., one for the chorus rhythm guitar and one for the verse), so that you can fine-tune those levels without automation. (The most recent version of Pro Tools added a "clip gain" function that allows users to adjust levels of audio clips quickly and easily in the edit window. This permits automation-type level adjustments in certain instances more easily than with the automation system and leaves the primary output fader available for overall adjustments in level without using automation—a great new feature!)

5.1 Online versus Off-line Automation

Many of the capabilities of DAW automation will become clear as we explore the differences between online and off-line automation. *Online automation* refers to changes made in real time. That means that faders or rotary knobs or other controllers are moved as the music plays, and the automation system remembers whatever moves are made. This operates on the recording model; movements are "recorded" as they are made and then played back on subsequent replays. DAWs usually use the term "write" for record—writing automation data as controllers are moved and then "reads" them upon playback. The process often resembles recording, in that the automation function needs to be armed and the "write ready" mode is often represented by a flashing red light, just as with the "record ready" mode for audio recording. Online automation follows the model established by the high-end analog recording consoles with integrated computers for automation.

Off-line automation refers to changes made independent of playback (the music isn't playing), usually utilizing a graphic interface. Off-line automation functions similarly to the editing process and generally uses many of the audio editing tools in slightly altered fashion. Although the automation is controlled off-line, there can be immediate playback auditioning of the changes made. Some analog consoles have limited off-line functions, but the DAW has vastly expanded the capabilities of this approach to automation. Before delving into the specifics of these two systems, however, let's explore the pros and cons of each.

Online automation has the advantage of real-time input that allows the recordist to be responding to aural information, and it has a tactical component that means you can use the fine motor control in your finger for automation moves. Online automation has the disadvantages of being dependent on physical response time, which can be a problem when trying to do things such as raise the volume of one word in a continuous vocal line. In order to take advantage of the finger's motor control, online automation also requires a hardware interface for your DAW (control surface or mixer). Moving controllers with the mouse does not provide nearly enough fine control for most of the kinds of changes you would want to make during the automation process.

Off-line automation has the advantage of exceeding fine control over both the position and amount of controller changes—for example, raising the volume of one word in a vocal line by exactly 1.2 dB is very easy with off-line automation. Off-line automation also has the advantage of certain kinds of automation moves, such as time-based auto-panning, that are impossible using online automation. (I explore these in more detail in the section "Details of Off-line Automation," below). Off-line automation has the disadvantage of not having a physical component (finger movement) and being a completely different process for those used to working online.

I spent many years using the automation systems on SSL consoles, which had taken analog/digital online automation systems to new heights of functionality and user friendliness. Nonetheless, I now do all of my automation off-line in Pro Tools. The ability for precise control of parameters has proved to be a big advantage, even over the familiarity of the online model. Some recordists find that they prefer to control certain functions online—fades, for example—but most functions are faster and more accurately done off-line (and many are impossible online). Many recordists do not have a hardware interface for their DAW, and the constraints of mouse movement mean that they will naturally use off-line automation; but many of those with access to physical controllers are still tending toward off-line automation for most functions.

5.2 Details of Online Automation

The basic "write/read" functionality of online automation is enhanced in many ways, though the details vary among DAWs. In most systems you would begin with a write pass during which you would create some of the basic automation moves that you want to hear. Once you've made one basic "write" pass with online automation, you will probably work in one of various updating modes.

A typical update mode might be called "touch." In touch mode, the previous automation is read until you move ("touch") a fader or other controller and then new automation begins to be written. There may be two types of "touch" mode; in Pro Tools, touch mode retains all automation written after you release the controller you touched to begin rewriting, and "latch" mode erases all the automation past the point of the touch update. The choice of which of these to use depends on whether you are updating a section in the middle of some established automation (touch) or working across a timeline from beginning to end (latch).

Another common online automation mode is "trim," which updates already written automation. If you had a bunch of automation moves on the lead vocal of a song's chorus, for example, but you decided the whole thing needed to be a little louder, you would use the trim mode to increase the volume ("trim up") the entire section. The trim function would change the overall volume while retaining the previous automation moves.

SCREENSHOT 5.1

An automation menu.

Details and further functionality of online automation will vary in different DAWs and with different hardware controllers. If you have access to physical controllers, I recommend that you familiarize yourself with their use, but that you also explore off-line automation for increased automation accuracy and functionality. Screenshot 5.1 shows a typical online automation menu.

5.3 Details of Off-line Automation

Off-line automation, using a graphic interface, allows for very fine control of automation data and the opportunity for some unique automation effects. Off-line graphic automation uses a horizontal line to represent a scale of values. The higher the line on the graph, the greater the value of the parameter setting. For volume or gain, the horizontal line represents the fader setting: all the way up is the maximum fader level (+12 dB on many systems) and all the way down is −∞ dB (equivalent to off). Screenshot 5.2 shows some volume automation created by raising and lowering certain parts of a vocal take. The line represents volume, with greater volume (output fader position) indicated when the line is higher and less volume when lower. In the background you can still see the waveform of the vocal, allowing you to pinpoint the places that you wish to raise

SCREENSHOT 5.2

Volume automation on a vocal track.

or lower volume. Although the actual movement of the volume by raising or lowering the line on the graph is done off-line (the music or program material is not playing), you can immediately audition the results by having the curser placed just in front of the passage being automated and playing back the results immediately after making a change.

As mentioned previously, the big advantage to this kind of off-line automation control is the ability to easily select the exact portion of audio that you wish to control and then to make very precise changes in parameters. Most systems allow control to one-tenth of a dB (.1 dB increments) and this allows for very fine adjustments. After using this technique for a while you will begin to become familiar with the likely results from certain degrees of parameter changes. I have a good idea of what a 1 dB or 2 dB (or 1.5 dB!) change in volume is going to sound like, so on the first try I can often make exactly the right automation move for what I'm wanting to hear. In any event, I can easily revise a move by whatever increment I want in order to achieve the result I want. Some systems show both the new absolute level as you move a portion of the vertical line and the change in level. In screenshot 5.3 you can see the readout is showing the revised level (–15.5 dB) and the change in level created by the automation move (+1.5 dB) is shown in parenthesis. The change in level is preceded by a triangle, which is the Greek symbol for change (delta).

Level changes in auxiliary sends can also be created off-line, allowing for easy implementation of special effects, such as a repeat echo on one word within a vocal line. By accessing the effects send level in the graphic automation mode, you can take a send that is set to 0 dB (so no effect is heard) to whatever level you wish in order to create the special effect (see screenshot 5.4). Because the graphic representation of the program material waveform is visible in the background, it is easy to isolate the effect send on something like one word.

"Breakpoints" indicate the spots where the graphic line moves in position. In screenshots 5.2 to 5.4, all the movement between breakpoints created

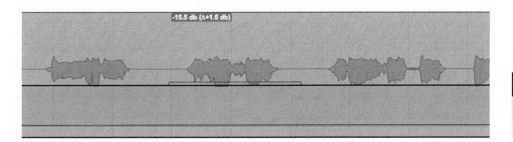

-15.5 db (Δ+1.5 db)

Vox

SCREENSHOT 5.3

Off-line automation readout.

SCREENSHOT 5.4

Automating a send so that one word goes to an effect.

127

by off-line editing is linear. Online automation will create nonlinear data, which is reflected in the graphic readout by multiple breakpoints. Many DAWs provide tools that allow you to draw nonlinear or free-hand style automation data off-line (see screenshot 5.5). In order to prevent problems with overtaxing the computer's CPU, you might be able to thin nonlinear automation data.

These same tools might be configured in various other graphic arrangements such as triangles or rectangles. The graphic shapes are typically used in one of the editing grid modes. Grids set in musical time—for example, a quarter-note or an eighth-note grid—allow for some great special effects done in musical time. The following screenshot shows two different panning effects—the first using a triangular shape to create smooth movements between hard right and hard left, and the second using a rectangular shape to jump from right to left and back again. This effect will be "in time" if it is created using a grid set to a subdivision of the tempo of the music.

Effects such as this that are timed to be in sync with the music reinforce the rhythm. If effects such as these don't conform to a subdivision of the beat, they can be very disruptive to the musical feel. The general effect is often referred to as "auto-panning" as it is the automatic and regular changes in panning position (see screenshot 5.6).

The following effect uses the same triangle-based automation editing tool on off-line volume rather than panning. When created in sync with an appropriate gird this creates a tremolo effect in musical time (tremolo is created through cyclical changes in volume). See screenshot 5.7.

SCREENSHOT 5.5

Nonlinear automation data as written, below as thinned.

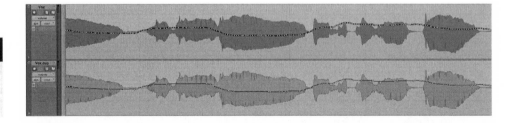

SCREENSHOT 5.6

Variations in auto-panning type effects using off-line panning automation.

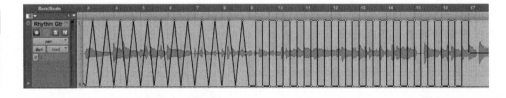

SCREENSHOT 5.7

A tremolo effect using off-line volume automation.

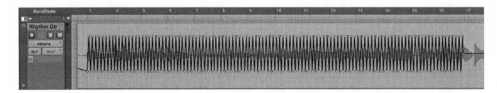

5.4 Timeline of Automation

As recommended in the beginning of this chapter, I try to avoid automation as long as possible, but you may have created some automation moves during recording, editing, or making rough mixes and you need to decide whether to erase those or integrate them into your final mix. Generally I integrate them, but recognizing that they are likely to change—or even be eliminated—as I put all my attention toward the mix.

Where there is already volume automation that you want to keep, it is good to remember the trick for "fooling" the automation. This simply means that you can use the output gain from one of your plug-ins to change the overall level and retain the automation moves already in place. Often compressors work well for this, but you can use almost any plug-in, and many DAWs have a dedicated "trim" plug-in for adjusting overall track volume as well.

Generally the progression of automation work proceeds from the macro to the micro. That is to say, I begin with large-scale moves to try to get things closer to where I want them. This may mean things like adjusting the rhythm guitar (or other rhythm instrument) to different levels in different sections—e.g., louder in the verses where there isn't much else playing and quieter in the choruses where one or more additional elements enter.

WHAT NOT TO DO

Don't nitpick automation until the very end.
Don't spend too much time in the early phases of automation trying to get things to be "just right," as your perspective is likely to change over time. You are may lose your perspective on the bigger picture—how are all the relative volumes?—once you start adjusting the level of one lick or one word. Try to keep your ear focused on big picture until you feel confident about how the mix is sitting before you start the nitpicking!

Once I'm happy with the general sound of each section of the music, I start the process of fine-tuning. This almost always begins with the lead vocal and can end up being very detailed. I focus my attention on the vocal level on a line-by-line basis, often adjusting lines, phrases, words, or syllables to provide greater consistency and intelligibility. I keep emotional content in mind—some words or phrases are meant to be louder or quieter than others. I'm not trying to make everything equal, but I want to keep the lead vocal present at all times. I find this is easiest to do by making several passes through, doing adjustments as I go, rather than trying to get each element where I want it in one or two passes.

I try to fine-tune the lead vocal first because it is central to the music experience, and most other elements will serve the music best by being in proper relationship to the lead vocal. Other elements that often need close attention are fills (such as a track of guitar or sax fills around the vocal) and vocal ad-libs. I often adjust the level of every fill or ad-lib separately to get it to sit just right in relation to the lead vocal.

I find that fills that are a part of more basic elements, such as drum and bass fills, or fills that are a part of a rhythm track, often sit just right without any adjustment. That's because a musician will typically add a bit of emphasis on a fill as part of the performance, and that is just what is needed. However, I listen for all these fills and will sometimes adjust them either up or down as I see fit.

Although I may make panning adjustments as part of the automation process, I am more likely to use extra tracks to reposition separate sections of a single performance—such as a guitar solo that was played in the middle of a rhythm track. This allows other adjustments (EQ, effects, etc.) as well as a change in panning. Where panning automation is particularly effective is in creating the kind of special effects described in the previous chapter on panning and in some of the combined automation effects covered in chapter 6, on mixing individual elements.

It is unusual for me to automate EQ, dynamics, and effects parameters except to produce special effects. If I feel a section needs different processing treatment, I usually split it out to a separate track. The most common exception is in regard to effects sends. I may well decide that the lead vocal on the chorus could do with more or less reverb, or perhaps a long delay that isn't there on the verse. In these cases I create and/or automate an effects send to add or remove an effect from one part of a performance (see the previous section on off-line automation for details).

As outlined in chapter 2's Quick Guide, revise, revise, revise is the essence of good mixing (but also check the What Not to Do on page 46 regarding excessive revisions that get you caught in an endless mixing cycle). The details of the process will be different for every mix, but if you work from the big picture on down to the details as systematically as possible, you will have the best chance for realizing your creative vision.

5.5 From Simple to Complex Mixes

The difference between a three-element mix and a mix of 23 (or more) elements has more to do with specifics than with general principles. *The process of fine-tuning from macro to micro, and the concepts of foreground and background and fits best versus sounds best, are still the guiding principles of mixing.* Nonetheless, the specifics do demand some very different considerations in the ultimate creation of the final mix.

Simple mixes, with relatively few elements, allow the mixer to focus on the richness of sonic elements and the complex soundscape often made from multiple effects on each element. The "sounds best" principle can often take the upper hand, as there aren't so many conflicts requiring a "fits best" approach. The question of perspective is naturally more concerned with foreground, as there isn't the need to force elements into the background in order for foreground elements to have sufficient space.

The automation for simple mixes may be considerably less intensive than for complex mixes. On one hand, it may be possible to allow a simple mix to sit relatively true to the way that it was originally played and have a satisfying result. On the other hand, subtle changes in the balance between even a small number of elements may be a part of an ongoing process that is continually refined over the course of many revisions. While it may be simpler to model the live experience with simple mixes, it should be remembered that they are still recordings, and as such they are to be judged on their success in fulfilling the vision for a recording that may or may not bear a very close relationship to how the music might sound in a live, performance context.

Complex mixes, with many more elements, are likely to require considerably greater intervention on the part of the mixer. Tracks with many elements almost always require that you focus your attention on how to fit elements together that often have many overlapping and potentially conflicting frequencies and timbres. The exceptions may be choral or orchestral recordings where the instruments and voices are intended to blend into a whole, as opposed to popular music constructions where elements need to have considerably more autonomy. *With complex mixes, we often find ourselves tilting toward the "fits best" approach* so that all the elements retain their own identity and are allowed to fulfill their functions without getting lost or blurred by the conflicts with other elements that share frequency content.

With complex mixes, the need to establish foreground and background elements is essential. Creation of various levels of interest drives not only panning and level decisions but also EQ, dynamics processing, and the addition of effects. Background elements need to support the foreground elements, but they also need to have their own integrity. (If you mute a background element and don't immediately notice the difference, it should either remain muted—you don't need it—or it needs to be rethought in turns of level, placement, and processing.) Subtle and thoughtful use of panning placement and EQ'ing approaches that are heavily influenced by the sound and positioning of the other elements are essential.

Automation on complex mixes is also likely to be considerably more involved than with simple mixes, and not just because there are more elements. Providing autonomy and identity for each element will probably mean a considerable amount of adjustment from section to section, and even within each section. Vocals are especially likely to warrant careful automation on a line-by-

131

line, and even word-by-word, basis in order to allow the vocal to remain clearly audible without having to raise it too far above all the supporting tracks. Automation will need to be used to establish the proper foreground and background perspective that is set by the creative concept you have imagined for your mix.

5.6 Fades

Every song needs to fade, even if it has a "natural" ending you will want to fade to digital silence at the appropriate point. What that appropriate point is, whether at the end of a traditional fade during a vamp (an ending with the music still playing) or at the end of a natural ending where the music has stopped and the ambience is fading, involves some creative decision making. How fast to fade down that final, ringing guitar? When to begin the fade on the vamp? How fast to move the fade down? How to choose the musical element to be heard at the bottom of the fade (and even considering placing an element there to add interest)? All these questions need to be answered and are usually at least initially created by the recordist. Sometimes the artist or producer will have an idea for how to construct the fade, but typically the engineer will create a fade and ask for feedback (or just wait to see if anybody has a comment).

There are many styles of fades, from the famous "Atlantic fade" that was featured on many early releases from that label and involved a very quick fade-out, to some very extended fades that can make it difficult to determine where the fade started. Whatever the fading concept is, the practical application of a fade is made much simpler by using automation on the stereo buss (or master) channel.

There are many possibilities for when to start, how fast to go, and when to end the fade, and these three considerations all interact. Even if it's just a fade of the final reverb tail on the final note of a natural ending, you will need to balance what sounds natural with keeping too much very low level audio that can make it sound like there's too much space between selections on the final master. On fades that interrupt the ongoing performance (of vamps and the like), you may discover that what you hear as the best start and the best end of the fade instead end up creating a fade that feels either too long or too short. A certain amount of experimentation is almost always needed to find the best fade for a song.

In practical terms, you may want to create the fade with either online or off-line automation. I have been surprised to discover that different material seems to respond better to different techniques. Frequently I find that a straight linear fade actually seems to work best, and this is most easily and accurately achieved using off-line automation. However, sometimes I find that a nonlinear fade with a consistent curve works best and sometimes I tweak the linear curve with additional linear or nonlinear components to create what sounds the best to me. If you have a control surface, you may find the tactile experience of on-line automation preferable for final fades. Screenshots 5.8 through 5.11 are a variety of final fade automations showing various approaches.

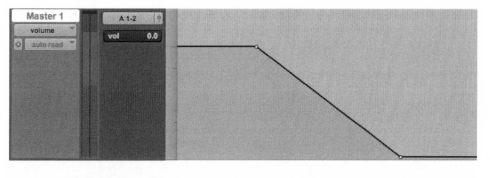

SCREENSHOT 5.8

A linear final fade.

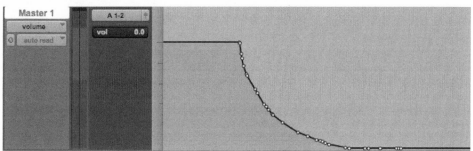

SCREENSHOT 5.9

A nonlinear final fade.

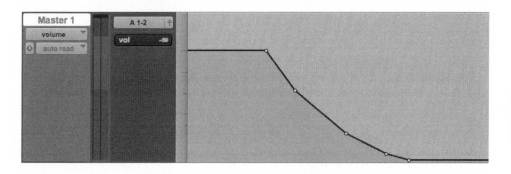

SCREENSHOT 5.10

A final fade with several linear steps.

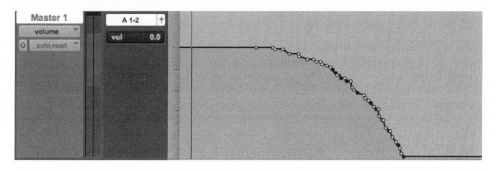

SCREENSHOT 5.11

A final fade created with online automation.

Sometimes I can't quite get satisfied with any of the fades I try, and I consider changing or adding elements. This may mean editing sections during the fade to get to a later section of the vamp that I want to hear but I don't want to have to wait until it happens to fade. It may mean just stealing a piece from later to put into the fade—it could be a vocal ad-lib or a piece of a solo, or even a backup vocal or horn section part. Fades can take on their own meaning because they are cueing an end to the song, so the rearranging of elements can add a sense of completeness to a fade or leave the listener feeling like the band was really taking off as they fade to silence (generally a good thing—leave the listener wanting more!).

5.7 Advanced Automation Techniques

Automation in DAWs allows access to virtually every parameter available in your mix. I've already talked about volume, panning, and aux. send automation, but there is also the capability of automating all the parameters in your plug-ins. Automating plug-in parameters offers a near endless number of possible real-time changes, so in most DAWs you need to make any plug-in parameter available for automation, rather than having it automatically available. This is an advantage, because many plug-ins have an enormous number of parameters, and if they were all automatically available it would clutter your workspace and tax your CPU.

There is the pitfall of making small adjustments to plug-in settings for parts of tracks using slightly altered EQ or effects parameters. These may be audible when the track is in solo, but may really be lost in the full mix. On one hand, lots of time can be taken making changes that don't really affect the listener's experience. On the other hand, subtle changes might combine to make subtle but meaningful differences.

Automation of plug-in parameters can be really useful for creating special effects, like the radical EQ'ing of a word or line in a vocal (perhaps the "telephone effect"), or the slow elongation of a reverb tail over the course of a long-held ad-lib note. I sometimes automate the threshold of my vocal compressor to accommodate a section where the vocal is delivered much more quietly, or much louder.

There are also volume automation techniques that can help make automation moves more natural sounding. Ramping changes in volume is often helpful in preventing transitions from sounding abrupt. Quick ramps may soften the effect of a loud consonant in a vocal, and slow ramps may create gentle dynamics changes in moving between sections (see screenshots 5.12 and 5.13).

Another volume automation technique that can be useful is what I call "manual de-essing." While a de-esser is often just the right tool to tame harsh sibilance, it doesn't always work exactly as you might want. Because of the ability to create volume automation moves in very small sections with extreme ac-

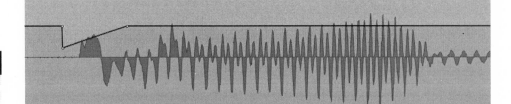

SCREENSHOT 5.12

A quick volume automation ramp on a hard consonant.

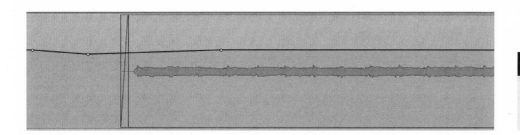

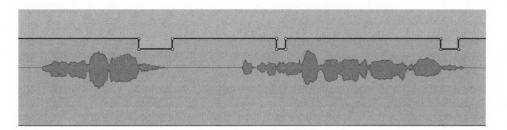

135

curacy by using off-line automation, you can do the same thing a de-esser does, but control the exact extent of volume reduction for each offending sibilance. This can be labor-intensive, so sometimes you can use a de-esser to take care of most of the sibilance issues, but use automation to alter the occurrences where the de-esser is not producing the most desirable results (see screenshot 5.14).

The depth of possibilities with automation provides wonderful creative opportunities, but they need to be balanced against maintaining a coherent vision of the overall sound being created. Sometimes mixes can be overworked to the point that the bigger picture is lost in the details, and then the mix doesn't hold together. *Sometimes simple mixes sound the best.*

5.8 Recall

As mentioned earlier, *recall* refers to the ability to recall all the parameters of a mix. This includes level setting, panning, plug-ins and their settings, automation, and anything else you have done to create your final mix. This used to be a very difficult, if not impossible, process when using analog equipment. Eventually elaborate computer-assisted analog consoles were developed that could remember the position of every fader and knob on the console and display those graphically. But recall was slow because an operator had to reset each parameter on the console by hand. In addition, someone (usually an assistant engineer) had to log all of the hardware outboard gear that was used—what the signal path was and the setting for each parameter on each piece of gear—and all of these had to be reset by hand. This was a long and tedious project, and as you might imagine with so many settings involved, not always successful.

While the debate over mixing "in the box" versus use of some gear outside of the DAW continues, in regard to recall, mixing in the box provides the ultimate in convenience and reliability. In the very short time it takes to open a session file, you can recall complete and perfectly accurate mixes. Many of us have come to rely on this capability, especially as remote mixing has become more common. *Remote mixing*—sometimes called "unattended" mixing—refers to working with clients in other locations by sending mixes over the Internet and taking feedback and making revisions after the client has had an opportunity to review the mix (see chapter 7). DAW recall has opened up the possibilities for these kinds of mixing strategies that rely on easy, accurate recall at the click of a mouse! Whether remote mixing or not, knowing that you can easily return to mixes to make even the smallest desired revision has changed the way we all work. (See more on recall in the Quick Guide, chapter 2.5).

Chapter 6

Mixing Piece by Piece

How to Approach
Individual Elements

This chapter surveys the primary instruments in popular music and the various approaches and techniques used to place them in a final mix. Specific approaches to individual instruments are balanced with an understanding of how they may interact with other instruments and how all elements may work together. Paying attention to the qualities of the recording of each instrument—what does it sound like before you start any of the processing and mixing—is also an important part of finding the best approach to placing the elements in a mix.

While it's not possible to cover every instrument or every mix situation, this chapter is comprehensive enough to give you some starting points for most instruments and most situations. While the principles here may be used in similar situations, an instrument may require very different approaches depending on the genre and desired aesthetic (e.g., mixing a set of vibes has a lot in common with mixing an acoustic piano, whereas mixing drums for a punk band is going to be very different from that for a traditional jazz band). The categories covered are drums and percussion, bass, guitar, keyboards, vocals, horns and strings.

WHAT NOT TO DO

Don't forget about the interaction between elements.
Mixing presents a classic "forest and the trees" problem in perspective. As you go through individual elements, it is most important to remember that

all elements interact in a mix. It is necessary to consider each element separately, but ultimately it is the interaction among them that forms your final mix. This is especially apparent with instruments that use multiple mics (the sound of the snare drum is a combination of all the drum tracks, not just the sound of the snare drum track). How is the EQ of the rhythm guitar affecting the way the lead vocal is EQ'd? How is the reverb on the organ affecting the clarity on the piano? Each tree in the forest must be tended to, but the overall health of the forest is your primary concern.

6.1 Drums and Percussion

The editor of a well-known recording magazine once told me that he could run an article on recording drums in every issue and the readers would be happy. Mixing drums is equally as challenging, and for many, just as mysterious. The key to mixing drums is the same as the key to recording them: it's recognizing that the drum set is actually many separate instruments that are extremely varied in frequency; they need to be dealt with as individual elements first, and then made to work together to form the whole. Of course, many of the specifics of the mixing of drums are going to depend on what the drums sounded like originally—how they were recorded—and what the goal of the mixer is (which is often influenced by the style of the music).

CREATIVE TIP

Use drum groups.
Before you get started with mixing drums, you will save time if you create groups for all related elements and for the entire set. On an elaborate drum recording with multiple tracks for kick and snare, your drum groups might consist of kick, snare, toms, overheads, and room, as well as the drum group that includes all of the tracks. You will need to be able to disable the groups in order to alter the level or panning of one specific element (your DAW should have a quick key for enabling/disabling groups); but most of the time you will want to be able to alter the level of (or solo or mute) each group as a unit.

Drum Panning

Generally, panning drums begins with replicating the panoramic spread of a typical drum set setup—although the first question is whether you are replicating from the drummer's perspective or the audience perspective. It doesn't matter which you do, as long as you're consistent (e.g., if you have stereo pairs for the overheads and/or room mics, the hi-hat mic needs to be panned consistent with the placement of the hi-hat in the those pairs, and of course those pairs need to be panned consistent with each other). If the hi-hat were placed on the left of the drummer, then it would appear left if applying the drummer's perspective and right if adopting the audience perspective.

Most people pan from the audience perspective, but because I was a drummer for so long it always sounds a little odd to me, so I pan from the drummer's perspective. Of course, everything is reversed if it's a left-handed drummer who has set up the drums in the mirror image of a right hander, but it's unlikely that the listener is going to know that (underscoring the fact that it really doesn't matter which perspective you use as long as you're consistent).

I do tend to use audience perspective if I'm mixing a concert that will have accompanying picture, so the drums sound in the same relationship as the camera perspective; but even then, sometimes the camera shoots from behind the drummer and the perspective is reversed—you can't win and you don't need to. Just settle on a perspective and make sure each element of the set is consistent with it.

Panning strategy also depends on how the drums were recorded—the more individual drum tracks, the more panning options you will have. Here's a panning strategy for a drum set that was recorded using 13 mics—a fairly typical configuration for contemporary studio drum recording. If you have fewer mics (very common), you would still likely pan the ones you do have in a manner the same or similar to this. This panning strategy is from the audience perspective. Comments regarding common variations follow this list.

Kick drum (inside the drum)	Center
Kick drum (outside the drum)	Center
Snare drum (top)	Center
Snare drum (bottom)	Center
Hi-hat	100% Right
Small rack tom	35% Right
Middle rack tom	35% Left
Floor tom	85% Left
Overhead left	100% Left
Overhead right	100% Right
Ride cymbal	60% Left
Room left	100% Left
Room right	100% Right

Note: The bass drum is more typically referred to as the "kick" in the studio.

There are endless possible variations on the above strategy, but this should serve as a starting point. A common variation is to pan the snare slightly left, maybe 10 percent. This is closer to reality for many drummers' setups, but be-

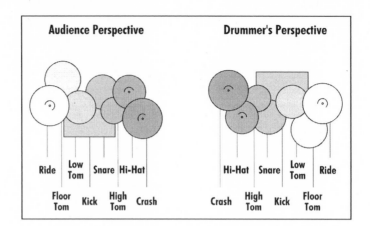

DIAGRAM 6.1

Diagram of a typical drum setup for a panning strategy

cause the snare occupies such a critical role in much of popular music, it might make your mix sound like it's leaning unnaturally if you pan the snare very much. The hi-hat mic supplements the hi-hat that is heard in the overhead and room mics, so its position really depends on its spread and volume in those stereo pairs.

It is fairly typical for me to use the individual hi-hat mic to push the hi-hat a bit farther in the direction of its natural position. I often find that by panning the hi-hat all the way hard left or right (depending on POV), it serves to move the sense of the hi-hat to a place that I like, because the overhead and room mics tend to leave the hi-hat more centered-sounding than need be. It is for this same reason (the relatively gentle panning placement created by overhead and room mics) that I tend to keep those pairs panned far left and right. Individual tom mics and ride cymbal mics also interact with the stereo pairs, so they can be used, in part, to push the panning in one direction or the other once the overhead and room mics are set. See diagram 6.1 for a typical setup.

Drum EQ

EQ'ing drums can dramatically alter the sound of the drum set. As with panning, there is considerable interaction among all the elements, so they must be EQ'd as individual pieces—but then often need adjusting as all the elements come into play. In what follows I describe the important considerations when EQ'ing, while avoiding judgments about what sounds "best," as different genres vary so greatly in drum sound aesthetics. Referencing favorite recordings that might be a good model for the mix you are working on is one of the best ways to getting assistance with drum EQ decisions.

Drums have two distinct parts to their sound: (1) the attack made as the stick or beater strikes the drum head, and (2) the resonance or sustain made by the vibrating top and bottom heads, as well as the interaction between the sounds of the two heads inside the drum (if the drum has two heads; sometimes the kick drum has had the back head removed, and some drummers even remove the bottom head of their tom-toms—nevertheless, there is still resonance within the drum shell with just one head). Cymbals have the same two elements—attack and sustain.

Kick Drum (inside the drum)

If you have two mics for the kick drum (an inside and an outside), this is the track that you will use to define the attack portion of the sound. I've found that boosting or dipping at two different frequencies (3K and 5K, for example, or 2.5K and 6K) gives the most control over shaping the exact sound and level of the attack element of the kick drum. Dipping mids may help clear space for other sounds but beware—a little bit goes a long way (meaning .5 or 1 dB may be plenty); you don't want to rob the kick of its heft.

   If you're using a second outside mic to provide most of the low end, you may want to dip lows on this track—if this is the only kick drum mic, you may want to add lows. Some mixers like to copy the kick drum onto another channel, and use one channel for shaping the attack and the other for shaping the low-frequency resonance.

   Shaping the low end of the kick must ultimately be done in conjunction with shaping the low end of the bass, so that they retain their distinct places in the frequency spectrum. Typically it works best for the kick to have more low-frequency presence in the prime low-frequency area (around 80 Hz) than the bass guitar.

Kick Drum (outside the drum)

If you have this element, it is typically used to supply some or most of the low-frequency content. You may want to low-pass this channel to clear it of high-frequency content. Shaping the low frequency will depend on the initial recording—you may either boost or dip the lows—but in any event you will want to shape the low end in conjunction with the bass part.

   You may only have an outside mic for your kick drum, and in that case you may use some high-frequency boosting to balance the attack with the low-frequency sustain. The high-frequency content of an outside mic may not reach much beyond 2 or 3 kHz, so your ability to create a kick drum sound that cuts through will be limited.

Snare Drum (top)

Typically, the top snare drum mic provides most or all of the direct sound of the snare drum. I've found EQ'ing snare drums to be an area that is most variable in approach, depending on the original sound of the drum and the desired result. Sometimes some pretty radical EQs have given me the best option in the mix—I've used as much as +6 to +9 dB in two different high-frequency bands. At other times I've felt the need to dip the highs to avoid too much "splat" from the drum. The low-frequency content of a snare drum is generally found centered

141

somewhere in the low-midrange (200–400 Hz) and can be boosted to add weight to the sound or dipped to keep a more "popping" kind of snare sound approach. If you are not sure where you're headed with the snare sound, reference someone else's mix that you feel is an appropriate model.

Snare Drum (bottom)

Typically, a bottom snare mic supplies a little extra snare sound (high, rattling part of the snare), if you feel like it needs it. When I've had a bottom snare drum channel, I've most often ended up not using it, but occasionally it provides some needed sizzle. If used, it will probably need some high-pass filtering to clean out the low end.

WHAT NOT TO DO

Don't neglect the phase relationship between the top and bottom snare mics.
The top and bottom snare mics are facing each other, so they are close to being completely out of phase; therefore, the bottom mic needs to be phase-reversed from the top snare mic. Reversing the phase is usually done in the recording so you don't need to do it during mixing; however, you'll definitely want to test the relationship to make sure the two mics are in phase.

To test for phase, take the two elements—top and bottom snare channels—and pan them hard left and right. Then dump the mix to mono; you need a mono summing control for this, which you may have on your outboard mixer, control surface, or interface. While in mono, switch the phase of the bottom mic in and out. Whichever setting provides the loudest output is the most in phase.

Hi-hat

The hi-hat mic is usually a supplement to the overhead mics, which typically include quite a bit of hi-hat. For this reason it needs to be set in conjunction with the overheads. The individual hi-hat channel can assist in providing a crisp sound to the hi-hat, since the overhead mics will inevitably have been some distance from the hi-hat and its sound will be more diffused. You might want to high-pass the hi-hat track to reduce low-frequency leakage from the kick and tom-toms, but take care not to rob the cymbals of the meat of their sound.

Sometimes the snare drum leakage in the hi-hat track will be loud enough so that you will need to pay attention to what the EQ is doing to the snare drum sound on the hi-hat channel as well. I've received tracks where the snare drum is louder than the hi-hat on the hi-hat channel—the result of poor mic placement—rendering the hi-hat channel essentially unusable.

Tom-Toms

Tom-toms share qualities with the kick drum in that they have two distinct elements to the sound—the attack and the resonance. A small amount of boost in the presence range (2–4 kHz) will help bring out the "stick," or the attack of the sound, and some low-mid boost (200–400 Hz) will increase the resonance. Depending on the consistency of the drummer, you may find that the sound of the toms can change pretty dramatically from one instance to another: the harder the drum is hit, the more transients or "stick" sound; also, where the drum is hit can made a large difference in sound. Tom hits that are weak or otherwise "different sounding" can be replaced with other instances where the drummer has hit the same drum. But remember that the sound is on other channels as well (overheads and room mics, especially), so you won't get the same overall tom sound unless you copy and paste all of the drum tracks for the replacement tom-tom hit.

Overheads

While the overhead mics are there primarily to capture the cymbals, they (of course) include the entire drum set. Before EQ'ing for the sound of the cymbals, you should listen to the sound of the other drums (especially the kick) and decide whether the sound is pleasing or problematic. You can diminish the amount of kick, snare, and toms in the overhead mics by EQ'ing out low frequencies or high-passing the track; but this should be done with caution, as the sustain of the cymbals contains some pretty low frequencies and you probably don't want to make them too thin. You might want to add some sizzle to the cymbals by boosting the highs—but a little goes a long way.

Ride Cymbal

If you have a separate channel for the ride cymbal, this can be an opportunity to increase the level and clarity of the ride cymbal without bringing up the crashes and hi-hat. As with the hi-hat, you can choose to exaggerate the EQ and panning of the single channel, and then blend it with the ride cymbal that is also present on the overhead mics to create your final ride cymbal sound.

Room Mics

Just because room mics were recorded doesn't mean that you have to use them—you need to like the sound of the room. Not all rooms sound good with drums in them, and of course, mic selection and placement affects what is captured as well. When I have nice-sounding room mics and feel that the ambience of the room suits the track, I often do not EQ the room mics at all, preferring to let them add the most natural element to the combined drum sound.

Drum Compression

In many popular music genres, it seems as if drums and compression were made for each other—the explosive drum sounds associated with a lot of popular music comes primarily from compression. It is not uncommon for drum mixes to use compression on each individual track, as well as on the overall drum set, via a stereo drum submaster channel (and the entire mix is probably compressed, too).

A common and useful tactic for drum compression, especially when fairly extreme compression effects are desired, is to use parallel compression. Parallel compression is the practice of duplicating some or all of your individual tracks and/or your drum sub, and compressing one of the tracks and not the other. You can then blend the compressed signal in with the uncompressed signal and balance them to achieve your final sound. In this way you can use extreme compression settings that create very powerful and explosive drum sounds, but you avoid being stuck with the somewhat unnatural nature of those sounds because you can blend them with the much more natural-sounding uncompressed tracks. Of course, the final result may not be very "natural" sounding, but that is not the point—the point is control, and parallel compression dramatically increases control over the compression effect. ("Natural" may or may not be the aesthetic you're going for.) Some compressor plug-ins have a "mix" control that allows you to mix the compressed and the uncompressed signals, providing parallel compression from a single track.

Here are some basic guidelines for using compression on drum sets:

- *Use slow attack times*: Drums have a lot of leading-edge transients created by the stick's striking the drum or cymbal. Fast attack times will significantly dull the sound of drums and cymbals.
- *For the most explosive drum sounds*: Use limiting (ratio of 20:1 or higher) on the overhead and/or room channels. You can also use limiting on the drum sub (entire drum set), though you're generally best off doing this with parallel compression so that you can mix in the limited drums and balance the heavily compressed signal.

VCA- and FET-style compressors will generally yield the most obvious effects on drums, but all styles of compressors can be used for either gentle or aggressive compression and limiting. The most famous drum compressors are probably the VCA compressors that are built into the channels of the classic SSL consoles, as well as the Quad Compressor available on the SSL stereo buss and the "Listen Mic" limiter that was used for talkback but was also available via the patch bay.

Drum compression can be dramatic, and it reached a peak in rock production in the 1970s and '80s. Over-compression might have been the single greatest cause for the return to the more naturalistic styles of roots rock.

The following audio clips offer examples of EQ, panning, and compression for percussion.

Artist: Rick Hardin CD: *Empty Train* Track: "Next Best Thing"

Audio Clip 6.1 Drum mix with EQ and panning but no compression.

Audio Clip 6.2 Same drum mix with compression on individual tracks.

Audio Clip 6.3 Same drum mix with compression on individual tracks and compression on the entire drum set (the drum sub).

Drum Effects

While drum effects might include reverb, delay, modulating effects, and so on, the most common drum effect is simple reverb. The most important reverb parameter is "length," or time; and because of the rhythmic and repetitive nature of most drum tracks, it is essential that the reverb be timed in such a way as to reinforce the rhythmic structure. Because timing depends on your perception of the reverb tail (the louder you're listening, the longer the reverb will seem), you need to set the timing by ear and at various volumes—making adjustments until the reverb seems to "breathe" best with the rhythm of the drums.

The genre and tempo of the music will dictate certain likely approaches. For example, alt rock, punk, and rap will probably be relatively dry (little or no reverb), whereas traditional rock, pop, and country will probably be wetter (more reverb—though the continuum will still run from a little to a lot). Slow tempos probably want more and longer reverb than faster tempos.

Drum reverbs may be halls, chambers, plates, rooms, or whatever other kind of simulation or sample (impulse response) you have available. Brighter reverbs, especially plates, have been favored on rock tracks, whereas a concert hall might sound best on a pop ballad. Nonlinear (gated) reverb was popular with disco tracks and '70s-style rock—it is reverb that doesn't conform to the linear decay properties of reverb in its natural environment. That is, rather than decaying, nonlinear reverb ends abruptly, often created by taking a long reverb algorithm or sample and stopping it before it has the chance to start to decay in volume. (The method was created by using noise gates on a standard reverb.) This lends the sense of a very big space without the long decay that can wash through tracks and create a muddying effect. Using a room reverb on drums creates a similar effect to nonlinear reverb—it has a natural decay but it is short enough to stay out of the way.

145

CREATIVE TIP

Use two reverbs for drums.
One tactic that I often use on drums is to have both a short reverb (typically a room) and a longer reverb (chamber, plate, or hall, depending on the music) available to combine. The short reverb might be between .5 and 1 second, and the long reverb between 1 and 2 seconds depending on the tempo of the song. I then blend the two reverbs on each individual drum to fit the song. An up-tempo song might use the short reverb only on kick and tom-toms with the snare getting both the short and long reverb. A mid-tempo tune might still only use the short reverb on the kick, but use short and long on snare and tom-toms. A ballad might use both reverbs on each of these elements. So, the type of reverb, the exact length of each, and the amount of each used on each element combine to create the drum ambience (as well as the natural ambience, especially from over-head and room mics, if they are used).

Long doubling (25–40 ms) and slap-type delays (125–175 ms) can work on drums, but they need to be quite subtle or they are likely to be disruptive (of course, disruptive can work sometimes, too). Modulating effects like flanging can work on drums, too (made famous by the drums in the '60s novelty song "Itchycoo Park"). Flanging reverbs, ping-ponging delays, long repeating echoes—the whole range of available effects are all possible drum-set effects when you're looking for the unusual.

Drum Mixing Concepts

There are endless drum concepts, from the most naturalistic to the most sur-real. Drums may sound thuddy or sharp, fat or snappy, bombastic or delicate. You may mix the hi-hat track relatively loud to keep the pulse prominent (often considered the "English pop" approach), or you may keep the cymbals very quiet but bright (on some recordings, Peter Gabriel famously didn't allow the drummer to play any cymbals). The drums may be in front of the mix (on some rock and rap mixes they are the loudest element, by far), or just chugging along way in the background (like some pop and country tracks). The drums might be huge, with tons of compression and lots of reverb(s), or they might be dry as a bone. There's no end to concepts for how to process and mix drums.

As I have noted elsewhere in this book, what is important is to *have a con-cept.* This might be your vision from the start, or it might come from referencing other mixes (or a combination of the two). It might require some experiment-ing (and some referencing of information in this book), but if you hear it in your head you should be able to create it (that's how you learn!)

WHAT NOT TO DO

Don't become too enamored of the illusive "analog" drum sound.

An enormous number and variety of analog modeling processors have come into the world of plug-ins. The processors attempt to recreate the kinds of distortion produced by analog recording and processing that many feel desirable, especially on drums. I've found that there is a fine line between the "fattening" effect of analog simulation and the "muddying" effect of too much "warmth" (the most common euphemism for analog modeling). Other kinds of distortion (using guitar amp simulations or using lo-fi techniques such as bit reduction) are also possible approaches to drum mixes. Experimentation is the key; I encourage a no-holds-barred approach to drum mixing (or any mixing, for that matter), but don't let the mystique of analog distort your critical listening chops!

CREATIVE TIP

Just because it was recorded doesn't mean you have to use it.

Sometimes, when you get to the mix stage, you find that your drum concept is best achieved without the use of the all the available drum tracks. I've found that I often abandon the "snare under" track, as the close sound of the snare rattle adds nothing to my overall snare sound. I might also abandon the second kick drum mic (outside the drum) because I don't like the quality of the "woof," or the hi-hat track because I have enough hi-hat at the level that I want to run the overhead tracks, or the room tracks because I don't think the sound of the room adds anything. On the other hand, I may take my entire drum mix from just the room mics. The point is simply to think of the sound you want, rather than how to find a way to use all the tracks that might have been recorded for the drums.

Drum Machines and Drum Loops

Of course, the drums in your mix might not come from the original recording of a drummer for the particular music you are mixing; they might have been generated by a drum machine or taken from samples of previous recordings (or drum machines or whatever). The part may be a programmed performance or a single one-bar loop that plays throughout (see screenshot 6.1).

Generally, drum tracks that come from these other sources are simple stereo tracks, with all the drums already mixed. This critically limits your options,

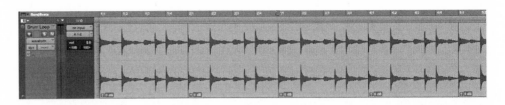

SCREENSHOT 6.1

A one-bar drum loop.

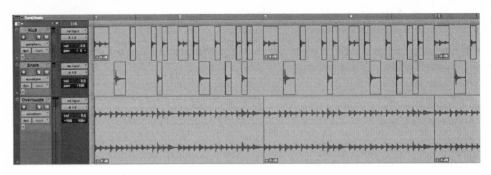

SCREENSHOT 6.2

A drum loop with the snare and kick on separate tracks. (Note: The hi-hat is played with both the snare drum and the kick drum, so if you do too much with EQ or effects you may create a very uneven hi-hat track.)

but it also usually means that the drums were chosen for their sound and the artist or producer isn't looking for them to be altered very much in the mix.

You can use EQ and dynamics, and even reverb or delay, on these stereo tracks, but the capabilities will be considerably reduced when compared to working with individual drum tracks. You might want to brighten or fatten with EQ, but a little will go a long way because all the elements are affected. It's similar with dynamics—and there's a strong likelihood that the track you are dealing with has already had compression added on the individual tracks, the stereo sum, or both.

Reverb and delay are particularly problematic because they will wash across all the elements (and some tracks may already have those effects added individually). More often than not, I find myself doing no processing at all to the stereo loops that are a part of the track I'm mixing. If anything, it's usually just a touch of EQ I add to rebalance things—a little bit of highs if I'm looking for a slightly brighter sound or a small boost in the lows for a bit more bottom on the kick drum.

If you are craving the ability to do more processing or mixing than is possible on the stereo drum track, it may be possible to split the elements out and place them on their own tracks for individual processing. This depends on what elements are playing together and whether there are overlapping sounds (like the ring of ride or crash cymbals). But it's not uncommon for something like the snare drum part to be pretty isolated and independent, so you could cut the snare from your loop track and place it on a separate track, allowing you to set the level and process the snare independently. There are any number of variations that may be accessible via chopping up your loops—something to keep in mind (see screenshot 6.2).

"Fixing" Drums: Timing, Layering, and Replacement

Altering drum tracks by either moving elements to deal with issues of timing, or layering or replacing drum sounds with samples to deal with drums that don't sound good (or how you want them to sound) falls into the gray area that exists between recording, editing, and mixing. One can argue that any of these practices should be part of the editing process, but every mixer will encounter circumstances where they either want to or are expected to do some fixing or sample enhancement as part of the mix process.

All of these practices are both aesthetically and technically challenging, but they can also make an enormous difference in the drum track in the mix. They can also be very time-consuming, so if you're getting paid by the hour for mixing, you will probably need to discuss this additional work with your client (especially if you're being paid a set amount for mixing).

Fixing matters of timing can vary from moving one slightly awkwardly placed snare drum (quick and easy, and probably not an issue with anyone) to retiming the entire drum take, which can take hours and wreak havoc with the timing of many other elements in the mix. It's generally advisable to keep this activity out of the mix session unless it's really just a very few fixes. (Note: to fix the timing of a snare drum beat, you must move all the drum tracks together, as the snare drum sound will likely leak into every drum mic.)

Layering samples along with existing drums can be very tedious work. Outside of timing issues, there is the fact that drum hits at different volumes and different places on the drum head will have different characteristics; this also means that a sample my sound good when layered with some hits and not with others. Replacing any drums presents similar challenges because of the leakage of the original drums into other mics, especially overhead and room mics.

There are many programs that can help with the timing part—search "drum replacement software"—with new and revised algorithms appearing frequently. These make layering or replacement much easier, but there will still typically be problems with some of the hits and/or some of the fills that require individual note manipulation.

Layering drums will maintain more of the original drum performance while still offering considerable flexibility with the sound. Replacing drums gives the greatest potential for recasting your drum sounds, but is more likely to produce mechanical-sounding tracks (although that could be a desirable result, depending on your creative vision). As mentioned earlier, every drum hit sounds different, depending on where on the head and how hard the drum is hit. There are drum sample packages that supply multiple variations for drum layering and replacement, but they can never reproduce the same variety as comes from a human performance (though, of course, it may be the excessive variety of the original performance that is the problem!)

Some people always layer or replace the kick and snare drums, and some never do. I take it on a case-by-case basis, but I have to be pretty unhappy with the original sounds to go down the layering/replacement road. I often make a few timing adjustments and a few replacements on drums (meaning I will do something like copy a good snare hit and place it over a weak one, not using outside samples), but I rarely go beyond that.

Percussion

The percussion family encompasses a wide variety of instruments, and their use presents a lot of options for mixing. A critical part of mixing percussion elements is a panning strategy, and just like full-mix concepts, you will want to have a panning concept for your various percussion instruments before you start tweaking each part.

You have to keep the drum set in mind when panning percussion—for example, a shaker or tambourine part will probably do best if panned on the opposite side of the hi-hat, which serves a related function. Here are some suggestions for mixing different types of percussion.

Drum-Based Percussion

Percussion such as congas, bongos, and timbales share a lot of the qualities of the drum set's tom-toms. The sound has two basic parts: the attack, created by striking with the hand or stick, and the resonance, created in the drum cavity. EQ can be used to sharpen the attack (high-frequency boost in the 8 to 10 kHz range will highlight the slapping fingers on bongos and congas), and low-mids can add heft to the resonance.

Compression will even the performance and, if used aggressively, can make the drums more explosive (and perhaps more unnatural), but you will want to use a slow attack to retain the transients. Remember: just because your congas or bongos are recorded in stereo (or possibly with three or more tracks, if it's a large conga setup), you don't need to split them wide in your mix. In fact, usually the congas and bongos will be more effective on one side or the other, though you might spread them a bit (e.g., 35 percent left for the low drum and 55 percent left for the higher drum). If the track is crowded and the drum percussion is pretty secondary, they can go harder left or right.

Hand-Based Percussion

Hand percussion can be divided into two basic types: high-pitched and clacking. High-pitched hand percussion includes tambourine, chimes, triangle, maracas, and bells. Clacking percussion includes cowbell, woodblock, castanets, guiro, and other percussion that is struck and that produces sharp clacking or scraping sounds. These instruments all have a lot of high-frequency transients, so you will probably want to use a slow attack if you are compressing them. I'd advise some caution when applying high-frequency EQ boost, as these can become annoyingly bright quite easily. Depending on how the percussion was recorded and how thick with elements the final mix is, you might consider some low-frequency dip (shelving) to thin the sound somewhat and a high-pass filter to clear out extraneous low frequencies.

Reverbs and delays can be effective on all percussion instruments, though high-pitched percussion is often best without additional ambiences (if you want reverb on your tambourine, for example, I'd opt for something warm and short, like a small hall, but a long reverb on the tambourine can evoke the '60s sound). The drum-based and the clacking percussion will respond well to all kinds and lengths of reverbs. In general, you'll want the reverb return to be panned with the instrument, as stereo returns that are split hard left and right will smear the percussion across the panning spectrum.

You can also use timed delays to reinforce the rhythm. I've found that a quarter-note delay with some feedback (three or so repeats) can be great on bongos or congas if panned right with the original signal and used very subtly—but effects like that will quickly create rhythmic confusion if they're too audible.

6.2 Bass

Electric Bass

Chapter 3 of this book, pointing to frequent problems with mixes, starts with a discussion of poor control over the low end. Getting the bass right in your mix might be the single most challenging aspect of mixing. This, in part, is because controlling bass in your monitoring environment is difficult, but it's also because bass frequencies occupy a less obvious place in our normal world of hearing/listening. Once you've done all you can to control and balance the bass frequencies in your mix room, you will want to reference your mixes (and other people's mixes, too) in other environments, paying special attention to the level and quality of the bass. It may take a while to learn how to gauge how the bass in your room is going to translate into other environments.

Bass guitar is often compressed during recording, but regardless of whether or not it was, it is very likely that you will still want to compress it during the mix. Bass is the foundation that most popular music rests on, and so you will want it to be very present—in fact, compression can be critical in keeping the bass consistently felt throughout your mix. A slow attack (50 to 75 ms) is essential to retain the attack of the instrument, but release times are less easily defined. If the part includes held notes, then a slow release will prevent pumping; but if it contains staccato parts, a fast release works best and a slow release can cause unwanted compression on notes that quickly follow one another.

Having a compressor with an auto release function is an advantage for bass compression, as it allows you to handle the varying demands of short and long notes. Typical compression ratios are from 2.5:1 to 4:1, but for bass I often opt for the higher ratios, and may even push the compressor to 6:1 or beyond if I feel like the bass dynamics really need to be tamed in order to remain present.

EQ'ing the bass can be pretty *counterintuitive*. For example, you'll often want to roll off the low end if you want to avoid a boomy, muddy track, and that might also help retain distinction between the bass and the kick drum. The bass and the kick drum occupy similar frequencies, so they need to be considered together in your mix. In fact, boosting the same frequencies in both bass and kick is a recipe for disaster. I find it usually works best for the kick to be more prominent in the very low frequencies (60–80 Hz), so I might roll off the bass there and boost the kick. Of course, sometimes the original bass recording is lacking in lows, so a boost around 100 or 125 Hz may be in order.

The upper register of the bass guitar often needs some boost in order to cut through the track. These higher frequencies (900 Hz–1.2 kHz) are really what allow us to "hear" the bass and define its rhythmic function. Fortunately the attack of the kick drum is typically higher (2–4 kHz), so there is room for both. When you listen to it in solo, your high-end boost on the bass might sound unnatural, but how it allows the bass to function in the track is what matters. See screenshot 6.3.

Most of the time the bass is panned dead center; any panning of the bass will make your mix sound a bit lopsided (though that may be a desired effect, at times). Typically, bass guitar will not have any additional reverb or delay, although some reverb on bass for a ballad might be lovely. Chorusing or flanging can be very effective on bass—a stereo chorus adds some spread across the panning spectrum and some movement and interest to long-held notes. Flanging

152

SCREENSHOT 6.3

Possible bass guitar EQ (recognizing that the original sound of the bass could conceivably dictate the exact opposite in terms of where the frequencies are boosted or dipped).

can serve to "toughen" up the bass sound, adding growl, and can be good on aggressive rock, rap, and R&B tracks, though it is "a sound" and might get old if used too frequently.

WHAT NOT TO DO

Don't immediately go for the low-end EQ boost on your bass guitar track.
There may be an inclination to boost the low end of your bass guitar track, and in solo it often sounds good. See the text for more detail, but know that with low frequencies and bass it may just be that less is more. In fact, less low-frequency may well allow you to have more bass presence in your mix.

153

Acoustic Bass

Most of the above is applicable for acoustic bass (string bass), as well. However, string bass might be more accommodating to reverb, and it's likely that you won't take quite as an aggressive approach to EQ as you might with bass guitar. Your approach to mixing acoustic bass will, of course, be affected by the musical environment and genre, and that may dictate a less invasive approach to processing. The instrument is also richer in timbre than an electric bass, and so you need to be more cautious about losing the richness with excessive processing, especially EQ.

There is often a mic recording of the bass as well as a direct input from some kind of pickup that the bassist uses. The two signals are likely to be quite different, with the mic channel providing the fullest and most realistic sound and the pickup providing a thinner but brighter sound that can be used to supplement the sound of the mic. Be sure to check the phase between the DI (direct input) and the mic—sometimes the DIs are wired backward, and you will need to flip the phase on one of them to keep them in phase.

6.3 Guitar

Guitars come in all shapes and sizes—acoustic and electric, nylon and steel string, and so on. They're played with picks, finger picks, fingers, slides (and sometimes, teeth!). They use a variety of pickups and internal mic systems, and get played through innumerable kinds of amplifiers and speakers. Mixing tactics will vary depending on all of these factors, but without getting bogged down in excessive details, let's cover the essentials regarding electric and acoustic guitar mixing.

Electric Guitar

Panning electric guitar tracks is usually pretty intuitive: rhythm tracks get panned to one side or the other (usually opposite some other rhythm track, like another guitar or piano) and lead guitar tracks usually are center panned. If there are two rhythm guitar tracks, don't be shy about panning them hard left and right. That often works best and leaves the most room in the panning spectrum for other things (unless they are just about the only elements, in which case you might want to collapse them in a bit—maybe 80 percent left and right).

Electric guitar tracks are one of those elements on which I generally use very little processing. Guitarists are notoriously picky about their sound, and what is captured is often what is wanted or needed for the track (guidelines for more interventionist approaches will follow). Guitar amplifiers and speakers cause the guitar sound to be naturally compressed, if the response of the pre-amplifier and the speaker cone is overdriven, as it often is. For this reason, I often *forgo any compression on electric guitar* unless it's a very clean setting and it sounds like it needs some help with level consistency. With EQ, I usually also use a pretty minimalist approach. Typical EQ on an electric guitar rhythm track might include adding 1 dB somewhere in the high-mid frequencies (between 2 and 4 kHz) and perhaps a little low-frequency shelving starting in the low-mids (between 200 and 400 Hz), to clear out the low end a bit. It's this low-mid and low-frequency dipping that are most crucial to clearing space for the bass; you don't want to rob the guitar of its heft, but the low end of the guitar is often a factor in muddying up the low frequencies and masking the bass track.

There is an increasingly popular technique for mixing electric guitars that involves recording them direct (no amplifier), and then creating their sound using one of the many amp and speaker simulation plug-ins. The advantage to this approach is that you have complete control over the sound in the mix stage. As many will argue, the disadvantage is that even the best simulation plug-in cannot compete with the "real thing" of amp and speaker distortion captured with a microphone. Because you don't necessarily have the guitar player there to consult about his or her sound, you might also fail to satisfy those guitarists obsessed with their sound (most of them!).

CREATIVE TIP

Create the eclectric guitar sound with a microphone and a DI track.
With track count rarely an issue anymore, it has become increasingly common to record a direct input (DI) track of electric guitar along with the traditional miked amp. This gives the mixer the flexibility of sticking with the original amp sound, creating a new guitar sound by using an amp and speaker simulation plug-in on the DI track, or blending the two. You

can also "re-amp" the direct sound, sending it out to an amp using one of the level-altering boxes that converts the recorded signal back to guitar level for use with an amplifier.

That said, I recently recorded a "guest" guitar track for a well-known guitarist that was to appear on another artist's CD. I did this at the guitarist's studio and ftp'd the tracks to the other artist's engineer (as is so common these days). The artist's engineer asked me if I would record a DI track as well as the amp track, and I declined. I know this guitarist is very particular about his sound, and he wouldn't want someone else giving him a "new" sound with an amp and speaker simulation plug-in.

The effects on electric guitars will depend on their place in the mix. Typically, rhythm guitars are most effective with a short reverb to give them some depth, without washing their sound across the mix or distancing them too far from the listener. I've found that a room reverb (.4–.7 sec) is often effective; but be sure to pan the reverb return to the same side as the guitar. (For more on effects use and panning, refer to chapter 4). Lead guitar treatment may well depend on the nature of the track and the genre of the music. On a rock ballad, your lead guitar may have room reverb, larger plate reverb (1.2–2 seconds), a doubling delay in stereo (e.g., 12 ms and 7 cents sharp on one side and 24 ms and 7 cents flat on the other), a slap-back delay (130 to 160 ms), and a longer repeating delay (300–600 ms, but in time with the music, of course). Other situations may require anything in between, meaning some of these effects and not others.

As crucial as which effect is used is how much of the effect to use. You can use all of these effects (two reverbs and three delays), and if you use them all very subtly, the lead guitar will still sound very present. If you use a lot of any one of them, you might find your lead guitar awash in an effect that draws the listener away from the sound. See screenshot 6.4 for an example of multiple effects.

Listen to the following audio clips for examples of guitar tracks with effects.

Artist: Laurie Morvan CD: *Fire it Up!* Track: "Lay Your Hands"
Audio Clip 6.4 Electric guitar lick with each effect individually (first dry then room, reverb, doubling, slap delay, long delay).
Audio Clip 6.5 The same guitar lick with all 5 effects in solo.
Audio Clip 6.6 The same guitar lick with all 5 effects in the track.

Acoustic Guitar

Acoustic guitars are very different instruments from their electric counterparts and their treatment in a mix is likely to require some different tactics. Panning tactics are not going to vary much, and the guidance on effects for electric guitars

	TL Space	IR-L	Doubler2	Slap Dly II	H-Delay

SENDS A-E	SENDS A-E	SENDS A-E	SENDS A-E	SENDS A-E	SENDS A-E
Bus 19-20					
Bus 21					
Bus 22					
Bus 23					
Bus 24					

I/O	I/O	I/O	I/O	I/O	I/O
no input	Bus 19-20	Bus 21	Bus 22	Bus 23	Bus 24
A 1-2	A 1-2	A 1-2	A 1-2	A 1-2	A 1-2

AUTO	AUTO	AUTO	AUTO	AUTO	AUTO
auto read	auto read	auto read	auto read	auto read	auto read

no group	no group	no group	no group	no group	no group

pan ▸ 0 ◂	◂100 100▸	pan ▸ 0 ◂	◂100 100▸	pan ▸ 0 ◂	pan ▸ 0 ◂

S M	S M	S M	S M	S M	S M

vol -2.7	vol -13.9	vol -17.1	vol -11.3	vol -19.2	vol -15.0
dyn ▸▸					
Ld Guitar	Gtr verb	Gtr Room	Gtr dblr	Gtr slap	Gtr delay

SCREENSHOT 6.4

A lead guitar track with 5 effects (room, reverb, doubling, slap delay, long delay).

can also be applied to acoustic guitar in an ensemble situation. However, approaches to EQ and compression may be quite different for acoustic guitars.

Acoustic guitars can have trouble competing with all of the aggressive sounds that are typical in a lot of popular music, and so they might require some pretty aggressive EQ in order to fit into your track. This often means a fair amount of high-frequency boost in order for them to cut through the track. If they were strummed using much of the lower frequency strings, they might also

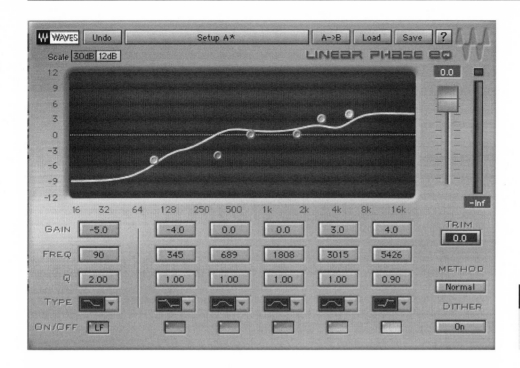

SCREENSHOT 6.5   157

Possible EQ for acoustic
guitar in a rock track.

want quite of bit of dipping in the low end to keep them out of the way of the bass and, in general, to prevent them from muddying the mix.

I've found acoustic guitar to be the element that most frequently requires a "fits best" approach that is quite far from a "sounds best" approach, which might be the case when you listen to that guitar in solo. Screenshot 6.5 shows an EQ curve I used for an acoustic guitar on a rock track. Then, check out the audio clip of before and after EQ in that track.

> Artist: Dave Murrant CD: *Goodbye Kiss* Track: "Snow Angel"
> Audio Clip 6.7 Acoustic guitar recording with no EQ.
> Audio Clip 6.8 The same acoustic guitar with the EQ shown in
>   screenshot 6.5.
> Audio Clip 6.9 The same acoustic guitar with the EQ, included in a
>   full mix of a rock track.

Unlike the electric guitar, which is typically compressed by the action of the amplifier and speaker, acoustic guitars often benefit from compression in order to help them sit comfortably in a track with many other elements. Depending on the situation, you can hit them hard if you want them to be very present while competing with a lot of other elements (for example, a 6:1 ratio with as much as 8 or 10 dB of compression on the loudest points). Or you can make them soft to allow them to maintain more dynamic range because they are less critical to the overall sound or there are less elements in the mix (for example, 2:1 with only a couple of dB of compression at the loudest points). In any case, because the sound of the guitar is created by striking the strings, you will probably want to use a slow attack (50–100 ms) in order to prevent dulling the sound (a fast attack compresses the leading-edge high-frequency transients).

Of course, acoustic guitars come in many varieties, including steel string, nylon string, 12-string, resonator, lap steel, Weisenborn, and so on, and they are all different. Many of them either come with or can be fitted with pickups (similar to those found on electric guitars), or built-in microphones, or body sensors—any of which turn the instrument into an acoustic-electric guitar hybrid (with varying results). Mixing strategies will vary depending on the genre of music, the nature of the part played, the sound of the recording, and the details of the mix. While the preceding information on acoustic guitars may serve as a starting point for any of these instruments, certain genres such as traditional folk will probably call for less processing, and certain instruments such as lap steel guitars, which are very bright to begin with, will probably not benefit from much, or any, high-frequency boosting.

Solo and Small Ensemble Guitar Mixes

Mixing is about what there *is* to mix, so when there are many fewer elements, the choices made on any given instrument might be very different from when that instrument is part of large ensemble. "Sounds best" may take precedence over "fits best" in most of these circumstances, but what sounds best is subjective. For acoustic guitars, the kind of aggressive processing that may be needed to fit the instrument into a heavily populated mix is probably out of place in a solo or very small ensemble mix. Also, effects such as long repeating delays that can create heroic-sounding electric guitar solos in a band context will probably seem gimmicky and obvious when exposed in a small setting.

The biggest help for solo and small ensemble mixing is multiple mic tracks (using great signal path and appropriate mic positioning). Having many sources to mix and balance will often provide the richest, most detailed mixes—and in these small environments, richness and detail can be emphasized in a way that isn't possible when many elements compete for space on the frequency spectrum.

6.4 Keyboards

Of course, "keyboard" instruments are now capable of creating just about any sound imaginable, thanks to sampling and advanced synthesizing technology. And I place the word *keyboard* in quotes here because so much of the world that was formerly housed in hardware keyboard synthesizers and samplers is now available in the "virtual instrument" world of software. For the most part, these sounds are still triggered by a keyboard, but it is also simple enough to trigger or program virtual instrument performances without any physical keyboard involved. Here, I organize the vast world of both physical and virtual keyboards as follows: acoustic keyboards (including piano, vibraphone, marimba, and others); traditional keyboards (including the Hammond B3 organ, and the Fender Rhodes and the Wurlitzer electronic pianos); synthesizers, samplers and keyboard roles (lead instrument, rhythm instrument or pad), and solo and small ensemble acoustic keyboard recordings. I don't differentiate between physical and virtual keyboards in this discussion, as their role in the mix is likely to be the same regardless of their source.

Acoustic Keyboards

Acoustic keyboards encompass a huge array of instruments, from piano, to harpsichord, to glockenspiel, and they play a variety of roles in different arrangements. In regard to panning, I find that despite the fact that the instruments often occupy a large part of the frequency spectrum and are usually recorded in stereo, I often do not pan the L/R keyboard recording hard left and hard right—it just takes up too much room in the stereo field and makes the instrument less focused in the mix. (Exceptions are covered in the "keyboard Role" section below.) I may spread the L/R instrument tracks across one side or the other, from fairly wide (for example, 5 percent left and 80 percent left, or 20 percent right and 100 percent right) to right on top of each other (both L/R set to 35 percent right, for example), depending on how many elements there are in the mix and the relative importance of the keyboard. I usually make the more centered track the low end of the keyboard and the one panned farther out from center the high end, to keep the low end focused in the center and the high end more clearly audible.

Screenshot 6.6 shows the panning I used on a recent jazz record with vibes (could be the same for acoustic piano). I used three tracks to record the vibes—left, right, and a center track created using a mic set a bit farther back from the instrument. I also show the guitar track panning, as it was the primary instrument that needed to be offset from the vibes in the panning spectrum. The guitar had two mics on the amp (a Royer 121 and a Shure 57).

EQ on acoustic keyboards will also vary depending on the role. The rich timbre of acoustic keyboards will suffer under too much EQ, so depending on the recording and context, a typical tactic might be to roll off a bit in the low end to keep things clear for other instruments and a small boost (usually no more than 1–2 dB) in the high-mid frequencies (2–5 kHz) to add a bit of presence. Crowded tracks in which the keyboard must fit may require more dramatic EQ, both in low-end roll-off and high-frequency boost. In solo, the instrument may sound pretty thin and overly bright, but that may work best in the cluttered context of some mixes.

Keyboard instruments are percussion instruments (they're struck by hands, sticks, mallets, or hammers), so they have significant leading-edge high-

SCREENSHOT 6.6

Panning for a 3-channel keyboard recording, set against a rhythm guitar.

frequency transients. This means that when using compression, you will probably want a slow attack (50–75 ms) to prevent excessive dulling of the sound of the instrument. The extent of compression will depend on the dynamic range of the performance, the number of elements in the mix (more elements usually suggests stronger compression so that each element remains present), and the genre (typically traditional folk, jazz, and classical music will be less compressed than other genres).

I find that the difference between how I might mix acoustic piano and how I might handle vibraphone (vibes) or marimba has much more to do with the context than with the instruments. These three instruments share so many qualities that they can be treated very similarly in whatever the context. One small difference is that the marimba lacks the sustain of the other two instruments, so you would likely use a shorter release time for compression.

Traditional Keyboards (B3, Rhodes, Wurlitzer)

The Hammond B3 organ, the Fender Rhodes piano, and the Wurlitzer piano are still used in a lot of music, and there are endless hardware and software synthesized and sampled versions of the original instruments. While mixing these instruments depends primarily on their role in the mix (see the next section), there are few things to keep in mind for each of these classic keyboards.

The B3 organ is closely associated with the sound of the Leslie rotating speaker that provides a Doppler kind of effect. If recorded (or synthesized or sampled) properly, the stereo effect of the Leslie speaker is very important, so I try to maintain hard right/left panning on the B3 to maximize that effect, unless the mix is extremely crowded and contains other, similar sounds (such as synthesizer pads).

The Rhodes piano frequently has a stereo vibrato effect, but it is less critical that it be spread wide. The primary attribute of the Rhodes piano is its bell-like quality, so be careful not to lose some of that with a fast attack on a compressor. You might want to enhance the bell a bit with some mid-high to high-frequency boost, but be careful not to make the transients too harsh or too thin.

The Wurlitzer piano has a distinctive and very bright sound, but it has often been played through a guitar amp and overdriven like an electric guitar. You can use some distortion from a guitar amp simulation plug-in on your basic Wurlitzer sound to give it that authentic edge, though it also works well without amplifier distortion.

CREATIVE TIP

Using the Leslie sound

You don't have to have a B3 organ track to use a Leslie speaker effect. It can be used on any kind of organ recording and is sometimes used on guitar and other instrumental parts as well. Any instrument that uses a fair amount of sustain or held notes (legato) in their part is a candidate for a Leslie effect, including vocals. There are many plug-ins that offer Leslie simulation; sometimes the preset is clearly labeled and sometimes it is called "Doppler" or "rotating," or some related term.

The original (hardware) Leslie had two speeds for the rotating speaker (fast and slow), whereas most of the plug-ins allow continuously variable control of the speed of the Doppler effect. Some of the plug-ins allow you to time the rotating Leslie speaker effect to the tempo of the music. The original Leslie speaker also includes an amplifier that has its own characteristic distortion, and there are some plug-ins that include Leslie amplifier distortion simulation as part of the Leslie sound.

Synthesizers, Samplers, and Keyboard Roles

There are endless "keyboard" sounds made with hardware and software synthesizers and samplers. I put *keyboard* in parenthesis here for a reason; many of these are keyboard sounds only because generally a keyboard (or virtual keyboard) is the easiest interface for playing (or triggering) the sound. The actual sounds created may simulate or sample a known instrument or be a completely original sound that doesn't model any previously existing musical sound.

What is most important with regard to mixing all of these sounds is the role they play in your mix. If the sound is the lead instrument, a rhythm instrument, or a pad function, you may use a very different approach—even to the same sound. See the section titled "Your Mix as a Movie" in chapter 2 for more ways to consider the various roles that these elements play in your mix.

Solo and Small Ensemble Acoustic Keyboard Mixes

As discussed in the similar section concerning acoustic guitars, solo and small ensemble mixes provide opportunities for some of the most naturalistic mixes and have the potential for using audio with as much detail as possible. This is in contrast to crowded mixes, where too much detail can be a problem because elements are competing for frequency space and panning position.

I have used as many as ten mics for a solo acoustic piano record, blending them to produce a very rich tonality. Similarly, multiple effects—as many as four or five separate reverbs and delays—might be blended to create a very subtle and complex soundscape on a solo recording, where the details of such a complex ambience would be lost in a more populated environment. Don't skimp on the time you spend on solo and small ensemble mixes; they are great opportunities to delve deeply into some very subtle sound and ambience possibilities.

Screenshot 6.7 shows a solo piano mix of a recording that used eight mics (three stereo pairs—close, mid, and far—plus a footer mic and a mic over the head of the pianist), with four effects for mixing (three reverbs—small room, medium plate, large concert hall—plus one stereo slap delay).

SCREENSHOT 6.7

A solo piano mix layout as described above.

6.5 **Vocals**

It doesn't get more important than mixing the lead vocal—or any vocal, for that matter—as the vocal is what the listener's ear naturally gravitates to. In this section, I consider mixing lead vocals, doubling lead vocals (physical and mechanical), harmony vocals, background vocals, ad-libs, and rappers.

Lead Vocals

You need a pretty compelling reason to place a lead vocal anywhere other than center panned; generally the lead vocal will be in the center. But you may have such a reason—for instance, the two lead vocals in one tune, as discussed below, might suggest something other than center panning. Most times, though, the old adage "front and center" couldn't be more applicable than with the lead vocal. Keeping the vocal in front of the band, without its sounding dislocated from the music, is probably the central challenge in mixing lead vocals. So here, I deal with this first, and then discuss vocal EQ and vocal effects after that.

WHAT NOT TO DO

Don't let the lead vocal get lost.
The relative level of the vocal to the band is a matter of taste, and it is somewhat dictated by genre (traditionally pop lead vocals are relatively louder than rock lead vocals, though there are plenty of examples where this is not the case). That said, I have very rarely had feedback on a mix asking for the lead vocal to be turned down. Instead, I have (especially earlier in my career) had folks ask for the lead vocal to be turned up— often because someone the artist played the mix for said he couldn't understand the lyrics. When I provide a louder vocal mix, the artist often decides it was better where it was—there is an uncomfortable quality to having the vocal so loud that it feels separated from the music. I call this latter result the "Frank Sinatra effect"; if you listen to many of his recordings, you'll hear a very prominent vocal and what sounds like a tiny orchestra in the background. Musical tastes have shifted since then, and the public ear is more attuned to vocals that sound like they are at least relating to the band. That said, most listeners still want the lead vocal to be prominent.

WHAT NOT TO DO

Don't rely on compression alone to keep the lead vocal in front.
A lead vocal often gets compressed as much as 15 to 18 dB at its peaks, usually about half of that during recording and half during mixing. I generally use a 3:1 or 4:1 ratio with a fast attack and a soft knee, hitting as much as 7 to 9 dB of compression at the vocal peaks of a crowded mix (less compression where there's more room for the vocal to sit comfortably without as many competing elements).

Compression is our friend but not our savior, so even with a lot of compression the vocal may not sit comfortably in front all of the time. That's especially the case now that most lead vocals are comp'd from many different takes; there is the likelihood that various words, phrases, or lines will be delivered at volumes that compression alone can't balance. Some engineers have resorted to using a brickwall limiter on the lead vocal to force a more balanced volume relationship from word to word. This works pretty well for maintaining consistent level, but it also flattens all the dynamics in a way that can take a lot of the musicality out of the performance. A combination of compression and automation (discussed below) is usually the best tactic for placing the lead vocal level.

I start by compressing and EQ'ing the vocal (more on vocal EQ next), and then try to place it so that I feel like most, or at least a good portion, of the vocal is sitting where I want it, relative to the level of the band. I then go through the vocal line by line and decide if any part of it (word, phrase, or whole line) needs to come up or down relative to the rest of the vocal. I use the graphic interface for automation, which allows easy and accurate access to volume for any part of the vocal (even one syllable). See screenshot 6.8.

This can be tedious and time-consuming, but with practice it can go reasonably quickly (you learn what 1 dB, or 1.2 dB, or 1.5 dB, and so on boost or dip sounds like, and that speeds up the process). I usually do this once through the whole song, and then over the course of the ongoing mix I revise bits as I continue to hear them in context. There is a constant need to balance the desire for the expressiveness that comes from variations in vocal volume with the desire for the vocal to be "front and center" and still a part of the band. Again—*there's nothing more important than getting the lead vocal to sit properly in the mix,* so it's worth the attention!

EQ'ing a lead vocal requires sensitivity to the complex nature of vocal timbre. From a high female voice to a low male voice, there is enormous variety in the frequency range and sound. Some voices are thin and some are very thick. Some have a lot of low-mid woof in them and some have a lot of high-mid nasal quality. As a result, it is very difficult to provide any generalizations regarding how to EQ a vocal. Some voices will want low-mid roll-off to counter a very thick quality, and some will want low-mid boost to counter a very thin quality.

SCREENSHOT 6.8

A typical lead vocal automation, using the graphic mode.

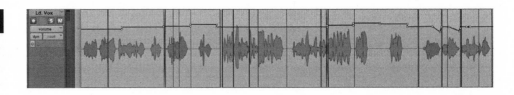

Some voices will benefit from high-mid boost to help with clarity and presence, and some will benefit from high-mid roll-off to counter an excessively nasal or shrill quality.

One rule of thumb from a technical standpoint is that generally your highest quality, most transparent EQ plug-in is going to be best on the very sensitive and complex timbre of a voice. And even with your best EQ, generally the less EQ you use, the more natural and detailed your vocal is going to sound. However, certain "soft"-sounding voices (those that don't have much high-frequency content) may shine with some very aggressive EQ when you're trying to fit it into a hard-hitting track, and some very bright voices may want considerable taming in quiet environments.

Of course, your goal may not be naturalistic and detailed—sometimes it's quite the opposite. A "telephone speaker" vocal effect is popular for certain sections of some songs (see screenshot 6.9), and radical EQ of all different types might fit your particular creative concept. Vocal effects using guitar amp and speaker simulation plug-ins are also popular for decidedly unnaturalistic vocal sounds. It's surprising how radical an EQ setting is needed in order to create the very small speaker effect.

Virtually every type of traditional effect (reverbs and delays) is fair game for vocal enhancement. It is common for a vocal to be treated with a couple of different reverbs: a short-room type (.4–.9 seconds) and a medium or long plate, chamber, or hall (1–3 seconds), and a couple of different delays: a short, doubling effect (12–30 ms), a medium slap-back effect (110–175 ms), and/or a long echo with repeats (eighth or quarter note, possibly dotted or as a triplet). If each is used subtly, the combination needn't sound like an over-the-top production. In fact, if used very subtly, the result can still leave the vocal sounding very

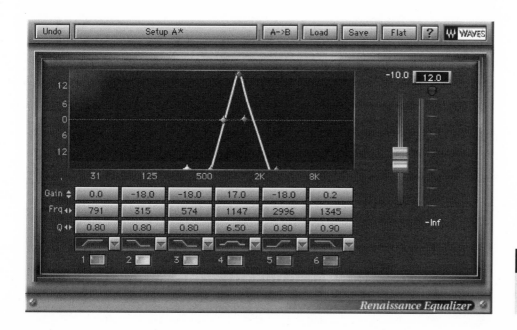

SCREENSHOT 6.9

The "telephone speaker" vocal effect.

much "in your face" but with a complex and interesting ambience that provides delicate color to the raw voice.

Effects can also be used more obviously to create a lush environment that gives the singer a majestic quality. As with all the elements in your mix, the tempo of the song will be an important part in choosing the length of the reverb and delays, as well as the amount that you want to use—slower tempos provide more space for longer, louder effects. Reverbs can't be mathematically timed like delays and echoes can (and should) be, but you'll want to use your ear to determine whether the reverb feels like it's supporting or fighting the beat.

Other special effects can be used on vocals as well, such as the "telephone speaker" effect and the use of an amp simulation plug-in already mentioned. Phasing, flanging, and chorusing of vocals can add either some subtle interest in moderation or some pronounced and gritty effects if used strongly. Reverse or flanged reverbs can create some otherworldly spaces, as can backward reverb effect, where a backwards reverb precedes each vocal word. A reverse reverb preset (found on many reverb plug-ins) creates a reverse reverb following each sound that it is processing, but you can also create a reverse reverb that *precedes* each word, creating what sounds like a swooshing sound that quickly crescendos into each word. To create this effect, do the following:

Backward Reverb Effect

1. Duplicate your vocal track (or part of it).
2. Reverse the vocal on the duplicated track (most DAWs have an off-line processing effect that will do this). Make sure to add a bit of additional time before the first word of your vocal before you reverse it so that the reverb will hang over past the reversed first word. See screenshots 6.10 and 6.11.
3. Process the reversed vocal with a reverb using an off-line reverb plug-in. Be sure the reverb is set to 100 percent wet. You can experiment with length but start with a medium length reverb (1.5–2 sec).
4. Reverse the processed reverb clip and play the reversed reverb along with the original (forward) vocal, adjusting the amount as desired. You can also use just the reversed reverb (without the original vocal) for a very unusual effect. See screenshot 6.12.

Review this audio clip to judge the results of using the pre-reverb and reverb effects.

Artist: Rachel Margaret CD: *Note to Self* Track: "Right Between the Eyes"
Audio Clip 6.10: Clip of a vocal in solo with a pre-reverb effect.
Audio Clip 6.11: The same vocal clip and reverb with the track.

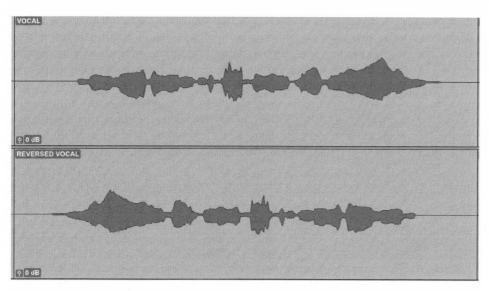

SCREENSHOT 6.10

Regions selection of the vocal before it is reversed.

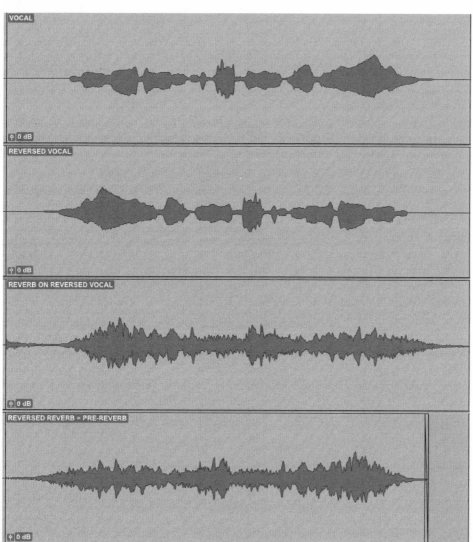

SCREENSHOT 6.11

Reversed vocal.

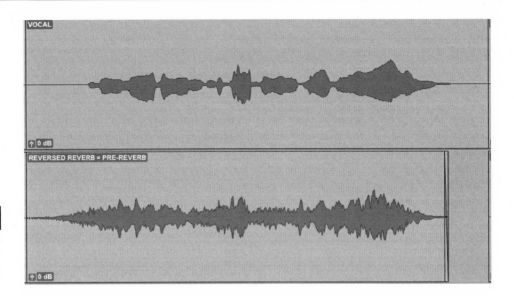

SCREENSHOT 6.12

Reversed reverb placed next to the original vocal track.

Two Lead Vocalists

Occasionally you'll encounter a song (or perhaps a whole group of songs from one band) where there are two lead vocalists. They may be singing at the same time, or alternating lines or verses, or some combination of both. In this case, you may want to offset them slightly in the panning field (maybe 15 percent left for one and 15 percent right for the other). If they are singing unison (the same notes) or alternating parts, you will want to run them at the same volume.

The latter can be very tricky to determine because voices sound very different; what "the same volume" is may be very subjective. If, for example, one voice is female with a lot of high-mid presence and the other is a lower pitched male voice that is broad but without a lot of presence, it can be hard to decide when they are balanced appropriately. EQ can help—you might soften the female voice a bit or boost the presence of the male, or both—but ultimately, you will just have to make a judgment as to what sounds balanced to you.

This is a circumstance where listening at different volumes, from very quiet to quite loud (although always a valuable part of mixing) is especially useful. If the two vocalists are singing together, but one is singing the melody and the other a harmony (be sure you know which is which; if you're not sure, then ask one of the singers), you will want to run the melody at least slightly more prominent than the harmony. The proper degree of difference is one of those creative decisions that you will need to make, though you'll probably want to work with the singers on arriving at a proper balance.

Doubled Lead Vocals

You may mix a song where the lead vocal has been doubled (performed twice) or even tripled. This is a common tactic in pop and rap (Elton John, Eminem, and many others use this technique frequently). You have various options as to how to use a doubled (or tripled) vocal. The subtle approach is to use one vocal prominently (as *the* lead vocal) and the other(s) subtly to thicken the original vocal but without such an apparent doubling effect. In this case you might pan both vocals center to minimize how audible the effect is. The more obvious use is to run them like the two lead vocal approach discussed above, split slightly left and right and balanced to be equal (it's much easier to balance the same singer than different ones). You might be surprised to find that even when used in this obvious way, most listeners will not be aware that the vocal has been doubled, though if you point it out they will probably be able to recognize the effect as they are listening.

Lead vocals can also be "doubled" by using a short delay effect, as already discussed. We call this "mechanical doubling" as opposed to the "physical doubling" created by actually performing and recording the vocal more than once. Mechanical doubling has a slightly synthetic quality that is much less noticeable when the effect is used subtly (but it may be used prominently if the mechanical effect is a desirable part of the mix concept).

Harmony and Background Vocals

Harmony vocals sing along with the lead vocal, only harmonizing with different notes, whereas background (or backing) vocals sing at different times (call-back lines, etc.) and/or different parts (such as ah's or ooh's). Background vocals are typically harmonized by several singers (or one multi-tracked singer). Harmony and background vocals may receive a variety of possible treatments, and different artists seem to have very different ideas about how they should sit in a mix. They may be featured prominently—almost as loud as the lead vocal (or even equal in volume), or they may be quite faint and just suggest the added layer or response to the melody.

If left to my own devices I mix harmony and background vocals to be quite prominent—some say that the primary appeal of popular music comes from harmony singing, even though there's a lot of very successful popular music without harmonies. In any event, I find that this is one thing that I need to get clear with an artist when we start working together. Does he or she like the harmony and/or background vocals prominent or not? This may vary on a song-by-song basis to some extent, but I have found artists to be relatively consistent on their preferences for the positioning of additional voices.

The harmony and background vocal tracks can be dealt with similarly to how you deal with a lead vocal in regard to compression and EQ. With effects, I tend to keep them simpler—not quite as "dressed up" as the lead vocal. Often I just use one small to medium-size reverbs on the harmony and background vocals. It's best if the reverb on the backing vocals is true stereo (see "True Stereo Reverbs" in chapter 4) so that the reverb reflects the panning position of the direct vocal track.

169

With panning, I generally nestle the lead vocal in the harmony and background tracks so if it's one harmony or two background vocals, they will probably be 15 to 30 percent left or right (the two backing tracks usually split left and right). With great numbers of background vocal tracks (I've had as many as 20 for one song with a lot of parts and a lot of doubling and tripling of parts), I venture farther along the panning spectrum if there is room, sometimes running multiple background tracks from hard left through to hard right. On a crowded track, you might end up wanting to focus all your background tracks in a relatively small part of the panning spectrum (e.g., from 15 percent right to 40 percent right). I tend to place lower harmonies more toward the center and higher harmonies farther out toward the edge of the panning spectrum, but there is certainly no rule in this regard.

For ease of operation, you will definitely want to group all your harmony tracks together (and where there are doubles or triples, those should be subgrouped). Balancing the harmony parts can be very tricky and require a lot of small shifts in panning and volume until you're really happy with how they are sitting. If you haven't already, you will soon discover that lower harmonies tend to disappear in the track, so what sounds perfectly in balance in solo may sound terribly out of balance in the track. You need to be able to hear each backing vocal part and adjust its level while playing in the track in order to ultimately get the background vocals sounding good. The ability to hear each part in context requires some concentrated ear training!

Ad-libs

Ad-lib vocals are a frequent part of a lot of contemporary music, and they provide the opportunity for some creative mixing. Sometimes ad-libs are simply a part of the lead vocal track and you might deal with them no differently from the rest of the vocal. When ad-libs are in addition to the lead vocal and/or sung by someone other than the lead vocalist, however, you will want to consider them as a separate element.

You can treat additional ad-libs simply, starting by finding an appropriate place in the panning spectrum—usually out of the way of the lead vocal and harmonies if there are any (perhaps between 45 and 80 percent left or right). Because ad-libs are often delivered with more emphasis than a typical vocal (they are generally meant to punctuate the music), you may find that some aggressive compression will help keep them present in the mix. Similarly with EQ; you may want to be more aggressive than usual with presence boost (high-mids) to make the ad-libs pop out from the track.

Ad-libs also provide an opportunity to bring some more interesting effects into your mix. You can treat them simply—with a bit of reverb, for example—but you could also consider some wilder effects to complement the intensity of

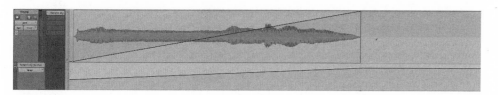

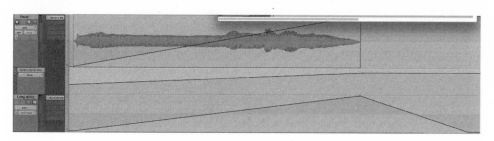

171

the ad-lib. Using repeating delays (in time to the music, of course) or long reverbs might work well. You might also want to add some movement to the ad-lib by automating the panning. (Automation is covered thoroughly in chapter 5.) Screenshots 6.13, 6.14, and 6.15 show how a long held note on an ad-lib might move across the panning spectrum and at the same time you might increase the feed to a long delay, culminating in a pronounced repeating echo (that is also bathed in reverb) and then the repeats pan back in the other direction.

Now listen to the following audio clips for real-time examples of this treatment of ad-libs.

> Artist: Sista Monica CD: *Can't Keep a Good Woman Down* Track: "Crockpot"
>
> Audio Clip 6.12 Clip of a vocal ad-lib with the panning, send automation, and effects described above—in solo.
>
> Audio Clip 6.13 The same ad-lib and effects—in the track.

6.6 Horns

Horns in popular music encompass a lot of territory, from brass to reeds, and from solo horns to horn sections. From a mixing standpoint, there isn't a lot of difference between brass and reeds, so I start with solo horns and then discuss horns sections.

The most common solo horn is a tenor sax, but it could easily be an alto or a soprano sax, a trumpet, flugelhorn, or whatever else. Mixing a solo horn isn't that different from mixing a lead guitar track. However, horns don't benefit from the natural compression created by distortion and speaker reproduction, so you're likely to want more aggressive compression than for a lead guitar.

Like lead guitar, I rarely use very much EQ, but with horns it is for different reasons. With a lead guitar I don't want to stray very far from the guitarist's "sound"; while the same is true with horn players, there's the additional issue of the complex acoustic nature of a horn. The delicate balance of overtones that create the horn player's timbre is easily upset by much EQ (lead guitar is generally more resilient). I might add or subtract as much as 1 dB of presence boost or low-mids warmth if I really feel like the sound would benefit, but I'm just as likely to do no EQ'ing (depending on the quality of the recording).

Effects on solo horns can range, again similarly to what you might do to a lead guitar. That means anywhere from completely dry or with just a touch of room-size reverb all the way to a short reverb along with a long reverb, a doubling or chorusing effect, a slap-back length delay, and a long (perhaps quarter-note) delay with multiple repeats for a solo horn. I'd be very careful with the doubling or chorusing/phasing/flanging type effects as they really alter the tonality—but anything is fair game. You might even find yourself using an amp distortion plug-in on your tenor sax solo to give it a truly unusual quality!

Horn sections play a very different role from that of the typical solo horn. Decisions about how to mix horn sections depend on the size of the section (typically from two to five horns), the role of the section, and the density of other elements in the track. You won't have much trouble finding a place for a two-piece horn section in a sparse track, but if the horns are doubled and the track is dense with elements, it becomes more complicated.

You can split doubled horn tracks left and right (as much as hard left/right), but they will sound more like two sections than one thick section. You can spread each of the elements across the field, such as trumpet right 60 percent, sax right 35 percent, doubled trumpet left 60 percent, and doubled sax left 35 percent, but they will occupy a lot of space in the panning spectrum. This might work well if the track is sparse, but with a dense track you might well want to isolate all the horn tracks (including doubles or triples) on one side of the panning spectrum, though you might still spread them a bit—such as trumpet right 70 percent, sax right 45 percent, doubled trumpet right 60 percent, and doubled sax right 55 percent.

With effects, I am likely to once again go with minimal or none, and keep the effects generally simple. If the section is playing more short notes and stabs (*staccato*), I use a room-size reverb, though I might add a short delay if I want a more "dressed-up" sound. If the section is playing mostly long tones (*legato*) for a pad-like effect, I might opt for a longer reverb (1.5–2.2 seconds). Because you have many elements and they are generally panned from relatively close in to very broad across the spectrum, it's helpful to have a true stereo reverb that retains the panning position of each element in its accompanying reverb (see chapter 4, "Processing Effects").

6.7 Strings

Much of what I have covered already in regard to background vocals and horn sections can be applied to strings, so instead I focus on what is different about mixing solo strings and string sections. String parts are often intended as texture (in traditional popular-music arranging, they are referred to as "sweetener"). If this is the case, then mixing them with quite a bit of reverb and spread in the panning spectrum, as you might with any "pad" type part, is often the best approach.

It's when you really want to hear the string parts that mixing them can become more complex (as in "Eleanor Rigby"). It's no accident that there aren't a lot of elements besides the strings in "Eleanor Rigby," just as it's no accident that there are many multiples of stringed instruments compared to the other instruments in a typical symphony. Getting strings to sit in the front of a mix can be a real challenge without making them unnaturally loud and sounding out of place. Unfortunately, EQ isn't an option, either—a little bit could be fine but much high-mid (presence) boost of strings will bring out the scratchy quality and will seriously compromise the sound of the instruments (or sample).

Of course, compression can help keep the strings present in the mix, and a good amount of compression—similar to what you might do with a vocal—is a good start toward allowing the strings to be clearly heard. In a crowded environment, panning will be your most powerful tool, and creating a space or stretch along the panning spectrum that is unoccupied by any competing element will be essential. Allowing string parts to really "speak" calls for some careful positioning and, even with significant compression, probably quite a bit of automation maneuvering so that the level of each phrase makes it present without sounding out of context.

Chapter 7

Mix Collaboration
The Mix Team

Mixing is rarely a solitary pursuit, though the nature of collaborations has changed with the advent of easy file transfer protocols on the Internet. What used to be a bunch of people with their hands on faders trying to make mix moves in real time because there was no automation has become individuals producing mixes of enormous complexity that are recalled and replayed effortlessly in the box. And what used to be groups of recordists and artists working together late into the night, trying to get a mix done before the next session came in to break down the console in order to start a new session, has become those same people producing a series of mixes and responses often sent via the Internet from remote locations and sometimes going on for weeks. These practices have created combinations of collaboration and communication that operate in new ways to complete a mix.

This means that written communication is now commonplace in mix collaborations. As a result, feedback is not interactive in the moment, and the mixer is working more independently. Obviously, the new setup makes clear and concise communication about mixes all the more important, lest hours or days be wasted in rehashing or changing misperceived directions. And working in the box, where everything from pitch and rhythm fixing, to the recomposition of elements such as solos, to the reconfiguration of whole arrangements is easily and quickly accessible, mixers confront uncertainties about what actually constitutes mixing. Here, I cover some basic written and verbal communications about mixes, some subjective issues concerning the limits of mixer intervention, and the practical aspects of remotely managing mixing projects.

7.1 How to Communicate About Mixes

What follows covers some general areas of communication in regard to mixing, but first I need to make note of the increasingly common practice of using written communication (email or text messaging) to discuss the mixes a person is working on remotely, including sending files over the Internet. Written communication has advantages; for instance, simply having to put your mix notes into writing can make those revisions easier and clearer for the recordist to understand. However, doing so can also delay the process as you try to clarify what is needed and desired.

WHAT NOT TO DO

Don't send a mix without notes.
Although it may be tempting to send the artist a mix (either a first mix or a revision) without any notes, you're just avoiding matters that should be on the table at this point. For example, when I send the first pass of a mix, I always mention the things I anticipate might be issues: "I set the background vocals pretty high, but I'm not sure how you want them," or "I wasn't sure if the lead guitar should take over from the background vocals in the end vamp—it's doing that in this mix but easy to change."

You're making hundreds of decisions on a mix, and there are always some things that you are not going to be sure about. You want the artist to know that you're flexible and that you want their participation. On revisions, I always comment on what's been done and how it reflects the ongoing collaboration. I might say something like "The backgrounds are a little quieter now as requested—more so in the chorus than the end vamp, just because that sounded right to me—easy to adjust more." I also might mention actions I took that weren't anticipated earlier: "I also panned the rhythm guitar farther to the right—you didn't ask for this but it sounded better to me as I was working on the other revisions." Dialog is essential to the creative process; initiate it, don't wait for it.

CREATIVE TIP

How to collaborate when you're mixing your own music
You may find yourself mixing material that you wrote, played, and recorded. So, where's the opportunity for collaboration? This can be tricky, as you don't have anyone you need to consult. If other musicians played on the project, you can go to them for feedback, but musicians don't necessarily have an ear for mixing (and they might get distracted listening to their own parts). And, of course, you might have played or programmed all the instruments yourself.

There's no right answer here; some people are capable of mixing on their own, without a desire for collaboration. If you want feedback, though, you can play your mixes for a friend, family member, or someone else to obtain feedback. Usually the best you can hope for is something very general, like "I can't hear your voice well enough"; that is a common reaction that I addressed in chapter 6. If you crave feedback from pros, seek out local engineers and producers, but don't be surprised if they say they're too busy or ask to get paid; some of us get a lot of these requests. Or, take a class (many community colleges have programs that are reasonably priced) and ask your teacher for feedback (and give you some valuable training in other recording and mixing skills as well). In any event, be aware that you can find opposing views on virtually any mix issue (one person says the vocal is too loud and another says it isn't loud enough), so in the end you have to trust yourself (and develop your ear and your skills).

Acquiring the vocabulary for communicating about mixing is largely a matter of building up your familiarity with mix and sound issues. Some things are easy and straightforward: "I think the vocal needs to be louder," though this leaves unanswered the question of how *much* louder. "I think the vocal needs to be a lot louder" or "a little louder" helps clarify matters, but the exact degree of change that is going to satisfy that request is still a matter of trial and error. Collaboration with others is another reason I like off-line automation. I can adjust the vocal up 2 dB, and if my collaborator says that's too much I can say that I'll split the difference (up 1 dB), and we can work from there. That is, expressing these changes in numbers and definable degrees makes everything clearer.

Mix issues other than volume call for a vocabulary that can be readily understood by others. For instance, questions regarding frequencies, as controlled by EQ, have given rise to a huge number of descriptive words, some more easily understood than others. Words that rely on the scale from low to high frequencies are generally clear. These include:

Lows	*bass*	*bottom*
Mids	*midrange*	*middle*
Highs	*treble*	*top*

These might become more precise by adding subdivisions, such as:

Lows
Low-mids
Mids
High-mids
Highs

Other words that are used fairly frequently are suggestive but less precise, and therefore open to interpretation. Some useful words and their probable meaning or means of responding to them include:

Boom (may be either a desirable or an undesirable quality of the low frequencies)

Rumble (generally refers to a low-frequency problem)

Thump (usually a quality of the kick drum lows, which may be good or bad)

Fatter (generally satisfied with a boost in the lows and/or low-mids)

Warmer (most frequently requires low-mid boosting)

Honk (probably a quality of the mids and/or high-mids that needs dipping)

Thinner (again, usually achieved through dipping of mids and/or high-mids)

Whack (probably refers to the high-mid content of the snare drum)

Presence (the presence boost is generally found in the high-mids)

Crunch (usually referring to the high-mids, though *crunchy* usually means distorted)

Brighter (generally the high-mids and/or highs)

Edge (generally the high-mids and/or highs)

Sibilance (the "s" sound can become overloaded from high-mid and/or highs)

Brilliance (probably satisfied by boosting the high frequencies)

Air (probably referencing the top of the audible highs)

These words might be pretty easy to understand, especially if they become used often among frequent collaborators, but they can also mean very different things to different people. And even if the general understanding is the same, the exact frequencies, the amount of boost and dip, and the best bandwidth settings still require considerable clarification. For example, the low-mid frequencies in a female vocal are at a very different part of the frequency range from the low-mids of the bass guitar.

Other words, such as the inevitable color references ("more purple") or highly subjective terms such as "magical," really give the recordist almost nothing to go on. (I did work with one artist for whom, after some trial and error, I discovered that the request for "more magical" was satisfied with more reverb.)

The most precise language for EQ is actual frequency references, and with the proliferation of engineering skills among musicians and other contributors to the mixing process, the use of these is becoming more frequent. Suggestions such as "I think it needs a little boost around 8K" ("K" being short for kHz) or "Perhaps we could thin this sound a bit around 300" (meaning dipping at 300 Hz) are increasingly common in mix collaborations. The recordist may still need to adjust somewhat from the suggested frequency—it's impossible to know exactly what the effects of any given frequency adjustment are going to be without listening—but this vocabulary is certainly the most precise.

Communications concerning ambience and effects can be more obscure. A request for a sound that is "bigger" probably refers to a desire for increased ambience, but not necessarily. Suggestions that a more "mysterious" or "unusual" mix is desired leave the recordist without a good idea of how to proceed. With wider use of recording gear, however, specific suggestions and references will be more common. A guitarist may well suggest: "How about some long delay on the lead guitar?" The performer may even be more specific: "Can we try a quarter-note delay on the guitar?" The more exact *nature* of the delay (overall level, amount of feedback, etc.) may be left to the recordist or may be part of an ongoing discussion of details.

Some terms can clearly suggest changes in mix ambience. Certainly "wetter" and "dryer" are accepted ways of describing the relative amounts of reverb and/or delay, though how to implement a request for a wetter vocal or a wetter mix still leaves a lot open to the recordists—more reverb, an additional type of reverb, a different reverb, or perhaps more or additional medium or long delay. Similarly, requests such as "closer sounding" or "more spacious" generally can be interpreted as references to types or degrees of ambience. Less reverb and less delay definitely make things sound closer, while more ambience increases the sense of spaciousness—though again, the specific ways to accomplish such changes can vary widely.

It is very helpful for a recordist to master these terms to use in helping collaborators clarify what it is wanted. Sometimes, when a vocalist is struggling to describe what she wants for the sound of her song, for example, you can help define that by asking if the sound should be more "present" or "closer" or perhaps "bigger" or "richer." This can give the vocalist a term that you might be able to interpret technically. This is preferable to hearing her request "Could you change the way the vocal sounds?" Of course, you can, but *how*? In short, don't rely on your collaborators to clearly express their desires; develop the vocabulary to be able to discuss with them how to create the mixes that you all will love.

Finally, when you're working remotely, make sure you are listening to and collaborating on the same mix! I have experienced confusions with artists over the elements in a mix, only to discover that we were not referencing the same mix. This is why I number and/or date the files or CDs that I provide for artists. I can then refer to that information so that changes are agreed to, based on the correct starting point.

WHAT NOT TO DO

Don't play a mix for anyone without proper permission.
It is important to respect boundaries in regard to music productions that are not yet finished. This means that you should not play material for other people (friends, other clients, etc.) that isn't finished without the permission of the artist. It may be that someone other than the artist is paying for the recording—and that gives the individual certain rights, of course. But try to respect the artist's wishes in regard to when the music is really done and ready to be released to the world.

For example, I prefer not to play unfinished work for the record company or others who may have a vested interest but who are not a part of the creative process. I also reinforce this notion with the artist: outside of the people who they are working with and trust, I urge them not to play unfinished mixes for others. This is because of two common outcomes: either the listeners don't like the (unfinished) work, or they fall in love with the unfinished version. In either case, you have undermined the process and may even jeopardize the project, depending on who is involved.

7.2 Levels of Mixer Intervention

I mentioned in chapter 1, "Am I Mixing Yet?," that editing, tuning, and rhythm fixing are not mixing functions, but that mixers often find themselves doing a little or a lot of all of them. These adjustments should have been completed before you start mixing, but the DAW allows for fluid workflow, so sometimes these functions get "mixed up" with the job of the mixer. If you're working face-to-face with your collaborators, then anything is fair game if you agree it needs attention. But if you're working remotely, it's sometimes hard to know how far to go down that other road (fixing note placement on the drum track, for example)—or even if you should go down that road at all.

I am often encouraged to "fix anything that sounds wrong to you" or something to that effect. But there's a fine line between "wrong" and "expressive" in regard to both pitch and rhythm, and it isn't really your call as a mixer (unless you're also the artist or producer). I generally don't make changes unless I really think something is having a negative effect, and I always let the collaborators know what I've done. I am usually specific: "I tuned the word *love* in the second verse" or "I straightened the drums out a bit on the fill going into the chorus." And I always add, "Let me know if you think this is an improvement." If I've worked with the artist a lot and have a good sense of what he or she would want, I might just say that I tuned a few things and/or adjusted timing on a few things; the performer can always ask me for more specifics if desired. Again, though, I always add, "Let me know if anything doesn't sound right to you."

Even more problematic, but potentially more significant, is the decision to mute either a portion or all of some element(s) in the mix. Overly cluttered arrangements are a fairly frequent occurrence, and when you're trying to mix something you might become acutely aware that there are more things than can comfortably fit together. It's not the number of elements or tracks—you can have a hundred tracks that work together beautifully—it's the overabundance of parts that don't fit together and that might create a muddle. Again, this is technically an arrangement issue, not a mix issue, but in truth you cannot separate the two.

So, yes, I sometimes mute parts or even whole tracks; but unless I was asked to do it, I always send alternative mixes—one with the part muted and one without—so the collaborators can easily hear the difference. I might say, "I thought it sounded better with the third rhythm guitar part muted, so I'm made a mix like that, but I'm also sending a mix with it unmuted." Some artists don't want to consider losing anything from the original recording, while others are very easy-going about eliminating elements—and many are somewhere in between. You will generally get a sense pretty quickly for where the folks are that you are collaborating with, especially if you venture to suggest some kind of muting.

CREATIVE TIP

Keep muting in mind as an option.
As a mixer, you are responsible for the final sound of the music. Muting is a powerful tool for opening up mixes and creating a more memorable soundscape. So, whether you're working on your own stuff or on that of others, keep the muting option open. Take a few moments at various points in the mix process to consider, "Is there an element here that could be muted without losing something essential and at the same time creating something more powerful?"

As far as larger-scale intervention goes—actually rearranging elements in a solo, for example, or eliminating a third verse, or putting the bridge after the solo instead of before it—these are changes that I would very rarely make without their having been suggested by the artist or producer. If I really hear a change like this as potentially valuable (after trying it on my own, of course), I send it along to my collaborators with a very strong caveat—something to the effect that I had this pretty radical idea for a change, and I'm just sending it along for them to hear, but I certainly don't feel that it's necessary.

In truth, I wouldn't even send such a radical change (and one definitely outside the scope of mixing) unless it was going to an artist I had a considerable history of working with and mutual trust. Otherwise, such a suggestion in itself could sour a relationship in its early stages if the artist or producer sensed that you were undermining his or her authority in making critical and creative decisions.

7.3 Managing Remote Mixing Projects

If you are mixing something you recorded, then you have been in control of the "assets" (audio and DAW files) from the start and probably your only concern is making sure that you have everything backed up at the end of every workday. But if you are receiving files from some other source, then managing those assets can be more of a challenge. To begin, you will want to make sure that you have everything you need.

The Transfer

Sometimes everything is straightforward: you receive a hard drive, flash drive, DVDs, or a link to files stored online. You copy all the files to your working drive, open the files you need, and everything is there and ready for you to get started. However, often there are problems somewhere even in this beginning process.

Problem #1

The original media is not compatible with your computer.

Solutions: Make sure you mention to the person you're getting the files from what computer and what system you are running. This is mostly a compatibility problem between PCs and Macs. Macs won't read PC-formatted drives (hard drives or flash drives), and vice versa. There is one exception—Mac's can read PC drives formatted in Fat32, which is a PC drive formatting option. However, Fat32 is an older format and has some limitations, so most PC drives are not Fat32 formatted. If you reformat a drive to make it compatible, you will lose the data on that drive. There is also software that you can purchase that will allow you to alter your Mac formatted drive in a way that will allow it to be read on a PC.

It might seem that recordable DVDs would make things easier, but unfortunately that is not always the case. There are four recordable DVD formats: DVD-R, DVD+R, DVD-RW, and DVD+RW. Depending on the make and model of your DVD reader, as well as your computer and its operating system, you can have trouble reading any one of these DVD formats (dirty lasers in DVD readers are also a consistent problem). I've always managed to get the information off a DVD sent to me, but mostly that's because my wife and I have three different computers, so one of them has always worked (but fairly often one or more of them hasn't). If the formatting issues addressed above are resolved, then hard drives or flash drives are more reliable than DVDs.

181

Getting files through ftp (file transfer protocol) sites or other "cloud-based" storage services (which have become very common) is often the most reliable way to receive files. Although this process can be complicated by your Internet service and speed (it can take a long time, depending on the size of the files you're receiving and the speed of your connection), at least there are none of the formatting problems presented by drives and DVDs. I usually start the transfer before bed, and in the morning, if all has gone smoothly, I have all the files I need. However, slow Internet service and momentary disruptions in service can undermine this means of transfer.

Problem #2

The original files are not compatible with your DAW or DAW version.

Solution: Again, communication is the key to solving file compatibility issues. You need to confirm which DAW (including which version of that DAW) the original files were made on. You may also need to confirm the file format, as not all systems support all formats (e.g., many interfaces support only up to 96 kHz sampling rate, and if the original files were recorded at a higher rate they will need to be down-sampled before you can work on them).

There is little or no cross-platform compatibility, so you cannot simply open a Logic Pro, Pro Tools, Digital Performer, or Nuendo file in any one of these other DAWs. There are a variety of work-arounds, some easier than others. It may be possible to maintain region or automation information, but you will have to research the proper technique for the version of the DAW you are using and the one you are exporting to. You'll have to be careful; you will definitely want to make a test before you assume that it's going to work.

The most reliable way to transfer from one DAW to another is to bypass the original program file by making a copy of each one of your tracks as a complete file, with no edits and with each track having exactly the same start time. In this way you can simply import the audio files into the DAW you want to use, line them up at the same start time, and you're ready to go.

Even when you're moving from one computer to another that is running the same program, you need to confirm what version the file was used, and you may need to make a conversion. For example, if the original files were made using Pro Tools 10 and you are going to be mixing them on a system running Pro Tools 9, you will need to "save a copy in" and then select "Pro Tools 7 → 9 Session" in order to have a file that will open in Pro Tools 9.

Problem #3

There are missing audio files.

Solution: This is one of those potential nightmare scenarios that happen all too frequently. You go to open the file you've received to mix, and you get a message saying that some (or all!) of the audio files are missing. There are a lot of possible reasons for this, running from the easily fixed to the complete disaster.

In Pro Tools, you will have the option to search for the files on any available hard drives and this is the first thing to try. Sometimes, when the files have been copied to your drive, the program file is looking for the audio where it was on the original drive so it can't find it. If this is the case, usually just asking the program to search for the audio files will resolve the problem.

If all of the audio files were not included in the transfer to your system, you have to find those files and add them. This problem is usually the result of there being multiple sources for the original audio. For example, if some of the audio was recorded and some taken from a sample library, it's possible that you only received the recorded audio and whoever made the transfer files forgot to include the sampled files. Or, the original audio was recorded at one or more studios and the files were never consolidated to one system, so not everything made it to the transfer.

Finding missing audio is sometimes relatively simple; the client realizes what happened, where the audio is, and sends it to you (a cloud-based system is fastest, of course). Sometimes the missing audio is old stuff that is no longer relevant, and you can ignore the missing files. But sometimes the files can be very difficult to track down. You may need to educate the client about how files are stored and then help figure out where the missing audio might be (on what hard drive, or at what studio). Sometimes the audio is in the possession of someone who previously worked on the project, and it will be up to you to appeal to that person for the missing audio. (I've had that happen on more than one occasion.)

If you simply can't find the audio, then it's down to the last possibilities. The audio either gets rerecorded, the artist or producer decides that the mix can proceed without the missing elements, or the project has to be scrapped. I've never gotten to the final disaster, but I have come close. If you are responsible for the recording, keep track of your audio!

WHAT NOT TO DO

Don't let a client leave without opening the files he or she brought for mixing.

This may be obvious, but it's worth repeating. If someone gives you files to mix (or master, or whatever), do not let the person leave without opening the files, making sure that all the audio that you need is present and that the music is going to play for you as expected. There are any number of problems that can occur besides missing audio, such as playing at the wrong sample rate or corrupted audio files that look okay but won't play or are distorted. Besides being able to access what is needed, you will want to review the material and the file with the client anyway, so make no assumptions!

The Backup

Of course, all program and audio files need to be backed up. I think we've all lived in the computer age long enough to have lost something (sometimes something very important) without having had a proper backup. Audio projects can be very large, so how do you handle the backup situation? Typically, either you will have been working on the project from the beginning or you are just receiving the files to mix. If it's your project from the start, you will need to keep a backup as you go.

Ideally, the backup lives somewhere other than the original files, but that isn't always practical. The cloud will work if the project is small or if you have a lot of cloud storage, but many projects get pretty large and extensive cloud storage gets expensive. Hard drives are relatively cheap, so having a backup on a separate hard drive is usually the most practical. If you are always working with others, it might be possible for them to have the backup drive and bring it each time you work, so everyone stays current. If you do some work when they're not around, you can back up the things you do in the interim and transfer them when they return with the drive. If you're on your own, two drives at home will prevent most disasters (outside of fire, flood, etc.).

If you're receiving files to mix, then the original files are usually still with the clients so you don't need to make a backup. You will need only to back up your program files and any new audio you might make (usually from time compression/expansion, tuning, gain changing, etc.). Be sure to get those files back to the clients at the end of the project so they have a complete set of files.

Eventual Disposition

What happens to all the files when the project is over? This is a thorny question, and one that doesn't always have a satisfactory answer. If you were the mix engineer, are you supposed to keep a backup of the files? Typically the answer is no, but it is important that you make this clear to the people you are working with. If the project is destined for CD release, I usually say that I will keep the files until the CD has been manufactured. The reality is that I have kept almost all the files from projects I have worked on, which is why I own over 15 hard drives! I don't know if all of the old drives will even mount anymore, but I just haven't been able to bring myself to discard material (though I also haven't bought new drives to transfer material from old drives—there's a limit to protecting client's files that I am no longer responsible for!)

The larger questions of whether old files will open on new systems or new program releases, and what kind of storage is most robust and likely to be functioning many years later, indicate the fragility of our audio projects. Of course, tape disintegrates over time (which is why so many old tape projects have been transferred to digital), but digital has longevity issues as well. There's no simple answer for this, aside from continually updating and backing up old files and having multiple locations for backups—not a practical solution for most of us. Ultimately, we have to accept the transient nature of all things, and focus our attention on not losing the files that we are currently working on!

Chapter 8

Delivering Mixes
Formats, Mix Types, and Multiple Mixes

Delivery of mixes has come a long way from the ¼-inch 15 IPS analog tape master. While delivery formats have always been in flux, contemporary digital file formats offer a large number of possibilities. Fortunately, there is much less of a compatibility problem than when a particular piece of hardware was required for each possible delivery format; now, DAWs can usually handle most digital audio files. A larger question remains, however, on the best way to deliver your mix for mastering. I have covered elements of this in regard to brick-wall limiting in chapter 3. Ultimately, you need to become familiar with the mastering process, as covered in detail in this chapter, to best understand how to create the final mix file for mastering.

8.1 Digital Formats for Mix Delivery

The best way to deliver a mix depends on a couple of key of questions: to whom are you delivering it and for what purpose? The mix format must be appropriate for the purpose the recipient intends for it. Often you will need to deliver mixes in a variety of formats to different participants. For instance, in a commercial project, you may need to deliver one mix to the artist, one mix to the record company, one mix to the webmaster, and one mix to the mastering house. But for other kinds of projects—such as website audio, film or DVD audio, or video game audio—the delivery requirements may be somewhat different. The extent to which your files are going to be mastered for their final destination also dictates important aspects of how you deliver your mixes. Lastly, if your project is not going to be mastered beyond your final mix, then you need to incorporate at least some of the standard mastering processes as a part of your product.

Digital formats are a constantly shifting array of file types, sampling rates, and bit depths. Specific audio delivery demands reflect the ultimate use of the audio files. Here, I cover delivery for CD mastering; Internet, film and video, and surround sound applications; video games, Internet downloading, and streaming services. In many instances, it will be necessary for you to talk with the person who will be working with the audio that you are delivering, as different applications require different audio formats, even though they may ultimately be put to the same use (e.g., streaming audio on an Internet site can call for a variety of source file formats, but the particular webmaster you are delivering audio to may require a certain format for that application).

Delivery for CD Mastering

Although different mastering engineers and mastering houses will want different file formats, depending on the programs they are running, there are two primary considerations for delivering your mixed master to the mastering engineer (even if you are the mastering engineer, too). The first is to provide the highest quality file format possible. This generally means maintaining the bit depth and bit rate that you used for your individual files before you created the mixed master. That is, if you recorded at 24-bit, 44.1 kHz (as I usually do), you will want to deliver your mixes in that same format, if possible. If you recorded at 48 kHz or at a higher sampling rate, you will want to maintain that sample rate as long as you've cleared the format with the person who will be doing the mastering.

One of the keys to providing the highest quality files is to do as little file conversion as possible prior to the mastering. The final CD master will have to be 16-bit, 44.1 kHz because that is the CD standard, but assuming you started with higher resolution files, conversion to this format should be postponed until the very last stage of file processing.

The second requirement is to provide files without any brickwall limiting. However, as explained in chapter 3, because brickwall limiting has become such a prominent part of final music delivery to the consumer, and because it affects the sound so dramatically, I find that I must complete my mixes using a brickwall limiter so that I can hear the likely effects of its use. Nevertheless, when I do the mastering, I deliver (or use myself, if I'm doing the mastering) my final mix with the brickwall limiter removed so that it can be added back in as the final process before creation of the mastered mix. If I'm delivering files to a mastering engineer (not doing it myself), I provide a file without brickwall limiting, but also provide a version with brickwall limiting so the mastering engineer can hear what I considered to be the actual sound of the final mix, as well as what the artist and/or producer heard and signed off on as the final mix. In fact, the role of brickwall limiting in mixing and mastering has become so important that appendix B explains the extent to which it has radically altered the relationship of mixing to mastering.

187

Recently, there has been a trend to using stems for the mastering process, so you may be asked to deliver stems. Stems have been a staple of large-scale film mixing for a long time, and they have also become an essential element in delivery of audio for video game work, as described later in the "Delivery for Video Games" section (which also includes explanation of what stems are and how they are created). See that section and the What Not To Do section below for discussions of delivering stems for CD mastering.

WHAT NOT TO DO

Don't deliver stems for mastering if you love your mixes.
The recent trend toward stem, or separation mastering, is not really mastering per se but, rather, a continuation of the mix process done by the mastering engineer. Face it; when it comes to sound, most of us engineers are control freaks, so whatever mastering engineer thought up "separation mastering," it was actually a means of gaining more control in the mastering process. This comes at a price for the mixes, of course; they are very likely to be altered more in separation mastering than in traditional stereo mastering.

Stems are submixes, so using stems to master means recombining the submixes into a new mix. Yes, it does offer more control, and it can be done so that the results are still very similar to the original mix, but it is not really mastering—it is a continuation of the mix process. I had a recent project mastered using stems and in stereo (no stems); the mastering engineer preferred the separation master, but I preferred the stereo master.

On the other hand, if you are not confident about your mixes, if you are new to the mix process, or if the mixes you've gotten from your mix engineer don't really sound right to you, then you may want to consider asking your mastering engineer to do separation mastering as a way to further refine your mixes. It will cost more than traditional mastering, but it may be worth it if you want another person's input on the mixes.

Delivery for Internet Applications

The ultimate file format that will be used for Internet applications (such as streaming clips on an artist's website) may vary, but the delivery file is most frequently an mp3 that is then converted or reprocessed as needed by the webmaster. Protocols for downloading and streaming vary, and the webmaster may ask for files in another format besides mp3, such as M4a's, RealAudio, or Quick-Time Audio. If you are delivering audio for these kinds of applications, you may need to invest in software that will do file conversion to a variety of formats, or you can ask the webmaster if they can handle the conversion. I always try

MP3

Encoder

Encoding Speed: [Slowest   ▲]   Fraunhofer Institut
                                                Integrierte Schaltungen
                    320kbit/s (44100Hz)
Constant Bit Rate (CBR): ✓ 256kbit/s (44100Hz)   c File
                    224kbit/s (44100Hz)
☐ Enable MP3 Surround Encodin 192kbit/s (44100Hz)   pe: MPG3   Creator: mAmp
                    160kbit/s (44100Hz)
                    128kbit/s (44100Hz)
ID3 Tag Info   112kbit/s (44100Hz)
                    96kbit/s (44100Hz)
Tag Type: [ID3 v2.3 ⇕] 80kbit/s (44100Hz)
Title: 64kbit/s (22050Hz)
                    56kbit/s (22050Hz)
Artist: 48kbit/s (22050Hz)
                    40kbit/s (22050Hz)
Album: 32kbit/s (11025Hz)
                    24kbit/s (11025Hz)
Comment: 20kbit/s (11025Hz)
                    18kbit/s (11025Hz)
Genre: [Rock ⇕]   16kbit/s (11025Hz)
Track: [1   ]   Year:

[Defaults]   [Cancel]   [OK]

SCREENSHOT 8.1

An mp3 dialog menu showing file format and meta-data options.

189

to deliver the audio in the CD format as well, so that the client has this on file for reference or for use in later applications where higher quality audio might be used.

Many of these Internet file protocols, including mp3s, contain more encoded metadata information than a CD-R (see screenshot 8.1). A musical category can be designated, which will enable the music to be sorted and potentially recommended in consumer searches. Information about the original CD release, number of tracks, position of this track in the sequence, whether the CD was a compilation, and so on can be included with the file as well as provide a link to the artwork, if this has been posted at a particular Internet address. I expect digital file formats to continue to add metadata capabilities to further integrate music tracks into the media data stream that is contained on an individual's computer. (There will be more on meta-data as part of the mastering process in chapter 12.)

WHAT NOT TO DO

Don't take the quick and easy route to mp3 file conversion.
Not all conversion to the mp3 format is created equal, so don't just use the simplest route, such as allowing the default settings on iTunes do the conversion for you. There are options on iTunes for higher quality conversion, dedicated conversion programs that supply many more options, and many DAWs also have mp3 conversion available with greater options for

higher fidelity. The standard resolution of 128 kbps at 44.1 kHz is decent quality (for mp3s, that is—none of which are really very good), and it creates pretty small files, which helps for easy email attaching and relatively light CPU load when streaming. However, higher resolution mp3s (the standard goes to 320 kbps) provide better sounding audio and still create reasonably small files in today's world of high bandwidth and fast computer processors. Use the highest resolution possible for whatever your delivery requirements are (definitely worth discussing with the person you're delivering these files to). It is also becoming much easier to share full bandwidth wave files (the CD standard is 16 bit, 44.1 kHz) through various cloud services. I try not to deliver mixes as mp3s (sometimes it's unavoidable)—the CD standard sounds much better!

Delivery for Film and Video

Audio for film and video may require synchronization with the visual elements. Obviously, dialogue requires synchronization, but so do most sound effects and music cues. In order to work effectively to picture, you will need to import a movie file into your DAW. The movie file should be a "window dub," which means that the time- code location number has been burned into a small window at the bottom of each frame (see screenshot 8.2). Establishing and maintaining sync through the use of time code is beyond the scope of this book, and there are many variables to consider.

Audio that accompanies picture may end up in a variety of formats, from small-scale documentaries to big-screen movie projection, from YouTube to concert DVDs. The file format required will vary depending on the final release platform and which editing and/or authoring program is being used. Check for

SCREENSHOT 8.2

A DAW work environment including a movie window dub.

this information with the person responsible for authoring to the final delivery format. Surround sound (typically 5.1 surround) is increasingly common for film and video, so you may need to supply both stereo and surround audio files (see below and appendix A regarding the surround format). You will need to work closely with the other content providers, including the author, editor, and packaging people, if you are providing sound that is to accompany visual elements. Large-scale projects also employ stem mixing, as described below regarding mixes for video game use.

Delivery of Surround Sound Files

Surround sound comes in various formats, but the dominant format on DVD is 5.1 surround, made up of left, right, center, rear left, rear right, and LFE (low-frequency extension) channels. The two rear channels are often referred to as the "surround" channels—they feed the "surround" speakers in back or to the sides of the listener. The LFE channel is, in fact, a distinct channel, so there are actually six channels of audio; but because it is not full frequency (carrying only subwoofer information, typically from about 90 Hz and below), it is referred to as the .1 channel of 5.1.

Format requirements for delivery of 5.1 audio may differ, but the current standard for surround that is destined for DVD is 48 kHz, 16-bit AIFF files, as this is what is used in the most common authoring programs (authoring is the process of assembling and finalizing the visual and audio elements for a DVD). Surround for DVD is encoded as an AAC file for Dolby, or some other codec for a different surround format such as DTS. Usually the audio person supplies the 48 kHz, 16-bit AIFF files, and the encoding is taken care of at the DVD authoring stage. If you are required to supply encoded files, you will need to get either an application that does the encoding or an add-on for your DAW that allows you to do this encoding within the DAW (only certain DAWs support this option).

The standard order for 5.1 files is as follows:

Channel 1: Front left
Channel 2: Front right
Channel 3: Center
Channel 4: LFE (low-frequency extension)
Channel 5: Rear left
Channel 6: Rear right

It is critical that the files be in this order for them to encode properly. Very large-scale film projects and some large home theater installations use 7.1 surround files, with a variety of philosophies regarding speaker placement for the extra set of left/right surround files.

Delivery for Video Games

Formats for delivery of audio for video games may vary, but it is likely that you will be asked to deliver a stereo mix, stems, and possibly a 5.1 surround mix. Because video games require so much music to accompany the many hours of game play, the audio elements may get used in different versions at different times. In order to do this, stereo stems are made, taken from the final stereo mix. A stem is simply an element taken from the larger mix of the composition. Together, the stems form the original composition and mix.

A typical group of stems might include five categories:

1. drums
2. percussion
3. bass
4. guitars
5. keyboards

More complex compositions may require 11 stems or more, such as:

1. drums
2. high percussion
3. low percussion
4. bass
5. rhythm guitars
6. lead guitars
7. horn section
8. piano
9. keyboards
10. lead vocal
11. harmony vocals

Once the final mix is done, the stems are made simply by muting all other tracks and running a "mix" of each particular stem element. The video-game developers then use the stems to create musical passages that contain certain elements from the full mix but not others (for example, a percussion-only mix, or a mix with rhythm instruments and no melody). Remember that in all these collaborative projects that combine audio and other elements (dialog, effects, etc.), you will need to coordinate your work—delivery elements, delivery file format, etc.) with others working on different parts of the project.

Delivery for Downloading and Streaming Services

Different downloading and streaming services use different file formats, but to gain access to most of them (especially the bigger ones, such as iTunes and Amazon, or streaming services such as Pandora, Spotify, and MOG), you will have to deliver your music to an aggregator (such as CDBaby, Record Union, or

Ditto Music); they then deliver it to the service. In many cases, this is the only way you will have access to such services.

Where you can deliver files yourself, the service provides information on what kind of file it will accept. If you're using an aggregator, you may have several options as to what kind of file to upload, and they then make the appropriate conversion for whatever service they are delivering to. In this case, always deliver the highest quality file that the aggregator will accept.

CREATIVE TIP

Encourage high quality download options.
As bandwidth increases and Internet download speeds accelerate accordingly, it has become increasingly possible to make sense of high-quality music downloads for the consumer. Search "CD quality downloads"; this will yield many sites that aggregate CD quality music and also yield results for sites offering "better than CD quality downloads," meaning files with higher bit rate and/or bandwidth than the 16-bit, 44.1 kHz CD standard.

With a decent Internet connection, you can download a typical CD file-format song in just a few minutes, and the quality will be substantially better than an mp3, M4a, or other compressed format. Most music players (including smartphones and tablets) handle the higher fidelity files just fine. Of course, these files take up considerably more space on your hard drive (approximately 10 times as much as an mp3 for a typical song). But with drive storage also becoming much cheaper and larger storage becoming standard, the specter of "large" audio files no longer is much of an impediment. I encourage all artists to make their music available in at least CD-quality files (as well as mp3s for the impatient), and I urge all consumers to take the time to find and download their favorite music in at least CD-quality files, if possible.

193

8.2 Full Mixes, TV Mixes, and Clips

Variations on the full mix file have increased as technologies have evolved. For a long time we delivered a full mix file as well as a "TV" mix or a "karaoke" mix. These are mixes that are missing the lead vocal. The one is called a TV mix because it can be used for a singer making a TV appearance; the TV mix is played and the singer performs live for the camera. This idea is now common practice in some genres for live club appearances and is also for karaoke service, if you happen to need that.

In any event, it's a good idea to create a TV or karaoke mix with no lead vocal. Sometimes artists will want variations on this. For example, I make a "no vocal" and "no piano" mix for a vocalist who sometimes appears with just her piano accompanist and wants to have the band tracks for additional accompaniment.

With so many artists and Internet services offering streaming clips as a way to promote music, I am often asked to create such clips from my mixes for the artist's website. Sometimes I'm given instructions as to where to start and stop the clip, but often I'm left to my own devices. Although the copyright laws are vague on this application, generally you can use clips of cover songs as long as you keep the excerpts brief (certainly under 30 seconds) and they are used only to demonstrate what the song sounds like, not to "decorate" or provide accompaniment for a website.

Clips should fade in and out, but very quickly. I generally start somewhere in a verse and get through at least half of the chorus, though of course song structures differ significantly and you have to decide how best to represent the song when choosing the section to take the clip from. Although clips are typically done as mp3s, you will want to confirm the desired file format with whoever is responsible for posting the audio.

8.3 Multiple Versions of a Single Mix

We used to record multiple versions of a mix as a matter of course. Because it was so difficult or impossible to recreate a mix once the studio was reconfigured for another session, we would try to anticipate changes that we might want to consider later. The most common variations on mixes were ones with different lead vocal levels. For example, we'd take a mix and then a "vocal up" mix in case we wanted a louder vocal. We might also take a "vocal down" mix, or two mixes with different "vocal up" levels, or a "drums up" mix. The problem, of course, was that there were endless options and the time and materials it took to run these mixes started to defeat the purpose.

If you are mixing in the box, the only reason to take multiple mixes is to have different possibilities to review. Because I'm often working remotely and can't consult with the artist on the spot, it is fairly common for me to make a couple different mixes for review, so that certain options can be considered. As discussed previously in the section on collaboration, if I'm making a significant change, such as muting a part, I definitely make two mixes for review. If it's just the age-old question of vocal level, I send whatever I think sounds right and wait for feedback.

Even if you are not mixing completely in the box—if you're supplementing your mix with some hardware processing—it might still be easy to log the settings on a few external pieces to allow for pretty simple recall. Many recordists and artists have come to depend on ease of recall as a means of providing the opportunity to live with mixes for a while, or to work remotely, with easy revisions being an essential part of mixing collaborations.

III

MASTERING

The introduction to part I of this book defined mastering, and presented a Quick Guide to best practices. Part II covered the details of mixing. It is time now to delve into the mastering process. I begin in part III with the basic tools for mastering and the framework of file structures you will need to master "in the box." I then explore all the essential mastering processes from the standpoint of your ear, introducing the basics of singal processing for mastering from a conceptual standpoint. I go on to detail the mastering process, focusing on both the practical application and the accompanying aesthetic criteria of signal processing for mastering. Lastly, I present the end stages of mastering production and delivery, and discuss collaboration in terms of both the creative process and in regard to working with others remotely.

The Loudness Wars

Hovering over all the technical and theoretical knowledge that forms the basis for this part of the book is a major issue facing the contemporary mastering engineer: loudness. Digital audio allows for the extreme exaggeration of audio levels with the application of a brickwall limiter. This processor offers a trade-off between impact and breath (or dynamics) that, when used to the extreme (as has become increasingly common), causes a listener fatigue that threatens the ability to have a sustained relationship to the music. Loud music can have great impact, but that impact eventually wears the listener down, ultimately alienating the individual from that very same musical experience.

I introduced this matter in chapter 3 and discussed it in more detail at various points in part II, but there is more that has been said about the "loudness wars" in dedicated web pages, forums, and discussion groups on the Internet. I encourage everyone involved in mastering, whether you're doing it yourself or working with a mastering engineer, to become familiar with the concerns that have been expressed about overly loud mastering levels. I also point you to appendix B, "Why Mixing and Mastering Can No Longer Be Separated." There, you will learn how the tools for producing loudness have impacted what used to be the separation between mixing and mastering.

Chapter 9

Setting up to Master
Tools and Files

Getting ready for a mastering project requires that you first have the tools you need to do the job and second that you make a file or files that have all the elements needed for the final master. There are options for these elements, but in this chapter I consider the general tasks at hand and encourage you to explore the ever-changing world of options on your own.

9.1 **Tools**

Having defined what mastering is in the introduction to part I, and having introduced some of the basics in the Quick Guide, it is now time to consider the specific tools you need to accomplish the task. The first set of tools is your room and your playback system. In chapter 3, I summarized the major issues regarding frequency balance and I warned about problems created by inadequate monitoring. The better the monitoring, the more accurately you can assess the audio.

As indicated in chapter 3, control of the low frequencies is particularly challenging, so a listening environment and playback systems that are reasonably accurate and extend into the low frequencies is particularly important. As a result, either full-range speakers or a subwoofer are essential. For most of us, the subwoofer option is a cheaper alternative to speakers that extend into the very low frequencies; it also provides balanced monitoring throughout the frequency range. There is detailed information on room and speaker setup, as well as selection, in other portions of this book (use the index) and in my previous book, *The Art of Digital Audio Recording*.

You will note that the three topics that follow—level, EQ, and dynamics and effects—are also discussed in the next two chapters. These functions constitute the bulk of the mastering process, and I explore them thoroughly. Although many mastering engineers use hardware processors as a part of their mastering chains, this book focuses on work in the DAW; therefore, I discuss plug-in options and needs rather than hardware.

Level

The number one job of mastering is to match the levels of all the separate elements in the final master. The simplest way to do this is with the automation system in your DAW. You can adjust the output levels for each element by automating the level, or fader position. However, because of common use of brickwall limiting, controlling the level in mastering typically focuses more on using a brickwall limiter plug-in than on direct control of the fader position.

Because the brickwall limiter (defined and discussed in chapters 3 and 4) affects both level and dynamics, it is central to mastering's level and dynamics. Here, regarding tools, suffice it to say that you need a brickwall limiter plug-in to do most types of contemporary mastering. There are many to choose from, and new ones are emerging at a pretty rapid rate. Unfortunately, these plug-ins come with a variety of names, so you have to explore their capabilities to make sure you are getting the brickwall limiting function you need. There are also a number of "combo" mastering plug-ins that incorporate many mastering functions, including brickwall limiting. These can be fine—just be sure they have the functions you need.

Brickwall limiters can be very simple plug-ins, with just a couple of parameter adjustments, or they can have elaborate interfaces that offer a variety of strategies for limiting. Thankfully, most plug-in companies offer free trials so you can audition the various processors and decide which one works best for you. See screenshot 9.1 for a sampling of brickwall limiters.

SCREENSHOT 9.1

An array of brickwall limiters (including multi-processors).

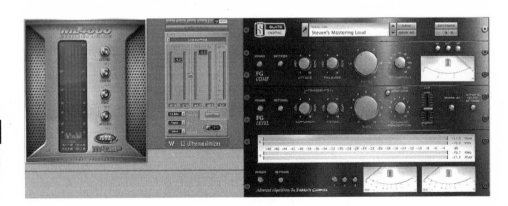

EQ

EQ adjustments are common in mastering. Typically, the mastering EQ includes a broad range of controls and is as transparent as possible, meaning that the processor has minimal effects, such as phase shift or distortion. Equalizers that are designed to add noticeable artifacts, such as analog-style distortion, are usually not considered best for mastering applications (though this may be desirable depending on the aesthetic goal). By a broad range of controls, I mean that you would typically want at least five bands of fully parametric EQ along with high- and low-pass filters.

There are many EQ plug-ins made specifically for mastering, and while they are often an excellent choice, they are not essential. Control and transparency are key, and many multi-purpose EQs possess those qualities as well and can be appropriate for mastering. Linear-phase EQs (as discussed in chapter 4) are often favored for mastering because of their particularly transparent qualities, but again, whether they are the best choice depends on the aesthetic. See screenshot 9.2 for a sampling of EQs for mastering applications.

Dynamics and Effects

Any processors that might be used in recording or mixing could also be useful in a mastering session, though typically mastering focuses on level and EQ adjustments. The same holds true for dynamics processors (outside of the brick-wall limiters already discussed) as for EQs: flexibility and transparency are generally the desirable qualities. As with EQs, phase-linear compressors may be preferable for their transparency, but they are not essential.

There are a whole breed of multi-band compressors that function more like EQs (see section 4.4 for details), and these can be life-savers for solving

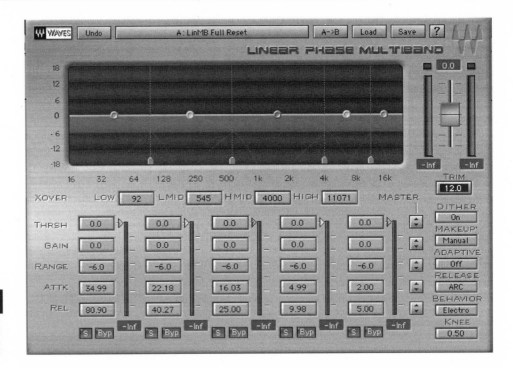

SCREENSHOT 9.3

A phase-linear multi-band compressor and expander.

200

problems (as discussed in section 11.3), but I don't recommend them as a major part of the mastering chain of processors. Many compressors can also function as expanders, and some mastering engineers favor expansion as part of a typical mastering session. A good (flexible and transparent) expander *should* be a part of the mastering toolkit, though I find I use it infrequently. Screenshot 9.3 shows a processor that can function as a multi-band compressor, or a multi-band expander; the fact that it is named "phase linear multiband" skirts the issue as to whether it is for dynamics or EQ.

Reverbs and delays may come into play in mastering when it's not possible or practical to return to the mix stage and it's felt that these effects will enhance the final recording. Whatever reverbs or delays you use in mixing will be suitable for mastering, if the situation calls for it.

Other effects processors, such as analog simulators, may useful during mastering, though this entails an aesthetic choice that may go beyond the wishes of the artist and/or producer if they were happy with the mix. In section 13.2, I consider the issues surrounding appropriate intervention in mastering.

Other Tools

With the wide variety of release formats for audio these days there are any number of other tools you may want or need to create appropriate masters. The most common master is probably still the one needed for CD manufacturing (also called "replication"). The default format for CD manufacturing is still a CD-R master, but DDP (Disc Description Protocol) files are increasingly common, even now often preferred by the larger replication plants.

In addition to, or instead of, a CD master, you may need to provide other file formats, including WAV (Waveform Audio File Format), BWF (Broadcast Wave Files), AIFF (Audio Interchange File Format), MP3 (MPEG-1 or MPEG-2 Audio Layer III), AAC (Advanced Audio Coding), and FLAC (Free Lossless Audio Codec). Although you probably don't own a lathe (which is required to cut the acetate master needed to create vinyl LPs), large, full-service mastering houses do. Details on creating and delivering these files are covered in section 12.2, on master delivery options.

9.2 Creating a Template

With many DAW programs you can create a template, which will shorten the setup time for a new mastering project. Programs differ greatly in how they handle individual track processing, so your template setup will depend on your DAW. If your program requires additional instructions in order to automate the settings for your brickwall limiter and your EQ parameters, then creating a template with these instructions will save time. For example, you will almost certainly want to be able to automate the threshold for your brickwall limiter, as well as separately set your boost and dip parameters for all of your available EQ bands for every track in your master. A template with these functions will enable you to get to work more quickly.

Your template might also include an appropriate workspace setup for mastering. In my case, because I master in Pro Tools, my template includes automation for many of my mastering plug-in parameters, as well as optimal track size and plug-in interface positioning (see screenshot 9.4).

201

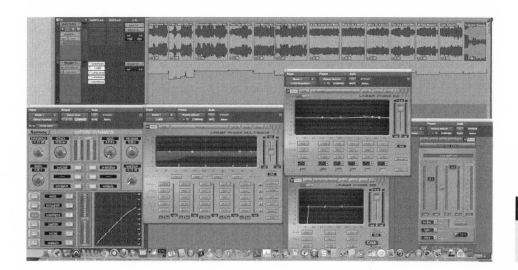

SCREENSHOT 9.4

A Pro Tools mastering template.

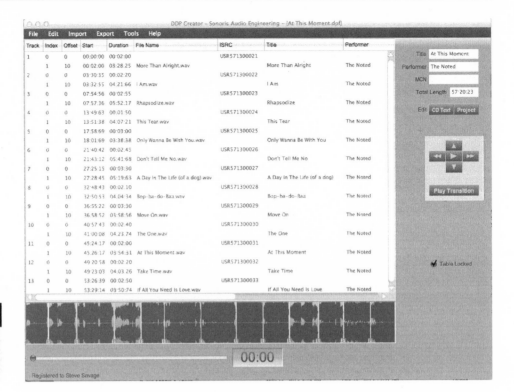

SCREENSHOT 9.5

A program for master CD-R burning and for DDP files set creation.

202

9.3 **Building a Time Line**

Because of the various kinds and capabilities of DAWs, and the many formats that music are delivered in, there are different kinds of masters and different ways to create them. In my case, I do most mastering in Pro Tools, but it doesn't have CD-R burning capabilities. So, after I've created all the mastered files in Pro Tools, I use a different program for burning a master CD-R or creating a DDP file set. So, I create a time line while I'm working on individual tracks in Pro Tools that matches the final CD sequence (see screenshot 9.5).

Theoretically, your master should work regardless of what order the tracks are in, but practically speaking, the order can affect your decision making. It's not uncommon, however, for an artist or producer to be unsure of the sequence, and it may change before the final master is ready. It may even change after the final is master is sent to the manufacturer, necessitating an alert to the plant to wait for the new master with the revised sequence. Still, I recommend working with a time line that reflects the current thinking on the sequence; it's the best way to gauge transitions from one track to the next.

Chapter 10

How to Listen for Mastering
From Your Ear to Action

In discussing mixing concepts, I described the difficulty some musicians have in listening to recordings for how they *sound*, without getting distracted by the musical content. While mixing benefits from the ability to separate your focus from the musical ideas and instead place it on to the sonic qualities, mastering absolutely requires it! Effective mastering entails focused listening on the audio event (song, etc.): What does it sound like? And how does that relate to the sound of the other audio events to which it is to be matched? This chapter focuses on how to adjust your ear to hear the fundamental qualities of the audio that may need attention in mastering.

Despite this principle, the mastering process cannot be completely divorced from considerations that go beyond pure sound. Musical genres have many conventions that show up in how the final masters generally sound. Even if your goal is to defy those conventions, you will have limited success in mastering styles of music with which you are not familiar. Here, I point to some of the genre conventions, and in doing so, also to the kind of listening you want to do when you have the perspective of the mastering engineer.

Finally, I discuss how *detailed listening* begins to be translated into making the adjustments needed for your master. This introduces many of the concepts and approaches that I cover in the more thorough discussions of processing that follow in the next chapter.

CREATIVE TIP

Use your favorite mastered tracks as models.
This is advice that I also give in regard to mixing. Using as a model the work that you admire is a great way to gauge your judgment of the elements discussed here. It is especially useful for referencing some of the idiosyncrasies of certain genres. Knowing those idiosyncrasies will help you decide how to fit (or not fit) into the genre's general practices. You're using those favorite tracks as models for your work because you love the way they sound (of course, it may also be material you love for other reasons); if you don't admire them from a sonic point of view, they aren't helpful mastering references.

WHAT NOT TO DO

Don't get caught in the "louder sounds better" trap.
There is always the danger of falling prey to the "louder sounds better" argument. Additional brickwall limiting, any EQ boosting, and even many effects processors, such as most analog simulators, all add volume. It's easy to immediately think "That sounds better!" But does it really?

Louder sounds better usually because it gets more of our attention. If two people are talking to you at the same time, you most likely will understand the one who is talking loudest. But it's more than that. Because of the Fletcher-Munson curve (discussed in section 2.2), louder also enables you to hear the high and low frequencies better, so the music sounds richer and more full frequency. (This effect reverses at very loud volumes, where your ear starts to attenuate frequencies.) So, small boosts in volume created by slight changes in processing may seem to sound better initially; but evaluate this in light of the volume shift. Sometimes it is worth listening, then processing, then listening to the processed signal turned down slightly, so as to compensate for the processing bump in gain.

10.1 Level

As mentioned earlier, job number one for mastering is to balance the levels for all the elements. This simply means that all the tracks should sound like they are at the same level. That's easy to say, but it's difficult to do and is a highly subjective process. Different tracks may have very different instrumentation and dynamic ranges, making them hard to match in volume. For example, the volume of a full electric rock band is going to be heard very differently from that of a single acoustic guitar and voice, yet the two elements may need to be balanced for level in your master.

There are two primary techniques for balancing the level of any material that sidestep the differences in density and dynamic range, allowing you to balance even the most disparate kinds of audio. As detailed below, the first is to pay particular attention to the lead vocal or lead instrument and the second is to focus on the loudest part of the track.

Listening for Level

Lead Vocal or Lead Instrument

In general, you will want to focus your attention on the lead vocal or lead instrument (in an instrumental track). Because arrangements and mixes can vary so much, one of the best ways to balance level from track to track is to try to get the loudest element (typically the lead vocal) to sound at relatively the same level from tune to tune. The listener's attention is almost always focused on this leading element, so if its volume sounds balanced from track to track, the listener is going to feel that the levels are well matched.

Loudest Part of the Track

At the same time you will want to try to balance the loudest part of each track. Tracks will likely differ considerably in dynamic range—some may go from very quiet to very loud, and some may just stay pretty loud throughout. For the listener, it is critical that one track doesn't jump up to a level that becomes uncomfortable; he or she generally sets the level of a player at the beginning and doesn't want to have to jump up and change the volume on some later track. But if all the loudest sections of the tracks are relatively balanced, then the overall listening experience should be consistent.

One track may get much quieter than another if it has a larger dynamic range, but that's just the nature of musical variation. Balancing the *perception* of level for the lead vocal with the *perception* of the loudest section is covered later in this chapter, with considerations of consistency.

Overall Level

In addition to setting the individual level for each track, you must decide on an overall level for the entire project. The issues surrounding brickwall limiting were introduced in the Quick Guide, section 3.3. Brickwall limiters supply the ability to limit the program material in a way that provides greater impact, but comes with a reduction in the musicality (natural dynamics) of the performances. It can be a very delicate balancing act: more aggressive limiting might provide a better "first impression," but it can have a negative effect on long-term pleasure.

Different genres will suggest different degrees of brickwall limiting, and some genres have aesthetics that may influence how you set your overall volume

205

and thus your use of brickwall limiting. On one hand, music that tends to favor more relaxed playing and listening environments, such as classical, soft jazz, folk, and other acoustic music, will sound inappropriately aggressive if you apply much brickwall limiting. On the other hand, very aggressive music, such as most heavy metal, punk, and various offshoots of rap, can withstand greater degrees of brickwall limiting and remain consistent with the genre. (One of the greater controversies on this subject came about over Metallica's 2008 release *Death Magnetic,* when over 13,000 fans signed a petition asking for the CD to be remastered with less limiting.)

Most rock, pop, hip-hop, world, blues, and so on fall somewhere between these two poles; you will need to find the line between the amount of limiting needed for the music to fit comfortably in the genre and the degree to which you maintain the tracks dynamics. Of course, the degree of compression used in the recording and mixing of the track also affects the extent you want to apply further dynamics reduction through brickwall limiting.

Perceptions of commercial ambition may also affect the application of brickwall limiting. If you are anxious for your music to "compete" with other releases, you may be inclined to aggressive limiting. I say "perceptions" since there is no proof that loudness affects sales. New consumer technologies, such as the streaming services provided by iTunes, Spotify, and Pandora, will adjust for variations in volume from track to track, beginning to neutralize whatever advantage you may have intended for "louder" tracks.

On a recent CD that I co-produced with the artist Bonnie Hayes, we put the following disclaimer on the jacket: THIS RECORD WAS MASTERED TO SOUND GOOD, NOT TO BE LOUD. IT IS UP TO YOU TO TURN IT UP! Of course, I did apply some brickwall limiting; I just didn't crush the life out of the music—and you can play a record as loud as you want, whatever the mastering level. But if a song with no brickwall limiting is in a playlist on an iPod, that recording will sound small, with very little impact compared to the others.

On the website I have the following clips from the Bonnie Hayes CD with three levels of limiting. I have adjusted the output to try to balance the clips so you can better hear the effect of the limiter—however, it isn't completely possible to set each clip to the "same" level because the dynamic range is altered and the level will be perceived differently no matter how they are set.

Artist: Bonnie Hayes CD: *Love in the Ruins* Track: "I Can't Stop"

Audio Clip 10.1 A clip of a section mastered with no brickwall limiting.

Audio Clip 10.2 The same clip with moderate limiting, as used on the final CD release (but output is lowered to better balance with the first clip).

Audio Clip 10.3 The same clip with aggressive limiting (and output is further lowered to better balance with the first two clips).

10.2 Frequency/EQ

After setting the level, your next most common process in mastering is frequency adjustment. There are two distinct reasons for adjusting the frequencies: to sound best and to match best (a variation on the "sounds best/fits best" issue in mixing). Overall sound quality and optimum matching qualities are equally important, but they require very different approaches, as well as different justifications for how to proceed.

Listening for EQ

Sounds Best

What "sounds best" when it comes to balancing frequencies is, of course, very subjective. But a good starting point is to go back to the meaning of EQ. *EQ* stands for "equalization"; when EQ processors were being developed, the concept was that all audio should be "equalized" in terms of its frequency balance. So EQ was invented with the purpose of creating balanced or "equalized" frequency response. It today's world, EQ is used for much more than just achieving balanced frequencies. In the part on mixing, I discussed a number of examples where EQ might be used to purposely unbalance the frequencies of some sounds to get them to fit best into a mix. Nonetheless, the goal of mixing is usually to create a final mix that is well balanced across the frequency spectrum, and therefore the goal of mastering is often to fine-tune those balances.

So, mastering often returns you to the original goal of the EQ processors—creating an equalized balance of frequencies from low to high. You need to focus your ear on the frequency spectrum and consider how well balanced each segment is. It is often convenient to think in terms of lows, low-mids, high-mids, and highs as a way to organize your listening, and ultimately your application of EQ (more on this in section 11.3). Of course, the musical arrangement is going to affect that balance, but this is another instance where you need to start by divorcing yourself from the musical content and just listen to the sound. As you start to hear the relative balance between frequencies, you can then consider how the arrangement might be affecting them and take that into consideration. For example, a simple arrangement with just acoustic guitar and voice is not going to have the same presence in the low frequencies as a piece that includes an acoustic or electric bass.

Matches Best

The other side of EQ'ing decisions for mastering is what individual adjustments in frequency will help all of the tracks match best, from one to the next. These decisions often are completely outside the "sounds best" point of view. Two tracks may sound just right to you, but when you listen to them back to back, you realize that the first track has less apparent low end than the second. They both may be perfectly acceptable on their own, but you will want to add low end to the first or dip the lows from the second so they sound more balanced going from one to the other.

In some instances, you may find that not only is "matches best" unrelated to "sounds best," but that the two are actually in conflict. If you make changes to create better matching, you may feel that you are no longer getting the best sound out of the track. In truth, you may not be able to fully accommodate both "sounds best" and "matches best"—you'll have to decide what is the best compromise. I discuss the best strategies for working with these conflicts and with the specifics of both "sounds best" and "matches best" processing, in the following chapter.

WHAT NOT TO DO

Don't rely on a spectrum analyzer.
This is a repeat of a What Not to Do from chapter 4 because, in the case of spectrum analyzers, the same principle holds true for mastering. I mentioned in section 2.1 that a spectrum analyzer could be useful for uncovering strange anomalies that might be out of the range of your speakers (or your hearing), such as infrasound (very low frequencies below the hearing threshold) or ultrasound (very high frequencies above the hearing threshold). It may also be valuable for beginners, helping them catch very out-of-balance frequency elements that might have been the result of poor mixes. It's worth checking your master on a spectrum analyzer, but other than as a way to catch the oddities, it's dangerous for anything more than a rough guide. You need to learn to trust your ear.

Genres have certain tendencies in regard to overall frequency balance, and this is another good reason to be wary of spectrum analyzers. Many contemporary R&B and rap tracks have a pronounced bump in the low end. A lot of rock & roll has noticeable boosts in the presence of high-mid frequencies. More pop-oriented mixes often have quite a bit of airy, high-frequency information. Of course, there are no hard-and-fast rules for any of these genres, but familiarity with convention is an important part of making the creative decisions that either conform or intentionally do not conform to genre expectations. In any event, responding to the dictates of a spectrum analyzer might produce more even, but less rewarding results.

10.3 Dynamics and Effects

Dynamics may be adjusted in mastering, for different reasons. Compression, expansion, and multi-band processing each have possible roles to play in the mastering process, though they are not necessarily part of a typical mastering session. As previously discussed, other effects also may be part of mastering, though this is relatively uncommon.

Compression and Expansion

Listening for dynamics in your tracks, and the decision to apply either compression or expansion, involves a variety of considerations. Buss compression (compressing the entire mix) is usually added in the mixing process (explored in section 3.3), so it is unlikely that you will want to use additional compression in mastering. Though if the track sounds particularly weak—that is, lacking impact—it may be a candidate for compression prior to brickwall limiting. Compression may also enter the picture in "matching" considerations as you listen from track to track. There is more on using compression in mastering in the next chapter.

Although I have covered brickwall limiting in several other sections of this book, and because of its direct correlation to overall level, it is important to remember that it is a dynamics processor. The likelihood is that you will be adding compression—reducing the overall dynamic range—with the use of brickwall limiting. This is another reason to be wary of additional compression in mastering.

Although I think it is rare on the whole, I know one mastering engineer who frequently uses expansion as part of mastering. Expansion increases the dynamic range, which adds expressiveness, but it is at the expense of presence or impact. Expansion is one tool that can combat overcompression, but compression followed by expansion does not produce the same result as skipping the compression in the first place. See the creative tip below for how to balance the compression/expansion in your mastering work.

CREATIVE TIP

Think of expansion and compression along the expression-to-impact continuum.

Musical dynamics are key to expressiveness. One of the most expressive live musical moments I have ever experienced was during a Buddy Guy show, where the band stopped and Buddy played so quietly (but intensely) that I could just barely hear the guitar. The audience got incredibly quiet and the room was quivering with musical presence. Of course, if you tried to reproduce this in a recording, you would want a fair amount of buss compression so that the quiet section didn't completely disappear at a normal, living-room playback level. Hence, the trade-off: more dynamics produces more expressiveness, but can lose impact as it compromises the listening experience. Conversely, less dynamics creates greater impact by maintaining a consistent presence, but compromises the expressiveness.

209

> *The reality is that it usually isn't a matter of adding expansion to regain dynamics but, rather, whether or not to use any additional compression prior to brickwall limiting—and if you decide to compress, how much to use. Keeping in mind all of the technical things already discussed regarding compression and brickwall limiting, you can aim your creativity toward hitting this balance between expression and impact. The particular genre (many rock and rap subgenres focus on impact, many folk and roots music subgenres focus on expression) will factor into how you achieve this result.*

Multi-band Compressors

Another tool often mentioned in regard to mastering is the multi-band compressor. As explained in section 4.4, multi-band compressors are also referred to as dynamic EQ, as they straddle the worlds of EQ and dynamics control. In most cases, you are simply trying to subtly enhance and match all the original mixes that you are mastering. Multi-band compressors create new, dynamic frequency balances, changing the shape of the mix from moment to moment. Generally you do not want to be this proactive in reshaping mixes if you (and those you are working with) are happy with the original mixes.

Multi-band compressors have their place in mastering, but as in mixing, they are most useful as problem solvers rather than as essential links in the chain of mastering processors. In chapter 11, I cover how these processors can help with certain problems. For now, I simply suggest you bypass the multi-band as a regular part of your mastering toolkit.

Effects

They are rarely used but sometimes are exactly what a mix needs. Effects such as reverb and delay should come into the mastering process only when you feel there is something significantly wrong or lacking in the mix and it isn't practical (because of time or money) to return to mixing and correct it. I get into the specifics of effects in the next chapter, but typically their use is not a regular part of mastering.

10.4 Consistency

Consistency might be the watchword for how the mastering engineer strives to adjust all the elements of a mix. But consistency can have different meanings in different contexts, and there is often tension between different kinds of consistencies, requiring creative judgment. The master should sound like all the elements belong together, offering a sense of wholeness evolved from the individual elements. Consistency—always thinking about what is going to help make all these elements work together best—should be the context for your listening and processing decisions.

What creates the proper consistency is highly subjective, though clearly the main considerations of level and frequency balance are a big part of bringing the project together. With the various tools to adjust the perception of gain, from simple volume adjustments, to compression with makeup gain, to brickwall limiting, you can not only change the perceived volume but also create new dynamic contours. And just about every other kind of processor that you might use, most especially EQ, will also affect level.

What's more, the perception and reality of level may not coincide. That is to say, you might perceive something as considerably louder even though it is measurably only very slightly so. You might also add considerable gain in a particular way or at a particular frequency, and barely notice the difference in the overall perception of volume.

As described above, in the section on level, you begin to negotiate these challenges by either focusing on the lead vocal (or lead instrumental element) or referencing the loudest section of each track. Using one of these criteria, you can then start to fine-tune the level matching. Unfortunately, these two elements may be at odds: with the vocal level balanced, one track might have a section that sounds much louder that anything on the other tracks. Or, with the two loudest sections balanced, the lead vocals don't sound relatively equal in presence. This is where the most creative elements of mastering enter the picture—you use the processing to achieve the best possible compromise, making the tracks sound consistent with the overall volume of the project.

Equivalent problems can emerge when you're balancing frequencies, overall dynamic range, or sense of width and space. Focused listening and expertise with a range of processors will move you toward reaching a consistent master. In the next chapter, I describe many practical applications within a typical (and not so typical) mastering session.

211

Chapter 11

Creating a Master
The Concepts and Tools
in Detail

Now it's time to get into the nuts and bolts of creating your master. You should have your file setup (in whatever software program you're using) with the tracks in sequence (to the best of your knowledge, recognizing that this might change and that it's an easy change if it does). You'll want to have access to automation for level adjustments, brickwall limiting (at least threshold and output), and comprehensive EQ (at least boost/dip and frequency select settings). You may also want to have access to other processors, such as compressors, expanders, multi-band compressors, and reverb, but you will bring these into the session only as needed. This chapter follows the process of a typical mastering session from the beginning all the way up to the sequencing and delivery process; the latter will be covered in the next chapter.

11.1 Creating a Reference Track

Although you will primarily be comparing elements, you need to begin somewhere. "Somewhere" means selecting one of the tracks to build upon and serve as an initial reference point. Typically, the track that sounds best to the mastering engineer, before any processing is done, works best for this. By "sounds best" for these purposes, the initial focus should be on frequency balance (you will then set level as described below). So, whichever track seems best balanced from lows to highs will make a good starting point. This doesn't mean that you won't do additional EQ work on that track as well. In fact, once you've selected your reference track, you will want to consider any EQ adjustments as discussed in the section on EQ processing.

Once you have selected a reference track, you apply any additional EQ to enhance that mix and create an output level for that track that will serve as a level reference. In most cases this means applying some amount of brickwall limiting to that track (parameters for this brickwall limiting are discussed in the following section).

Here's where you first face the question of how loud to make your master. To what extent will you succumb to the loudness war? As discussed in previous sections, brickwall limiting is endemic in popular music, and there is little doubt that excessive limiting is detrimental to the sound of the music and the listening experience. On the other hand, if you do no brickwall limiting your master is going to sound "small" compared to virtually everything else! So, in most cases it's not a question of whether to limit but of how much. And, in fact, some amount of brickwall limiting can produce very desirable results, especially in genres that are meant to be aggressive.

I discuss the issues concerning brickwall limiting with those I'm working with (artist and/or producer), and I generally suggest that we use a moderate amount—enough to be reasonably competitive with other masters, though usually a touch less than the standard for very commercial product releases—with the understanding that it's easy to adjust this later, if desired. Based on this discussion, and combined with my own sense of what will work best for the particular project since I have to translate "moderate" into actual settings, I then set a limiting threshold/output level for my reference track. Typically, this is somewhere between 3 and 6 dB of limiting on the peaks.

I now have a level and frequency balance reference to use in comparing the tracks. I often then work systematically track by track, starting with the first track. I playing bits of the reference track (including the critical loudest sections) and compare that to bits of the first track, adjusting level (brickwall limiter threshold) and frequency balance (using EQ) to try and best match the tracks. When I feel they are reasonably close, I move to the second track, now referencing the new track to both the reference track and the adjusted first track. Then I'm on to the third track, using the three previously worked-on tracks as references—and on through the master. Of course, there will be many revisions along the way, including revisions that you might make to your reference track as you do more listening and comparing. There are other considerations besides level and frequency balance, but this is the general working strategy I use for creating the final master.

11.2 Processing: EQ

Although level is "job number one" for mastering, you want to address EQ issues prior to setting the final level, since EQ effects level directly. As discussed in the previous chapter, EQ considerations fall into two basic categories: sounds best and matches best. Having established a reference for frequency balance, you can approach the sounds best/matches best issues at the same time, because what matches best to the reference track should also reflect what you think sounds best overall.

It may be that I decided on some global EQ moves in the process of choosing my reference track; for example, I might have felt that all the elements could use a touch more sizzle in the very high frequencies or a slight dip in the lower mids. In that case, I will have set those parameters to what I thought best on the reference track and then applied them globally to all the tracks, but more typically each track requires a unique EQ approach.

Types of EQs for Mastering

Although some EQs are specifically made (and marketed) for mastering, any EQ can be a mastering EQ, and many of the elements from the discussion of EQ for mixing (section 4.3) are applicable to mastering as well. The main criterion for the best mastering EQs is that they be very flexible, which typically means than they have a large number of bands to work with. Because you are generally dealing with complex audio that is very full frequency (e.g., from the lows of a bass guitar to the highs of the cymbals), you may need to access many different points along the entire frequency range to fine-tune the frequency balance.

Besides flexibility, transparency (minimal distortion and artifacts) is often a desirable quality of mastering EQs, as you are generally trying to be as minimally disruptive to the original mix as possible. As discussed in section 4.3, linear-phase design EQs are particularly smooth and transparent, and as a result they are often chosen for mastering duties. Screenshot 11.1 of the mastering EQ suite from Waves shows their phase-linear EQ package that includes a flexible seven-band EQ with an additional three-band EQ that is focused on the low frequencies—where often the greatest degree of shaping is required in the mastering process. Limitations in playback systems used for mixing sometimes result in frequency-balance problems in the low frequencies that become more apparent on a truly full-range mastering playback system.

New EQ designs such as the Manley "Massive Passive" may incorporate a variety of EQ approaches from previous hardware and/or software designs. This

SCREENSHOT 11.1

Waves mastering EQ bundle.

plug-in has eight bands to work with and tremendous flexibility, making it a good choice for mastering with a different "flavor" from the linear-phase designs—and there are many other options (see screenshot 11.2).

It may be that you don't have a dedicated mastering EQ, or even a particularly "transparent" EQ, or you may decide that you want a more aggressive EQ for your mastering project. There are no hard-and-fast rules; whatever works for you (and to some extent, whatever you have available) may be fine for your mastering work. A good ear combined with a creative vision is going to be more important than the details of your processing options.

Extent of Mastering EQ

How much EQ should you apply when mastering? Of course, it isn't really possible to answer this question since it depends on the program material and how you determine that it should be shaped. However, the mastering mantra of "minimally invasive" should guide your EQ decisions. Also driving a "less is more" approach to EQ'ing for your master is the fact that, in the mastering stage, you are processing across the entire mix. As a result, EQ often affects a broad spectrum of elements in your mix, and a little bit will have a much more significant (and audible) effect. For example, if you boost in the upper-mid frequencies— say, 3 kHz on a typical popular music track—that EQ will have a significant effect on the lead vocals, any background vocals, most guitars and keyboards, the snare drum, and just about any other element in the mix. It might only have a small effect on the bass or the kick drum, but otherwise pretty much everything will be significantly affected. And the cumulative effect on all these elements means that even a 1 dB boost at 3kHz with a typical broad bandwidth setting (Q) will have a pretty dramatic affect on the overall sound of the mix.

Compare this to the same EQ boost on a single track (vocal, guitar, snare, or whatever): that will certainly be audible on that one particular element, but it will not have a large-scale effect on the overall mix, as it does when applied in a mastering setting. On the following audio clips you can hear the difference between a mix with no mastering EQ and one with a 1 dB boost at 3K.

Artist: Bonnie Hayes CD: *Love in the Ruins* Track: "I Can't Stop"
Audio Clip 11.1: A clip of a section mastered with no EQ.

215

Audio Clip 11.2: The same clip with a 1 dB boost at 3 kHz with a bandwidth setting (Q) of 1.0.

You may find yourself applying significant boost or dip EQ settings when mastering, but this would certainly be the exception rather than the rule. I rarely exceed more the 2 dB boost or dip in an entire mastering session; even then, the vast majority of EQ settings will probably be 1 dB or less. Even a boost or dip of .5 dB is clearly audible at most frequency settings, and I often end up using 1/10s of a dB as I fine-tune my mastering (adjusting an EQ setting from plus .5 dB to plus .7 dB, for example).

WHAT NOT TO DO

Do not be deceived by the "louder sounds better" fallacy.
As with mixing—and possibly even more so—there is the danger that the "louder sounds better" fallacy will negatively influence your EQ'ing choices. Even a small EQ boost in mastering will give the track a significant boost in volume, and because louder generally sounds better, there is a tendency to over-EQ. You can try adjusting the playback volume as you switch the EQ in and out (you should at least try this), but in general you will need to train yourself to hear beyond the volume increase and listen to the frequency balance and quality of the sound to determine whether the EQ is helping—that is, achieving something closer to your creative vision.

Approaches to Applying Mastering EQ

In practice, your EQ choices may conform to various EQ standards—some general and some specific to mastering. The smile EQ—covered in detail in section 4.3—is an approach to general EQ practice that may find its application in many mastering situations. Without repeating the various reasons that the smile EQ is a frequent approach in mixing, the fact that it enhances sounds for musical as well as physiological reasons means that it may offer enhancement possibilities in mastering as well. The danger is that the mix engineer is often applying smile EQ fundamentals—reducing mid-frequency content by boosting in the high and low frequencies and/or dipping in the mid-frequencies—and so the mix may already be pressing the boundaries of usefulness for the smile EQ curve. Losing too much midrange content can make music sound thin and weak—music needs midrange for warmth and body and depth. So—again, it is overall frequency balance that you seek. This may mean some elements from the smile EQ will enhance your masters, but it doesn't necessarily mean that it always will.

216

SCREENSHOT 11.3

Broad Q EQ application—set to –1 dB at 300 Hz with a Q of .8.

EQ tactics that are more specific to mastering include specific application of the smile EQ principle as it relates to lead vocal (or instrument) presence. Dipping in the mid-frequencies is common, but in mastering, when you are working on a completed musical palette, you might want to focus your mid-range dipping on helping to carve a more generous place for the lead vocal. Selecting the frequency to dip will depend on the range of the vocal (generally lower for male vocal and higher for female), but you can dip significantly and then sweep through the frequencies, listening for the place that opens up the vocal, giving it more space by dipping the competing frequencies just below the primary bandwidth that the vocal occupies. Enhancing the vocal presence without significantly robbing the track of body and warmth is generally the goal.

Along the same lines is a suggestion regarding the Q (bandwidth) settings. Just as you typically use small boost and dip settings in mixing EQ, you generally rely on low (or broad) Q settings in mastering EQ. Broader bandwidth settings are gentler and generally more musical sounding because they create a slow transition into EQ frequency shifting. High and low shelving (with a gentle slope, generally created by lower Q settings) are similarly less disruptive than traditional average or sharp Q boosting or dipping. Because you are usually trying to subtly shift the frequency balance of your master, a broader bandwidth setting will provide gentler results.

It isn't possible to define the exact implementation of specific Q settings, as different designers use different criteria, and Q values change as you move through the frequency spectrum. Screenshot 11.3 is an EQ set to a moderately broad Q setting as might be typical of a mastering EQ application. Relating what you hear to the graphic representation that many EQs provide is helpful as you refine your approach to using broader bandwidth settings.

Dynamic EQs/Multi-band Compressors

When I discussed the multi-band compressor earlier in the book, I did so in section 4.4, on dynamics, because this processor uses dynamics controls (threshold and ratio), and I needed to be sure the reader was clear on dynamics processing before I introduced the multi-band compressor concept. I titled that section "Dynamic EQ" because the effect of this processor is actually closer to that of an EQ than it is to a traditional compressor. For this reason I cover its use in mastering as a part of this section on EQ.

217

Multi-band compressors or dynamic EQs create EQ-type effects because they alter the frequency content at different places in the frequency spectrum (as a traditional EQ does). However, by using dynamics processing, you get a resultant EQ that is not static, as would be with a traditional EQ; the effect on the various frequency bands changes depending on the extent of program content within that frequency band. Dynamic EQs are flexible, with the ability to combine dynamic EQ effects using compression and expansion techniques. Some dynamic EQs can go beyond the basic downward compression or upward expansion based on frequency content that I described in section 4.4. By combining a threshold control with gain and range controls, it is possible to achieve "frequency conscious" upward compression and downward expansion as well. Gain supplies a consistent boost at the selected frequency and range controls the compression or expansion of those same frequencies when they cross the threshold. Some examples follow.

Upward Compression

For upward compression at the low- and high-frequency bands, set the gain for these bands to a positive value (say, +5 dB) and the range to an equal but opposite value (say, −5 dB). Set the threshold to a relatively low level (perhaps between −40 and −60 dB). The entire program is raised 5 dB in that frequency range, but when the signal crosses the threshold, it starts lowering the level of that frequency back toward its original level.

When the signal is far enough over the threshold to cause the full 5 dB of compression (the maximum set by the range control), the effective level is the same as the starting point (it has been raised 5 dB using the gain control but turned back down that same 5 dB by the compression). In this way the low-level signals in any given frequency are boosted, whereas the high-level signals remain the same. This effect is that of a smile EQ boost (increase in the low and high frequencies), but the dynamic quality of the processing allows for the already prominent lows and highs to remain unchanged while the lower level elements in those frequency ranges get boosted. See screenshot 11.4.

Downward Expansion

For downward expansion at a mid-frequency band, set the gain for this band to a negative value (say, −5 dB) and the range to an equal but opposite value (say, +5 dB). Set the threshold to a relatively low level (perhaps between −40 and −60 dB). The entire program is lowered 5 dB in that frequency range, but when the signal crosses the threshold, it starts raising the level of that frequency back toward its original level.

When the signal is far enough over the threshold to cause the full 5 dB of expansion (the maximum set by the range control), the effective level is the same as the starting point (it has been lowered 5 dB using the gain control but

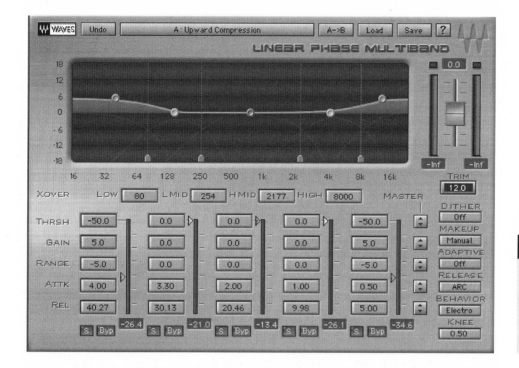

SCREENSHOT 11.4

Dynamic EQ set for upward compression to enhance low and high frequencies by increasing the volume of low-level program material in those frequencies.

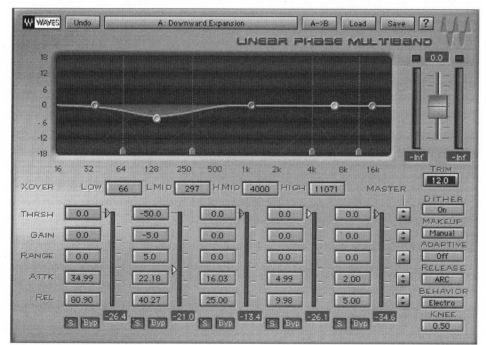

SCREENSHOT 11.5

Dynamic EQ set for downward expansion to enhance mid-frequency dynamics by decreasing the volume of low-level program material in those frequencies.

turned back up that same 5 dB by the expansion). In this way the low-level signals in any given frequency are lowered further, whereas the high-level signals remain the same, creating more dynamic range. This also creates a variation on the smile EQ, dipping low-level mid-frequency elements even further; see screenshot 11.5. (Note: Your dynamic EQ may not have this degree of flexibility.)

Don't start with a dynamic EQ.
Dynamic EQ creates tremendous control over frequencies based on their relative presence in the audio program, but it can have numerous unintended and undesirable effects. Because you are dealing with the entire audio program, all EQ boosting or dipping is affecting multiple elements of that program and you risk creating changes in the frequency balance that cause instruments to sound differently at different points in the mix, bringing about a lack of stability in the sound. You may be trying to correct for a disparity to start with, and the dynamic EQ can be useful for that, but at least with static EQ the effect is consistent over the entire timeline; generally this will be a preferred method of frequency alteration.

Dynamic EQs have their place, but I generally reserve them for problem solving rather than use them as EQ processors (see the section on "Mastering EQ Problem Solving").

Removing DC Offset

DC offset is a solvable problem involving the digital waveform where the center of the waveform has shifted to one side of the zero crossing point (see screenshot 11.6).

DC offset can get into a digital signal in two ways. You can "catch" DC offset by recording an analog signal that has DC offset (that may have been acquired in a variety of ways but primarily from faulty op amps). More likely, the

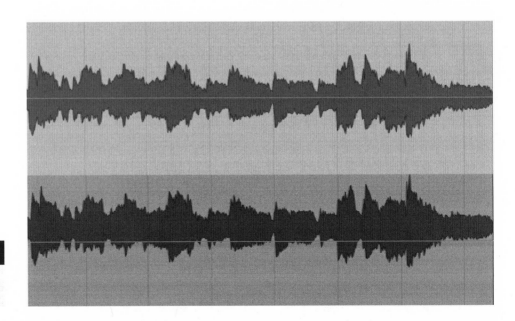

SCREENSHOT 11.6

DC offset (without - top, with - bottom).

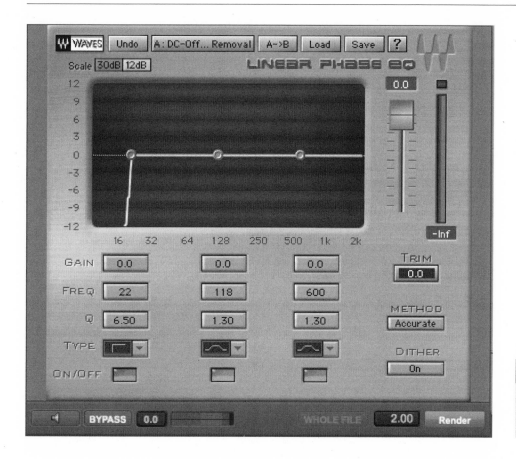

SCREENSHOT 11.7

EQ application for removal of DC offset: 22Hz, Q6.5, Variable Slope Hi-Pass.

DC offset has been caused by inaccuracies in the A/D (analog to digital) conversion process. In any event, even a small amount of DC offset can get significantly amplified by processing that increases gain, such as distortion effects. DC offset reduces dynamic range and headroom, which can be a significant problem, especially if severe. The presence of DC offset will often cause audible clicks between audio sections that have been edited together.

Many DAWS supply a plug-in to eliminate DC offset by analyzing and correcting the signal so that the center of the waveform actually sits at the zero crossing point. Many EQ plug-in processors (especially those primarily intended for mastering) include a preset for removal of DC offset. A steep cut at 20 kHz (as shown in screenshot 11.7) eliminates DC offset and also eliminates other subsonic problems that can occur from some signal processing. Even if you don't detect DC offset, it's a good idea to filter out these subsonic frequencies just in case there are hidden problems that are using up bandwidth.

You may need to remove other low-frequency artifacts besides DC offset when mastering. EQ plug-ins with a preset designed to contain DC offset and lower rumble introduced by mechanical components such as microphones or turntables may also be a part of your basic mastering EQ settings (see screenshot 11.8). This may affect the sound of low-frequency instruments such as bass or kick drum, but may still be necessary to tame unwanted rumble.

221

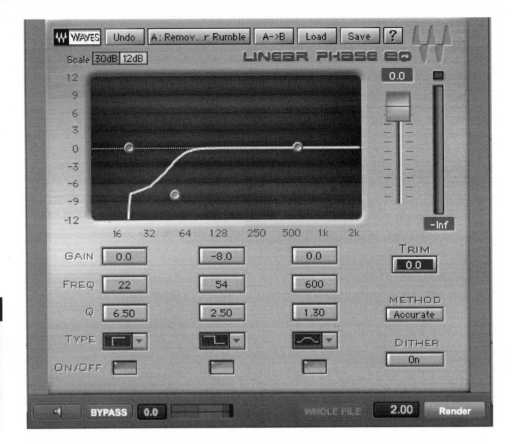

SCREENSHOT 11.8

DC offset removal and reduction in low rumble: Band A—Freq.: 22, Q: 6.5, Type: Variable Slope Hi-Pass. Band B—Freq.: 53, Q: 3.83, Gain: –8, Type: Variable Slope Low-Shelf.

222

EQ Strategy for Mastering

EQ strategy is in line with the overall strategy regarding mastering: the primary goal is to balance the master from one selection to the next. With EQ, this will probably mean using one of the tracks as a reference and working to achieve a compatible balance of frequencies on all the other tracks. Some enhancement to each track and to the master might also be part of the process, depending on your assessment of the mix. After picking what you think is the best track for overall frequency balance, you may still want to change certain frequencies or duck others to find the optimal frequency balance for the reference track. Once you feel that you have good reference point, the broader EQ process unfolds from there.

The primary working strategy is to move from track to track, listening to a relatively small amount of each track to assess frequency balance and making small EQ adjustments in an attempt to match each track to the reference track. As you go, you may end up continuing to make small revisions to the reference track as well; you may also decide on global enhancements at some frequency range (for example, adding a touch of high-frequency "sparkle" such as +1 dB at 10 kHz to many or even every track). There is typically a lot of back and forth, checking various places in each track, and you'll make numerous very small revisions of EQ boost or dip at various frequencies. Remember, matching is job one, and though enhancement may desirable as well, you want to keep the vision of the mix engineer (including your own concept, if you were the mixer) and not allow the mastering process to undermine the mixer's creative concept.

Sometimes there may be frequency balancing issues between sections of one track. As you listen, you might decide that the chorus of a song lacks sufficient low end compared to the verses—perhaps the bass is playing in a higher register on the chorus. Generally, issues such as this are a result of arranging and/or mixing choices, and if it really is a "problem" it should have been addressed at one of those stages. (I put "problem" in quotes because what may sound like a problem to you may have been a creative choice of the arranger or mixer.) Delving into the whole area of EQ changes on sections of a track, as opposed to only dealing with track EQ on a global basis, is up to the mastering engineer on the project. Keep in mind the vision of the arranger and mix engineer, and do not undermine their work. However, your job is to bring your creative imagination to the project as well, and if you feel that EQ changes on a section-by-section basis are warranted, plug-in automation can give you that capability.

Mastering EQ Problem Solving

Sometimes you will need to EQ to solve problems as well as for matching and enhancement. Some of these situations have been discussed above, such as DC offset removal and control of rumble. Other problems with unwanted noises and more subtle problems with specific elements that you will want to EQ can be addressed in mastering by using specialized tools such as notch filters, specialty plug-ins, and dynamic EQs. While these problems are more properly solved in the mix process, sometimes you find yourself at the mastering stage without the luxury of being able to revise the mix.

A 60-cycle hum (caused by bad grounding) sometimes finds its way into material that you're mastering, as does various forms of high-frequency buzz and hiss. Your ability to fix these problems largely depends on the extent of bandwidth they are affecting. A 60-cycle hum is typically contained within a very narrow bandwidth, so it can be virtually eliminated with a notch filter. A notch filter is simply a single band of parametric EQ that dips at the selected frequency with a very narrow bandwidth. If the hum is centered at 60 Hz with a very narrow bandwidth, then application of the notch filter EQ settings as shown in screenshot 11.9 will probably virtually eliminate it, with relatively little effect on anything else because of the narrowness of the bandwidth.

Other occurrences of hum or buzz may be more difficult to control, as they may occupy a broader bandwidth. Generally you need to determine the center-frequency of the problem tone (by using a narrow Q, exaggerating the boost or dip function, and then sweeping through the frequencies), and then see how great a dip at how narrow a bandwidth you can get away with, compro-

SCREENSHOT 11.9

An EQ set to a notch filter at 60 Hz: Freq.: 60 Hz, Gain –18 dB Q: 6.5 (narrowest setting).

224

mising between the amount of buzz or hum reduction and the degree of ill-effects on the rest of the material.

There are other, more sophisticated processors designed to eliminate un-wanted noise. These processers have been used most extensively for reducing surface noise, pops, clicks, and other problems from vinyl recordings when they are being transferred to digital medium for reissue, but they are also valuable for any kind of noise reduction (not to be confused with general noise reduction through processors made famous by Dolby). Such specialty processors have been developed to take advantage of the complex algorithms available through digital signal processing and certain techniques such as "look-ahead" processing that give the plug-in an expanded ability to solve difficult noise problems.

For these noise-removal processors to function you need access to a small portion of the noise as an isolated sound. This often occurs before or after the recording or in a break in the performance. The software analyzes the isolated noise and creates an algorithm to reverse the effect, using EQ-type process-ing but with more sophisticated parameters based on the exact profile of the noise that has been sampled. As with the gain control on an EQ, you can control the extent of processing; and as with EQ, the deeper the processing, the more noise is removed. However, at the same time, there is the likelihood of greater negative impact on program material that you are trying to retain. See screen-shot 11.10.

While most commercial mastering facilities have this kind of noise-reduction software, it certainly isn't necessary for most mastering projects—and its success is pretty variable depending on the nature of the noise. Just like the notch EQ approach, the broader the bandwidth of the noise, the more dif-

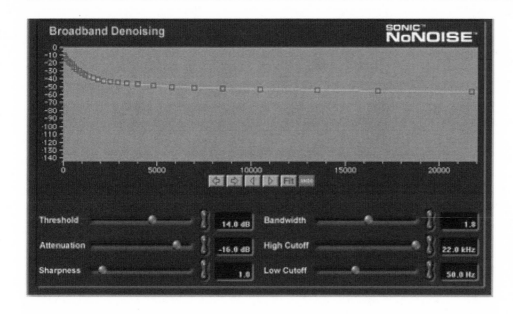

SCREENSHOT 11.10

Noise reduction software.

ficulty the processor will have in reducing it without creating noticeable and undesirable effects.

In contemporary recordings, the hums, buzzes, hisses, clicks, and such are often isolated from the original recording to one track, and it would be much better to attack the problem in the mix stage, where you might be able to get away with more aggressive notch filtering and/or more successful application of noise-removal software, with much less effect on the overall program material—but again, it isn't always possible to get back to the mix.

More subtle aesthetic issues can sometimes be effectively addressed in mastering using the multi-band compressor/dynamic EQ. An example would be a mix where you feel that the lead vocal requires corrective EQ. If the lead vocal is too bright (too much high-frequency information, perhaps harsh or brittle sounding), you would be inclined to roll off some of the highs. However, the rest of the track really suffers from high-mid frequency roll-off, so when the lead vocal isn't happening the reduction in those frequencies is making the track sound worse (dull or muddy). In this case, you might try using the dynamic EQ to reduce the high-mid frequencies only when the lead vocal is present. If you set one of the bands of the multi-band compressor with the center frequency at the point most problematic in the vocal, set the threshold so that you are getting gain reduction in that frequency band when the lead vocal is present, but little or no reduction when it isn't. Adjust the bandwidth to as narrow as possible to still tame the high-mids of the lead vocal and you might be able to improve the sound of the vocal without the negative effects on the track when the vocal isn't present (see screenshots 11.11 and 11.12). Certainly it's not an ideal situation—much better to address the sound of the vocal in the mix—but if that isn't possible, then the dynamic EQ option can provide significant improvement over traditional EQ.

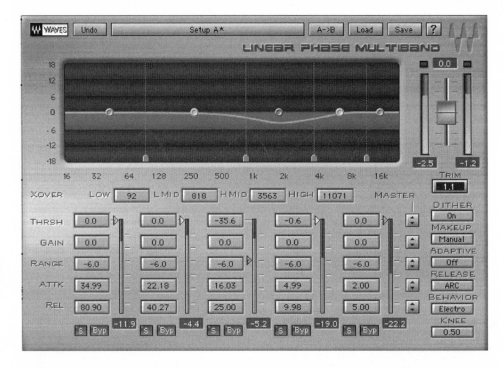

SCREENSHOT 11.11

A dynamic EQ showing significant reduction in the high-mids when the vocal is present.

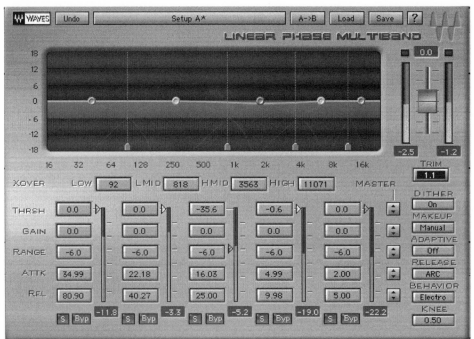

SCREENSHOT 11.12

The same track during a passage without the lead vocal, showing very slight reduction in the high-mids.

11.3 Processing: Level

Level setting is job one of mastering, though it isn't possible to do much fine-tuning of level until at least a major portion of the EQ decisions have been made, owing to the effect of EQ on level (as described above). Although I covered various approaches to setting levels in chapter 10, the reality in contemporary production is that the brickwall limiter is going to be your best choice for setting level in most circumstances.

Once you have come to grips with the thorny matter of overall level by setting the brickwall limiter on your reference song, you are ready to start balancing the level for all the remaining material. As suggested previously, the focus should be on the loudest part of each track, since that best represents the listener's overall experience. At the same time, you will want to pay attention to the level of the vocal or other lead instrument to see how those elements are matching the reference track. Here, I cover these detailed level setting strategies and some problem solving.

Types of Brickwall Limiters for Mastering

Brickwall limiters all end up with the same basic result—they set an absolute limit (brick wall) on the program material output, and when used to process material, they reduce its overall dynamic range. The techniques used to detect and process the gain characteristics of the source material can vary considerably. Because brickwall limiting is a relatively new technology, and because it has become such a fundamental part of almost all mastering, there are new processors with new approaches appearing frequently. Some are combined with other processors in a single unit that supplies all the basic mastering functions (EQ, compression, limiting, and brickwall limiting), some are part of a suite of processors designed for mastering, and some are standalone processors.

Although all of them will likely be described as capable of processing any kind of material (and they are), the reality is that some handle certain kinds of material better than others. Some are designed for aggressive limiting and maximum volume at high settings, and others are designed to be particularly transparent when not driven to high levels of limiting.

The list of available brickwall limiter plug-ins is enormous. Coming from large established plug-in developers, mid-size companies, and startups, these plug-ins include Waves L1, L2, and L3; Sonnox Oxford Limiter; Universal Audio Precision Limiter; McDSP ML-4000; Avid Maxim; Wave Arts Final Plug; TC Electronic Brickwall limiter; Brainworx bx_XL; Voxengo Elephant; FabFilter Pro L; Slate Digital FX- X; iZotope Ozone (system); Blue Cat's Protector; Massey L2007; Sonic Core Optimaster; Loudmax Limiter; TL Maximizer; T-Racks Brickwall limiter; Kreativ Sound Kjaerhus Master Limiter; RNDigital Finis; and the list goes on. Some of these have very few controls and some have banks of parameters. Some work only on certain platforms, though most are available for both Mac and PC, and for most major DAWs.

I haven't tried most of these, and the online reviews vary widely in terms of user preferences. Certainly, different limiters work differently on different kinds of material, and because there are parameter and preset choices, each plug-in is

227

capable of producing a variety of results. Although it may be ideal to have many different brickwall limiters to choose from, mostly that isn't practical. As with most plug-ins, almost all of these are available for trial periods (some fully functional and some slight disabled), but even that doesn't make choosing easy. On-line reviews at sites such as Gearslutz.com can help, and you might as well audition at least a few possibilities.

Finally, pick your poison; and use whichever you choose with a musical aesthetic and an ear for good audio while understanding that if you don't use any brickwall limiting on your master, it is going to sound so radically different from almost anything else out there that you do run the risk of seriously undermining the music's chances of being heard.

Extent of Mastering Brickwall Limiting

How much brickwall limiting should you apply when mastering? Of course, it isn't really possible to answer this question, since it depends on the material and how you determine it should be shaped. In chapter 10, on listening for level, I discussed issues of overall volume and offered some audio samples. Here, I reiterate my hope that we all will control our use of limiting in order to retain musical dynamics and allow our music to "breath!"

That said, I generally limit between 3 and 6 dB at the song's peaks (meaning the peak reduction meter will show between 3 and 6 dB of reduction during the loudest passages). Sometimes I use less limiting (for more "purist"-oriented folk or jazz recordings, for example) and sometimes more (when the artist and/or producer says he or she wants maximum impact). Then, when matching other songs to the level set for the reference track, I adjust the threshold to a similar extent of limiting—as a starting point. However, two songs that both hit 5 dB of reduction at their loudest point may still sound fairly different in volume (see screenshot 11.13). The nature of the frequency content

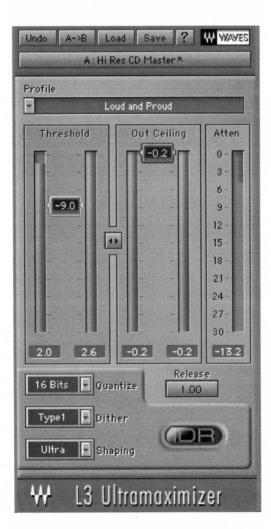

SCREENSHOT 11.13

A brickwall limiter showing 5 dB of gain reduction.

and dynamic range can cause tracks with the same amount of limiting to have pretty different "perceived" volume levels (that is, the impression we have of the volume of the track).

> ### WHAT NOT TO DO
>
> **Do not be misled by the "louder sounds better" fallacy.**
> *As with mixing and EQ'ing—and repeated here for the third time because it is that important!—there is the danger that the "louder sounds better" fallacy can negatively affect your brickwall limiting choices. Even a small increase in brickwall limiting will give the track a significant boost in volume, and because louder generally sounds better there, is a tendency to over-limit in mastering. You can try adjusting the playback volume as you change the limiter threshold to compensate for the added volume (you should at least try this), and there are a few brickwall limiters with a level-matching feature that attempts to balance the limited level to the original level for comparison. But in general you will need to train yourself to hear beyond the volume increase and listen to the effect of the limiter. You then must determine whether the additional volume is worth the sacrifice in dynamic range and low-level distortion (or more pronounced distortion and other artifacts when pushed to high levels of brickwall limiting).*

Mastering Level-Setting Strategies

I covered the essentials of listening for comparative levels of each element in your master in section 10.1. Once the fundamental degree of brickwall limiting has been set, the practical application of level adjustment involves working from song to song (or whatever elements constitute your master), balancing the level from one to the next.

For the most, part the level is adjusted by raising or lowering the threshold on the brickwall limiter—a lower threshold increases the volume and a higher threshold reduces it. Being able to automate the threshold setting is essential for your mastering workflow. In screenshot 11.14, the lower the horizontal position of the graphic displays the lower the limiter's threshold.

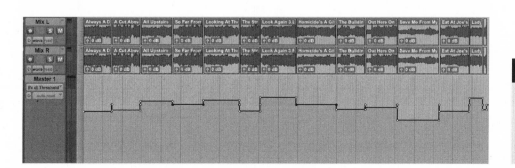

229

SCREENSHOT 11.14

A mastering session in Pro Tools showing the automation for the threshold setting on the brickwall limiter.

Generally, you will want to narrow your range of concentration by focusing on the loudest section of each element, while paying particular attention to the level of the lead voice (singer or instrument). While I like working in the sequence of the final master because it provides some sense of structure, the reality is that the sequence might be changed by either the artist or the consumer, so your goal is to balance the level regardless of sequence. I bounce around from song to song somewhat randomly—each needs to work in relation to any other. That's pretty much the entire process for setting level on many records where the material is fairly closely related—for example, the same basic instrumentation and approach on each track.

Balancing Different Kinds of Material

There are issues that arise in mixing that result from the need to match different kinds of material, and there are particular challenges that arise with use of brickwall limiting. One of the more common challenges is trying to balance relatively dense material—like full rock band tracks—with sparse material such as acoustic guitar tracks having no bass or drums. It's fairly common for a rock or blues band to include an acoustic track on its CD. Balancing the acoustic track with the band tracks is generally not something that can be accomplished by simply adjusting the threshold of the brickwall limiter.

Aesthetic decisions start to overshadow the pure level considerations when you're dealing with very different-sounding tracks. If you actually set an acoustic track to what seems like the same level as a band track (matching vocal level, for example), it is likely to sound "wrong" because a singer with a guitar shouldn't sound as loud as a band—it isn't "natural." On the other hand, you may want to have a similar amount of brickwall limiting on the acoustic track as on the full band tracks in order provide the same overall impact. If the acoustic track is also much more dynamic than the band tracks (and it will naturally be somewhat more dynamic because of the relative sparseness), it's going to be even more difficult to fit it with the other material. So, I have found that reducing the ceiling on the brickwall limiter for the acoustic track can be an important tactic in balancing the acoustic track to the band tracks. Different processors may have different names for the "ceiling" (such as "output level" or "peak"), but the meaning is the same: the maximum level relative to digital zero that the brick wall permits the audio to achieve.

Typically, the ceiling is set to something around –.2 dB (very slightly under digital zero to avoid errors in reading from the CD laser). If you maintain a threshold on your acoustic track that is consistent with your other tracks (meaning you get a similar amount of limiting), but reduce your output ceiling (I find that somewhere between –1 and –2.5 dB usually works), you can match the intensity of the other tracks while dialing back the level to a place that seems appropriate relative to how you want a band to sound versus a solo acoustic performance. Of course, this is very subjective, but beyond the point of the obvious (x is clearly louder than y), all level setting is quite subjective.

Similar level issues arise when working on masters for compilation records, where material is taken from many different artists, recordings, or mixers. Different arrangements and mixing styles create different experiences in regard to level. One track may have a rockin' sound with a very prominent rhythm section and the lead vocal tucked back into the track, while the next track might be folkie with a sparse arrangement, quiet drums, and a prominent lead vocal. Matching lead vocal levels of these tracks causes the first to sound much louder than the second, whereas matching the louder sections from each track causes the folkie track to sound inappropriately louder than the rockin' one. Thus, matching levels for these kinds of very different tracks calls for even more subjective assessment, as you have to try to get an overall sense for the impact of the track on the listener.

CREATIVE TIP

Be sure to use different monitoring levels for balancing track to track.
As discussed in section 2.2, the Fletcher Munson (equal loudness) curve can work to your advantage when making certain creative decisions. Trying to match levels on very different kinds of tracks can be easier when listening at very low levels. Low-level listening strips away a lot of the information and the prominent mid-range elements become more clearly distinguishable. As a result, you get a better idea of whether the overall volume on the folksy versus rockin' tracks (or any other elements) is balanced.

231

Balancing Different Sections of a Track

Another issue that may arise in balancing levels is the relationship between very quiet passages and louder passages in a single track. Since the brickwall limiter is reducing the volume of louder passages, there will be a smaller difference in volume between the loud passages that have been limited and the quiet passages that haven't. For the most part we accept this as part of the mastering process; we may even feel that this result provides a more consistent experience for the listener. But if you feel that too much is lost in these discrepancies, you can always consider less brickwall limiting—often the most musically satisfying solution. You can also consider lowering the volume of quieter sections. This can be done using expansion (discussed in the following section on dynamics processing) or by using automation to create a level change where desired.

The place where I find this level issue to most frequently need addressing is with the intros. It is fairly common for a song to start with one or just a few instruments playing prior to the entrance of the band. This may be just a few beats worth of music or several bars, but in any event, when the band enters, triggering the brickwall limiter, the relationship between the intro level and the band entrance is sometimes pretty dramatically altered from the original mix (depending on the extent of brickwall limiting, of course). This is one of many reasons I finalize mixes using moderate brickwall limiting, though I remove it in creating the final file for mastering. I find that using automation to lower the level on the intro, regaining the approximate relationship of intro to band entrance as in the original mix, is the best and easiest solution.

Mastering Level Problem Solving

Beyond the challenges mentioned in the section on strategies above, there are other problems that you might encounter in the mastering session. Probably the most common one is the loss of level on the kick and snare that occurs with a typical popular music mix when processed with a brickwall limiter. Because the transients on these elements tend to trigger the limiter, there can be a significant loss of their level during mastering. There are a variety of ways to counter this problem at the mastering stage through use of dynamic EQs to boost the upper-mids, or use of expansion to create more dynamic range.

Both of these kinds of processing tend to maintain better level on the kick and snare through brickwall limiting, but they are essentially rebalancing your mix to do so. Similarly, some new brickwall limiter plug-ins apply these kinds of processing algorithms to help you maintain more of the transient levels.

This problem (as with most balance issues) is better resolved in mixing than in mastering. This is a strong reason to finish your mixes with a brickwall limiter so you can adjust levels accordingly, though it's better to take your mix to completion without the limiter and then add that element and adjust as desired as the final stage (see section 3.3).

Other common problems occur with the original files that you have to work with. The files may be distorted, which leaves you no real option other than to transfer that distortion to the final master—doing the absolute minimum to make the distortion any worse. The mixes may be heavily compressed or heavily EQ'd in ways that are contrary to your aesthetic (and the artist's too, though he or she may not understand the technical problems involved). There are usually some things you can do with expansion and with EQ that might be able to counter some of the ill-effects, but you will probably not be able to get especially satisfying results. Expansion can restore some of the lost dynamics, but the ancillary effects such as pumping caused by excessive compression can't be removed. It's similar with EQ—you can reshape the frequency spectrum of a mix but, while significant harshness in the high end or boom in the low end can be softened with EQ, loss in fidelity from over-EQ'ing cannot be completely overcome.

A fairly common occurrence for me has been receiving mixes that have already been processed with a brickwall limiter. This may be because the mix engineer delivered it that way or because the material was drawn from a CD or some other source in which the mastering had already been done (not uncommon when dealing with older material that the artist or record label wants, but the only thing that remains is the CD version because the original mixes have been lost). This isn't necessarily a problem unless the limiting on the particular track you receive is greater than you want to put on the other tracks in the master. The one already limited track will sound louder than all the other tracks unless you give them a similar level of brickwall limiting. My solution has been to lower the overall output of the already limited track. It's not the ideal—and it never sounds perfectly balanced to everything else to me—but it allows me to use the track without having to add more limiting to the other tracks, and without letting the pre-limited track sound louder than anything else.

WHAT NOT TO DO

Don't be afraid to inquire about getting a revised mix.
If you're working on material that you didn't mix, and you encounter problems that would best be solved by either revising the mix or getting a different version of the music (such as a version without brickwall limiting), you should consider asking about the possibility. Sometimes the timetable is going to prevent revisiting the mix or alternate or adjusted versions are not available, but if you aren't sure, there's no harm in asking. What is important is that you ask carefully; you might feel that some element (the lead vocal, for example) has been made exceeding bright (in your opinion, unpleasantly bright), and you aren't happy with dipping out some highs on the master because of what it's doing to the rest of the elements in the track.

You might say something like "the lead vocal seems a bit bright to me." The artist or producer might say "I like it like that," and that's the end of the discussion. But the individual might say, "Yeah, I was thinking that it sounded really bright, too" and then you can see if it's possible to go back to the mix to change that before finishing the master. Of course, this will delay finishing the master so a lot depends on the circumstances—generally we want to finish without reverting to the mix stage, but sometimes doing so can save records!

Wither Dither?

Dithering is a process that lowers distortion when applying bit reduction. The most common application is during the final mastering bounce, when creating the 16-bit file to be used for the CD mastering from the 24-bit mixes used in the mastering session. Dithering was developed to counter the negative effects of truncation whereby 16-bit files were made from 24-bit files simply by removing the last 8 bits. Dithering is a complex process that randomizes the noise created by bit reduction. There are various kinds of dither that can be used, and noise shaping may be integrated with dithering to further reduce distortion.

While dithering can reduce distortion, the process also alters the audio in a way that makes any further processing problematic. Processing audio that has already been dithered can actually increase distortion. For this reason it is typical to use dithering only in the very final stage of mastering—the final bounce that reduces the audio from 24 bits to 16 bits and produces the files that will be used to burn the CD master.

There are a variety of strategies for dithering, and some plug-ins give you options for different types, while some others have options for different versions of noise shaping. If you have dithering options, refer to the user's manual for whatever software you're using to determine which type to use—it will depend on the sonic complexity of the material. Remember that you only dither once, at the final stage of your master.

Mp3s do not require dithering, as they use a completely different algorithm for file compression. There is no advantage to dithering when encoding the mp3 file format.

11.4 Processing: Dynamics and Effects

Dynamics processing (outside of brickwall limiting) and effects (such as reverb and delay) are not frequently used in mastering sessions, but they have their place. Both the demands of matching and the desire to enhance the sound can drive a mastering engineer to this kind of processing. Given the global aspect of processing in the mastering stage (everything is affected), dynamics would be a more likely candidate than effects.

Types of Dynamics Processors for Mastering

There are dynamics processors made (and marketed) as primarily buss compressors, meaning they are meant to be applied to the overall mix. However, most compressors can be used as a buss compressor, and your choice (if you decide to use one, see the following section) should be based on goals rather than marketing. That said, the most famous buss compressor comes from the classic SSL consoles that had the built-in quad compressor. (They were called "quad compressor" because the SSL consoles were developed during the brief period that quad, or four-channel, audio was being promoted. They retained their four-channel capabilities, though they were used primarily on stereo material—the quad format never caught on.)

The various qualities of different compressor design (and software applications providing emulations and extensions of those designs) are described in detail in section 4.4 and all are relevant to using compressors in mastering. The extent to which a compressor might be more aggressive (meant to impart a sonic signature) versus more transparent (meant to create the least alteration in original sound) varies depending on the details of the design and its implementation.

Generally the VCA and FET designs are more transparent, while the tube and opto designs provide more coloration (of a sometimes desirable, "analog"-oriented kind). RMS-level detection tends to be gentler than peak-level detection, which is good at taming sharp transients, so RMS is generally favored for buss compression. The SSL quad compressor, a VCA design that uses RMS-level detection, brought in a new era of mixes that were heavily compressed.

When to Use Dynamics Processing in Mastering

I discuss the pros and cons of using buss compression in mixing (or waiting until mastering) in section 3.3, and I side with those who consider it part of the mixing process. If there has been buss compression used in mixing, you probably won't want to do it again in mastering, though (as always) it depends on what it sounds like and what your goals are. Developing your ear to recognize the effects of compression is the first step toward making decisions about the application of compression in mastering. In the following audio clips you can hear a section of a mix with and without buss compression.

> Artist: Mike Schermer CD: *Be Somebody* Tracks: "Over My Head"
> Audio Clip 11.3: A clip of a section mastered with no buss
>   compression.
> Audio Clip 11.4: The same clip with moderate buss compression.

You can determine for yourself whether you like the effects of buss compression, but it has become a standard in almost all popular music production and is used frequently in other types of music as well, including classical. In the mastering stage, you may not know whether buss compression was used in the mix, and it may not be obvious from listening, either (especially if used subtly).

Aggressive buss compression provides additional impact and can transform relatively tepid mixes into pretty strong stuff—at a price. The perils of over-compression come in the extent to which musical subtlety is lost to increased impact. As more of the audio gets pushed to the forefront there is a loss in depth, and it is easy to move from increased impact to a sonic assault that may be impressive but is hardly inviting. If this language regarding buss compression sounds similar to some of the previous descriptions of brickwall limiting, it is because the two are closely related. Reducing the dynamic range of the final mix is a delicate trade-off, and buss compression and brickwall limiting need to work hand-in-hand to create a track with impact but that retains its musicality and depth.

If you want your mixes to be loud and are willing to accept the sacrifices caused by aggressive brickwall limiting, you will do well to start with aggressive stereo buss compression. Buss compression can help maximize volume with fewer artifacts than simply using brickwall limiting, so the combination yields more musical results than an aggressive version of one or the other. Even when a very gentle degree of limiting is desired, the combination of gentle buss compression and gentle brickwall limiting is preferable to a slightly stronger version of just one. In practical terms, this means most every production will benefit from some combination of buss compression and brickwall limiting. However, as a mastering engineer, you should assume that the stereo buss compression happened in the mix process unless your ear tells you otherwise.

Expansion in Mastering

In part because of the desire to grab people's attention and in part a result of increasingly compromised listening environments (such as earbud listening in public spaces), we live in an era of aggressive compression and brickwall limiting. The use of expansion in mastering is rare. EQ may be a kind of selective expansion by frequency—boosting at a selected frequency makes them louder than unboosted frequencies, thus "expanding" the distance between the two.

I explored the subtle variations of frequency-dependent expansion through the use of multi-band compressors earlier in the chapter. Global expansion tends to decrease overall impact, though it may create more expressiveness, which is what musical performers use dynamics for. Expansion may be used to counter the effect of over-compression on material you receive that has already been heavily processed, but it won't correct the pumping or distortion that may also have occurred. In any event, expansion will never yield the same results as the dynamics of musical performance, so it's best to refrain, avoiding the need for expansion by avoiding overly compressing or limiting the music.

Use of Effects in Mastering

Using effects such as reverb or delay is uncommon in the mastering stage. Adding ambiences such as these are generally best accomplished as effects on individual elements applied in the mixing. However, there are instances when effects do become an essential part of mastering.

The primary circumstance that is likely to make you reach for your reverb plug-in is when you are mastering stereo recordings. There is a whole world of recordings made with two microphones (or one stereo mic) that haven't had any prior processing. In many respects, mastering these recording is no different from mastering mixed material—you apply EQ and dynamics processing using the same matching/enhancing criteria as I have been covering. But they present a circumstance in which adding ambience may be an essential part of the mastering.

Two-channel recording techniques demand that the recordist balance the direct sound of the ensemble with the ambience of the recording environment. Generally, recordists want to err on the side of the direct signal because ambience can be added but cannot be taken away easily. For this reason many two-channel recordings benefit from added ambience in the mastering.

The following audio clips are from a two-channel recording of a drum and bugle corps. The first is an excellent recording, but it is dry; it lacks the ambience that suggests the kind of stadium environment that these groups most frequently appear in. The second recording has the addition of a large reverb ambience.

> Artist: The Blue Devils Track: "Current Year 2011"
> Audio Clip 11.5: A clip of a relatively dry 2-channel recording.
> Audio Clip 11.6 The same clip with the addition of a large reverb
>   ambience.

Reverb or delay might be a consideration on any kind of material, but generally this kind of processing is done in the mixing stage, and you will need pretty strong motivating circumstances to use it in mastering. You can add reverb or delay to an overall mix if everyone agrees that it could use some additional depth and it's really not possible to get back to the mix stage.

The greatest area of compromise in these situations is in regard to the low end—reverb or delay will muddy the bottom quickly. The best results will probably be had by using a high-pass filter on the send to the effect, the return from the effect, or both. Reverb will provide the most natural-sounding effect while delay can create a sense of depth while retaining greater overall clarity.

11.5 "Mastered for iTunes," Spotify, Pandora, etc.

Before finishing this chapter with a look beyond the traditional tools of mastering, it is important to address some of the new music delivery formats and the ways that they have (or have not) altered the mastering process.

Recently there's been an initiative from Apple called "Mastered for iTunes," which allows for high-resolution audio uploads to the iTunes service. They recommend files at 24 bit, 96 kHz, but they accept any file standard at 16 bit, 44.1kHz or better. Use of high-res uploads and improved codecs for creating compressed audio files means that the typical Internet download can sound much

237

better. It also means that services such as iTunes will have high-quality audio files available in case they decide to offer a higher standard in the future. Unfortunately, very few services for independent labels and individuals can take advantage of "Mastered for iTunes," so this feature is not widely available. Nonetheless, many of these services (aggregators) do offer standard CD quality upload (16bit, 44.1kHz) and use that to create the compressed file formats for download and streaming services including iTunes, Spotify, Pandora, and the like. To get your music to the Internet, always provide the highest quality file accepted by whatever service you are using. Because you will probably be using CD-quality uploads for eventual conversion and use on the Internet, it's helpful to reference the way the audio will sound after it has been converted (compressed) for these various delivery services. Apple provides free tools to reference the way the higher resolution audio is going to sound after it's been encoded to the iTunes format (M4a). Other companies offer similar software that will convert audio to formats used by iTunes, as well as those used by other services such as Spotify or Pandora. These are valuable references and I recommend your using the Apple tools or other codec referencing software before uploading your files.

11.6 What Else Is in the Box?

What else is in the box? Tons of stuff! Not only is there the huge array of signal processors but also the various editing and automation capabilities—any of which may be useful in a mastering session.

Other Signal Processors

Processing options in the digital domain are almost endless (with new ones appearing on almost a daily basis). Many processing options, outside of those already discussed, are either not relevant to mastering or would be considered only in unusual and rare circumstances. Some, however, might be useful on a more frequent basis—such as the addition of analog tape or vacuum tube simulations, or specialty low-frequency processing.

Analog simulation, generally modeled after the harmonic distortion created by analog tape recorders or vacuum tubes, has been one of the explosive areas of plug-in development in the past ten years. In section 4.3, I discussed the various effects of harmonics on sound and how the addition of even-order and odd-order harmonics in analog processing can either enhance or diminish sounds. Some simulation processors have elaborate controls over the addition of harmonic content and the effects it can produce, from the very subtle to the very pronounced. Many processors now have an "analog" parameter setting along with the more traditional EQ, dynamic, or effect-processing controls. Some of the most recent processors have elaborate simulations of many different analog tape recorders and the effects produced by different types of tape and different alignment settings (see screenshot 11.15).

As discussed in section 4.7, I have found these processors to be useful (pleasing) in a variety of mixing situations, including use on the stereo buss. They carry some downsides, too—especially in a tendency to muddy sound. And many can trigger the "louder sounds better" attitude, as adding these effects usually boosts gain as well. As with stereo buss compression, there is a good chance that the mixer has already added some of this processing to the overall mix, and in that case additional processing of this type at mastering may not be helpful. As always, you need to use your ear to determine whether there is an improvement in the sound beyond the immediate satisfaction of a small boost in gain. I rarely add analog simulation in mastering, but there are instances when it has clearly contributed something positive to the material.

Digital signal processing has permitted the development of some interesting low-frequency processors that take advantage of sophisticated digital algorithms to create new kinds of effects. One such process from the Waves software developers is used in their Maxxbass and Renaissance Bass processors (see screenshot 11.16). The patented algorithms can take fundamental bass notes and generate upper harmonics that can then be added back to the original signal. These added harmonics can make bass notes more apparent to the ear. In fact, when music is played on systems that aren't capable of reproducing low pitches (very small speakers), the harmonic is still audible and the ear fills in the missing bass notes because it recognizes the relationship of the harmonic to the missing fundamental note (you "hear" the low bass note even though it isn't being reproduced by the speaker). When the additional harmonics created by these plug-ins is added back to the original signal, the apparent low end can be dramatically increased without actually adding more low-frequency content.

Other kinds of processors also have options—anything is an option—but they are rarely employed. I have run entire mixes through amplifier distortion simulation or through a flanger, but always as a part of the mix process. Such decisions are generally not considered part of mastering unless you are the art-

The Waves Maxxbass and Renaissance Bass processors.

ist, producer, or mixer and have the freedom to take such radical steps during mastering.

Fades, Edits, and Automation

When it comes to working "in the box," there is an entire world of editing and automation that can be accessed. Typically, you don't get involved with any of these, but sometimes they can be essential tools for finishing the job. I have received some projects for mastering that didn't have any end-of-song fades completed, and I was asked to do those as a part of the mastering. Fortunately I was working with the artist at the studio, so I didn't have to decide on my own when to start the fade or how quickly to complete it.

As a mix engineer, I often decide on the fade and play my idea for the artist and/or producer, but sometimes the individual has a particular idea for how the fade should work. In any event, it almost always happens before the piece goes for mastering. If you are asked to do fades, and if you're working remotely, you might request some guidance from the others involved, or possibly send a couple options, if you're not sure what is going to work best. Although you can use fades created from the audio file—and most DAWs have a variety of fade shapes available—end-of-song fades are generally best created using automation. There are more details about fades in section 5.4.

I have already described two situations where volume automation may come into play in a mastering session—for creating fades and for balancing different sections of a track. Though these are the most common, virtually any automation could become useful. You might find that you want to EQ particular sections of a track differently and need to automate EQ parameters, for example. You might decide to add reverb to one section of a song and need to automate a send to a reverb. These are relatively uncommon occurrences, and are better dealt with in the mix stage, but all manner of automation can be used in mastering if the situation calls for it.

It's similar with editing. It's fairly rare to make edits during mastering, but it can happen. For instance, sometimes a fresh ear on a mixed track hears new possibilities, and this may include editing out a part. Edits can be easy to do on mixed material, and they can sound completely seamless, or you may be unable to get satisfactory results and find it necessary to return to the multitrack mix for a particular edit.

CREATIVE TIP

Don't always edit at the obvious edit point.

If you are attempting an edit in the mastering stage (or in the mix stage, for that matter, though there's more flexibility for global edits when you can adjust edit points on a track-by-track basis), the obvious edit point (typically the downbeat of the sections involved) is not always the best choice. The specifics of where to edit to remove an entire section (global edit) are usually guided by the drums (on tracks that have drums). A big downbeat with a kick drum hit is often a good place for the edit, but you should consider the drum fill or other elements going into the section.

For example, does the fill from the section prior to the part removed create the best transition to the newly adjacent part? Or might the fill from the section removed work better? Is there a vocal or instrumental pickup to the section that is to be removed that requires an earlier edit point? Of course, there are harmonic considerations that often mean such an edit couldn't work, but it isn't uncommon to have this option.

There are other possibilities, such as editing on the 4 beat before the transition, or even editing a bar or so into the new section, that sometimes sound more natural than an edit at the downbeat. One of the joys of editing on a DAW is that the creative options for global edits can be explored quickly and easily.

241

Chapter 12

The Final Master
Creating and Delivering

While some DAWs allow you to create a final CD-R master from within the DAW, many do not. If that's your case, then the final steps of sequencing, setting spacing between tracks, and creating the master for replication are accomplished using different software. I cover the software topics first, and then introduce the technical issues regarding creation of a sequenced master, including setting the time between songs (spacing) and any desired cross-fades between songs. I discuss the aesthetics of sequencing and spacing of songs, as well as offer techniques to help in that creative process.

There are a few different formats for delivering a master for CD replication, and there are other formats that may be required for uses such as download, streaming, or in film or video games. Most CD manufacturing plants accept a variety of formats, and there are also applications that create the master from different sources. There may be options for the actual delivery of the master too, with delivery over the Internet becoming increasingly common.

12.1 Creating a Master

Making the final sequence for a CD or complete album download requires the appropriate software (included in some DAWs) and the aesthetic decision on how to order the elements. Placing time spaces between each element is also done in this final stage. If you are delivering a single element, or elements not intended to run as a sequence, you don't need to consider these matters, and if you're assembling elements for a longer project, like a film, there are different protocols for maintaining synchronization.

If you are creating a CD master in the form of a CD-R, you have many options for burning your master. The only actual requirement is that the disc be burned in the Disc at Once (DAO) format, which means it is burned as one whole pass. The alternative is the Track at Once (TAO) format, which burns each track independently. The TAO format was used for CD-RW discs in order to add tracks to a previously burned disc, but that format has almost disappeared and many burn programs don't even offer TAO anymore. In any event, you will want to check that your burner is burning the DAO format for a master.

The differences in burning software lie in their ability to access more advanced capabilities and in storing meta-data on your final CD (more on what meta-data is in the following section). If you burn from the desktop using the operating system (Mac or PC), you will get an acceptable CD master that can be used for manufacturing, but you will not be able to manipulate the CD numbering, index markers, or cross-fades and it will not include meta-data.

DAWs that include burning capabilities and various dedicated software burning programs vary in their capabilities. Even the professional, dedicated mastering programs have different capabilities, though many of them include editing and processing functions, as well as burning protocols. I prepare my program material in the DAW to the point where I need only access functions directly related to burning the CD-R to be used in manufacturing.

It is becoming increasingly common to use a DDP file (Disc Description Protocol) for delivery of masters rather than a CD-R. The DDP files allow you to deliver the master over the Internet, and they also tend to be more reliable than a CD-R. Many manufacturing plants now accept DDP files and provide upload access at their sites, though some charge a premium for this service. A fairly limited number of mastering software programs offer both burning and DDP creation options, but I expect this to become a more common feature as the use of DDP files increases.

Basics for CD Masters

The digital format for CDs is called Red Book audio. It is unique to CDs, but it is relatively easy to create from many different types of audio files, such as AIFF, WAV, BWF (Broadcast Wave Files—the more recent and standardized version of WAVE files), and AIFF. There is a multitude of digital audio files, such as mp3, AAC and FLAC, m3u, AC3, OGG, and MOV. Some of these employ compression algorithms and some include graphic and/or film components. Different burning programs accept different formats for conversion into Red Book audio for CD playback.

Besides burning the tracks to the CD-R, every burning program also creates a CD number for each track, numbered sequentially, and places some space between each track. In the most basic programs (such as those that are a part of the computer's operating system), ordering the tracks may be the extent of your

243

control in this matter. With slightly more advanced software, you may be able to adjust the space (gap) between the tracks. Note that CDs require a minimum of a two-second gap prior to the first element on the CD, so burning programs have this as a default setting. If you try to shorten it you will get an error message and the CD-R will not burn.

Every CD includes PQ codes that direct the CD player to the various tracks and tells the CD player where each track starts and ends. These codes are embedded in the disc's table of contents (TOC). Most professional burning programs also create what is usually referred to as a PQ code file or sheet (as a text or pdf file) that shows the track list, the time between tracks, index times, crossfades, ISRC codes, and so on. The DDP file includes a PQ sheet, but for your CD-R master you'll need to print it out and send it along with your master for manufacturing. Manufacturing plants like to have a copy of this PQ sheet (see screenshot 12.1) to confirm what they are seeing when they analyze your master, but they will accept your master without the file.

PQ Sheet   All times are in M:S:F format

Title	: At This Moment		Engineer	: Steve Savage	
Performer	: The Noted		Studio	: The Rumpus Room	
MCN	:		Phone	:	
Printed at	: Tuesday, July 16 2013, 12:25:58		Client	: Daniel Work	
Created with	: Sonoris DDP Creator v3.0.1.1		Project	: At This Moment / The Noted	
Registered to	: Steve Savage		Source	: Digital	

T	X	ISRC / TITLE	PERFORMER	START	LENGTH
01		USR571300021			
	00	Pregap		00:00:00	00:02:00
	01	More Than Alright	The Noted	00:02:00	03:28:35
				TOTAL	03:30:35
02		USR571300022			
	00	Pregap		03:30:35	00:02:20
	01	I Am	The Noted	03:32:55	04:22:01
				TOTAL	04:24:21
03		USR571300023			
	00	Pregap		07:54:56	00:02:55
	01	Rhapsodize	The Noted	07:57:36	05:52:27
				TOTAL	05:55:07
04		USR571300024			
	00	Pregap		13:49:63	00:01:50
	01	This Tear	The Noted	13:51:38	04:07:31
				TOTAL	04:09:06
05		USR571300025			
	00	Pregap		17:58:69	00:03:00
	01	Only Wanna Be With You	The Noted	18:01:69	03:38:48
				TOTAL	03:41:48
06		USR571300026			
	00	Pregap		21:40:42	00:02:45
	01	Don't Tell Me No	The Noted	21:43:12	05:42:03
				TOTAL	05:44:48
07		USR571300027			
	00	Pregap		27:25:15	00:03:30
	01	A Day In The Life (of a dog)	The Noted	27:28:45	05:19:73
				TOTAL	05:23:28
		LeadOut		32:48:44	

SCREENSHOT 12.1

A typical PQ sheet (partial track listing).

CD Numbering, Indexing, and Offsets

While every burning program assigns a CD number to each track, only more advanced programs allow you to adjust the position of the CD number or to create more than one CD number for each audio file. Though you will want the CD number to correspond to the beginning of the track most of the time, there may be times where you wish to manipulate the position of the CD number. If, for example, you are cross-fading between two songs (see the upcoming section regarding cross-fades), you may want the CD number to correspond to the beginning, the middle, or the end of the cross-fade, depending on how things will sound if the user skips to that selection. Multiple track numbers for a single audio file are commonly used on classical recordings to allow easy access to various points in a long, continuous piece of music.

CDs can also include indexes for location points within a track, but most CD players are not capable of displaying or accessing these. Some professional players can read the index points, and they are sometimes used by radio stations to cue specific spots within a track. For these, the start of a track is Index 1, and the pre-gap is Index 0. You do not have to have a pre-gap if you don't want a gap between tracks—except for the very first index (prior to the first track on a CD), which must be an Index 0 and be a minimum of 2 seconds.

Some CD players, especially older models, have a delay when jumping from one track to another. This can cause playback problems, so some CD burning software programs have the ability to add a very small offset between the index point and the actual start of the audio. Typically this offset is between 5 and 10 frames.

Hidden Tracks

There are many techniques for creating what is called a "hidden track"—usually a track on a CD intended to be hidden under typical playback conditions (though sometimes the term simply means that the track is not listed in the credits but plays normally wherever it is placed on the CD). The most common hidden tracks are those that follow the last song on the CD but that don't play until after a long silence. They may or may not have their own CD number, though typically they don't, so the listener has to fast-forward or wait to hear them.

Some CDs have many short tracks of silence at the end so that the hidden track has a very high CD number (typically not listed). CDs are also capable of having audio placed in the pre-gap between songs or before the first song. Placing audio before the first song requires that the listener manually back up the player, and this is possible only on some CD players. Only certain burning programs allow you to place audio in the pre-gap. My favorite hidden track comes after about 5 minutes of silence at the end of a CD and is a recording of someone snoring!

245

Meta-Data

The inclusion of meta-data has become increasingly important in the digital/Internet age. Meta-data is information about the music that is coded into the digital audio file or onto a CD. The selling platforms, the streaming services, and consumers use this information to identify and organize the music. It is also used to identify music by copyright owners, publishing companies, and other parties interested in the commercial use and management of the music.

Typically, meta-data on CDs includes at least the name of the song or track, the name of the artist or performer, and the name of the disc (if the track is part of a disc release). It is also possible to encode the name of the songwriter(s), composer, and/or arranger, as well as any text message desired, but there is a maximum of 160 alphanumeric characters. With mp3 files, there are places for these same categories and also a field to code the year of release, as well as an option to code for a genre category with a large number of possibilities to choose from. CDs store the meta-data as part of the CDDB (CD Data Base), whereas the mp3s store the data as a part of the digital audio file. This is why you cannot access meta-data from an audio file formatted for CDs—it exists only in the data portion of the physical CD.

CDs can also be encoded with an ISRC code (International Standard Recording Code) and the MCN code (Media Catalog Number). The MCN code is the standard UPC/EAN number. ISRC codes are assigned to each track and they provide ownership information so that the track can be traced for royalty collection, administration, and piracy. There is a one-time registration fee to get these codes (currently $80) for all your projects. The MCN codes cover the entire disc and can be used for online payment information, but they are not in common use at this time.

Meta-data can be transferred from CD to mp3 (and back), depending on the conversion program. However, ISRC codes do not transfer, so, for example, when CD tracks are converted to mp3s, ISRC codes have to again be embedded in the files. The mp3s don't have a dedicated place to put ISRC codes, but they can be embedded as standard ID3 tags. Newer compression and file formats, such as AAC and FLAC files, also contain meta-data, but they have their own tagging systems. For these, the data won't transfer; it has to be embedded again when you're creating or converting to these files. See screenshot 12.2 for an example of these embedded files.

Level Adjustment

Some mastering or burning programs provide the ability to adjust the overall level of each element. In practical terms, this means reducing the level because if you have used any degree of brickwall limiting (or normalizing), you cannot increase level without creating digital distortion (pushing levels beyond digital zero). Since setting levels has been job number one in the mastering process, it

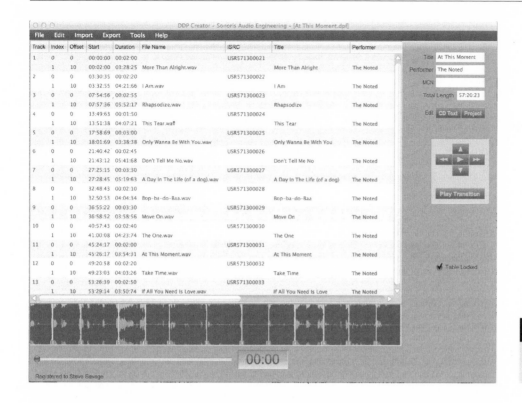

Track	Index	Offset	Start	Duration	File Name	ISRC	Title	Performer
1	0	0	00:00:00	00:02:00		USR571300021		
	1	10	00:02:00	03:28:25	More Than Alright.wav		More Than Alright	The Noted
2	0	0	03:30:35	00:02:20		USR571300022		
	1	10	03:32:55	04:21:66	I Am.wav		I Am	The Noted
3	0	0	07:54:56	00:02:55		USR571300023		
	1	10	07:57:36	05:52:17	Rhapsodize.wav		Rhapsodize	The Noted
4	0	0	13:49:63	00:01:50		USR571300024		
	1	10	13:51:38	04:07:21	This Tear.wav		This Tear	The Noted
5	0	0	17:58:69	00:03:00		USR571300025		
	1	10	18:01:69	03:38:38	Only Wanna Be With You.wav		Only Wanna Be With You	The Noted
6	0	0	21:40:42	00:02:45		USR571300026		
	1	10	21:43:12	05:41:68	Don't Tell Me No.wav		Don't Tell Me No	The Noted
7	0	0	27:25:15	00:03:30		USR571300027		
	1	10	27:28:45	05:19:63	A Day In The Life (of a dog).wav		A Day In The Life (of a dog)	The Noted
8	0	0	32:48:43	00:02:10		USR571300028		
	1	10	32:50:53	04:04:34	Bop-ba-do-Baa.wav		Bop-ba-do-Baa	The Noted
9	0	0	36:55:22	00:03:30		USR571300029		
	1	10	36:58:52	03:58:56	Move On.wav		Move On	The Noted
10	0	0	40:57:43	00:02:40		USR571300030		
	1	10	41:00:08	04:23:74	The One.wav		The One	The Noted
11	0	0	45:24:17	00:02:00		USR571300031		
	1	10	45:26:17	03:54:31	At This Moment.wav		At This Moment	The Noted
12	0	0	49:20:58	00:02:20		USR571300032		
	1	10	49:23:03	04:03:26	Take Time.wav		Take Time	The Noted
13	0	0	53:26:39	00:02:50		USR571300033		
	1	10	53:29:14	03:50:74	If All You Need Is Love.wav		If All You Need Is Love	The Noted

00:00

Registered to Steve Savage

SCREENSHOT 12.2

A mastering program with meta-data entered.

247

isn't too likely that you will all of a sudden decide to adjust overall level when mastering, but it might happen during the review phase.

For instance, after listening to your master with fresh ears and/or in different places, you may decide that one song needs to have the volume dipped a touch, and it might be easier to do that in the burning program than to go back to the original mastering DAW (although they might be one in the same). Lowering level globally produces different results from those obtained by raising the threshold on the brickwall limiter (though both reduce the perceived volume).

If you used your threshold control on the brickwall limiter when you were initially balancing the tracks (a common tactic), then you will probably want to go back to that stage to make any level adjustments. One exception, as previously discussed, would be to balance the elements with very different types of arrangements (acoustic solo tracks with electric band tracks, for example). In these cases, lowering the level of the softer track may solve the level issue in the most appropriate manner.

Overlapping Tracks and Cross-Fades

Some burning programs allow you to create overlapping tracks and/or cross-fades between songs. The most likely instance would be a simple overlap where the fade of one song is still audible as the next song begins, without any change in the gain of either. Other circumstances might include a fade-out and/or a fade-in between the two selections, usually creating a softer transition. In these instances, you need to decide whether the CD number should come at the begin-

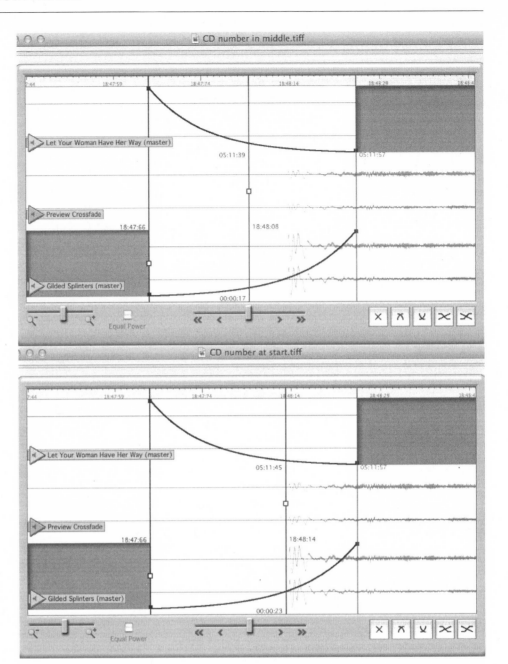

SCREENSHOT 12.3

A cross-fade between two elements with different CD numbering positions.

ning of the fade-up, at the mid-point between the fade-up and the fade-down, or at the end of the fade-down. See screenshot 12.3 for an example of this.

Creating a Sequence

Creating a sequence (ordering all the elements) is very simple technically, but often is very difficult aesthetically. The mastered files are placed in a burning program and can typically be dragged and dropped into any desired order. Reordering the sequence is usually as simple as dragging the file name to a new position. But setting the sequence of the tracks requires setting the spaces between the tracks (pre-gap). Once the final sequencing and spacing are done, the final CD-R master can be burned or a master DDP file created for delivery to the manufacturing plant.

Approaches to Sequencing Your CD: A Global Strategy

Of course, there is no "right way" to sequence a CD, but there are several approaches that you may wish to adopt (or ignore). You can seek to create a balance of material that attempts to engage the listener from the first song to the last, placing what you think is the most immediately compelling material strategically throughout the CD. Or, you can accept that it is less frequent for listeners to consider CDs as a whole work and simply front-load the CD with the material you think is most likely to grab the listener's attention, in the hope that he or she might be more likely to go deeper into the CD as a result. The prevalence of single-song downloading has meant that CD sequencing may no longer be as important as it once was. This has resulted in a second approach becoming the more common one.

Approaches to Sequencing Your CD: The Energy Strategy

How do you sequence songs so as to properly balance the relative energy of the material? Doing that is often a struggle. The tracks may lie along a spectrum that runs from highly energetic and up-tempo to languid ballads. In between are the mid-tempo tunes, the soft mid-tempo tunes, the power ballads, and endless other material that falls somewhere between fast and slow, aggressive and sweet.

One approach to sequencing is to begin with something energetic and keep the energy relatively high for a few songs, then break things up with a ballad. Then, you might follow the ballad with three or four mid- to up-tempo songs and intersperse another ballad, continuing with that strategy to the end. Of course, the exact number of up-, mid-, and slow-tempo songs on your CD will determine your options for interspersing slower material.

Another strategy is to create a place in your sequence for most or all of the slower tempo material placed together, creating an oasis in the broader upbeat sequence. This allows the listener to settle into a different space for a time, though it could also cause him or her to lose interest. As said, there's no "right way" to sequence. The good news is that re-sequencing is one of the easiest and quickest mastering functions to do, so you can create a variety of sequences as you decide which serves the music the best.

Approaches to Sequencing Your CD: Single Strategy

The notion of a "single" in popular music has changed somewhat, as playlists have shortened and iTunes, Spotify, and Pandora playlists have expanded. If you have a single release in the traditional sense, you will get a lot of input from your record label, marketing people, manager, agent, and so on. However, if you have—or want to have, or think you have—a single in the sense of one song that stands out as most likely to receive attention, that is a factor in sequencing your CD.

Singles used to be strategically placed in the second or third position on a record (and this extends well back into the vinyl days), but the competition to be noticed and people's shortened attention spans have caused singles to most typically be placed first in a CD sequence. As mentioned above, the prevalence of single-song downloading would also suggest that featuring what you consider to be your strongest song means placing it first in your sequence. However, if you are just releasing a single on the Internet, or to radio via download, it doesn't matter where it's placed on the CD (if there even is a physical CD).

Setting the Spaces Between Tracks

Setting the spaces between tracks—technically referred to as the "pre-gap," but also labeled "pause" in some programs—is often the last creative judgment to be made in preparing your master. A minimum of a two-second pre-gap before the first song is part of the CD Red Book protocol, but outside of that, you can put as much or as little space between the tracks as you want. You can also put audio in the pre-gap, as mentioned earlier under "Hidden Tracks," but this is rare.

The default spacing in most burning programs is two seconds between songs, and this often works pretty well. Some people just leave it at that, but it is worthwhile spending some time fine-tuning the spaces between the tracks as a part of the overall aesthetic. The biggest problem with setting the spaces is that they are heavily influenced by the playback volume. With loud-level listening, when you hear the very tail of the preceding song the space following it may seem quite short. However, when you're listening at a quiet level and you stop hearing the fade of the tail of the song before it is completely gone, that same space may seem overly long. Generally you'll want to listen at a moderate level and recognize that perception of the gap it going to depend on playback volume.

Some burning programs have a feature that plays the beginning of the first song for a brief amount of time (typically between 5 and 10 seconds), and then skips to play a portion of the end of the song (typically between 10 and 20 seconds) along with the beginning of the following song, then skips to the end of that song, and so on. In effect, the program is "playing the spaces" for you—with an appropriate amount of pre-roll and post-roll for each space. This is very helpful, but if you don't have this feature you can simulate it simply by skipping from the beginning to the end of each song and auditioning the spaces one at a time.

Some possibilities to consider in regard to creative spacing of songs include keeping the pre-gap spaces short for the first several songs to better keep the listener engaged; placing a longer pre-gap before a ballad or any song that you feel changes the general direction of the music, helping to "clear the air" for the listener; and running two or more songs with no audible gap to really keep things moving.

Burning or Creating the Final Master

There seem to be endless debates about what CD-R medium is best (which manufacturer, which color disc, etc.) and what speed the masters should be burned at. There has been a lot of testing done, and the upshot is that it really depends on your burner. No one medium is better than another, and no one burning speed is best. In fact, tests show that sometimes faster burn speeds result in CD-Rs with fewer error readings.

Most of the time, pretty much any CD-R, burned at any speed, will create a master with error rates well below the danger level. If you find a particular brand of CD-R that seems to work well with your burner, and you are getting good results at a particular burn speed, then you probably just want to stick with that for your master. You might try different brands of CD-Rs and different burn speeds, and do some listening tests to settle on a way to best create your masters with your system.

Once the master is burned, you need to listen to it before sending it off for manufacturing. It does no harm to a CD-R to play it as long as it's handled carefully, by the edges. Occasionally there are problems with a blank CD-R or with a burn, and there can be audible pops or distortions on a particular burn. You want to listen carefully to the master to make sure your master doesn't have any of these problems.

As mentioned earlier, DDP files are becoming increasingly common for master delivery, taking the place of CD-Rs. The DDP files offer the advantage of Internet uploading and they have greater reliability than CD-Rs. As more software programs offer DDP file creation, and as more manufacturers provide easy uploading of these files, there be increased use of this format for master delivery.

Be sure to burn a duplicate master (or single master CD-R, if you are delivering a DDP file) for yourself so you have something to compare to the manufactured CDs that will be shipped to you by the plant. *You should not be able to hear anything more than the very slightest difference between your burned CD master and the completed CDs from the plant.*

12.2 Formats and Delivery Options

There are an increasing number of format and delivery options for music, so you may be asked to prepare and deliver different kinds of files over various physical and virtual networks. What follows is a survey of common formats, but this is constantly shifting, so check with whoever is receiving your files to ensure that they are in the correct format.

Audio File Formats

There are many different audio file formats, but the most common are Red Book audio, which is for CD duplication, and mp3 audio, which is the most prevalent used for audio over the Internet. As discussed earlier, Red Book audio is created by CD burning or DDP file creation, and can be made from various file formats, depending on the software. Most DAWs work with BWF (Broadcast Wave File), a standardized version of WAVE files that is the dominant file format on PCs; or AIFF (Audio Interchange File Format), which was developed as the standard for the Mac. Both formats are usually easily handled on both platforms. Many DAWs can convert from known formats into either WAVE or AIFF files. While many DAWS can generate mp3 files, if you need another audio file format for a particular application, you may require a special plug-in or conversion program.

CD Masters

CD master formats and delivery protocols are pretty simple and have been covered earlier. A CD-R master delivered through the mail (or overnight) or a DDP file uploaded via the Internet are the two accepted delivery formats at the moment. In both cases, meta-data can be added and so delivering a PQ sheet is advised, to help reduce the possibility of confusion or errors in the duplication process.

Download and Streaming Masters

The ultimate file format that will be used for Internet applications may change. It used to be the pretty standard mp3 format, but the variety of music services and the desire for better quality have led to other formats that are now either accepted or required. Because of increased computer operating speeds and faster broadband connection speeds, it has become more practical for CD-quality files to be uploaded. File formats that lie in between the CD standard and the mp3 standard in quality and size are becoming more prevalent. Even higher than CD quality bit sampling depth and bit rate files (hi-res) can be found for downloading via the Internet.

As mentioned previously (chapter 11), there are some new services such as "Mastered for iTunes" that allow you to use high-resolution audio to upload. "Mastered for iTunes" recommends providing 24 bit, 96 kHz files. The files are then compressed by the content provider. This has the capability of improving the sound of the compressed audio that is ultimately delivered. It also means that the content provider has higher quality files that may become available at a later time. While not everyone has access to the "Mastered for iTunes" services that accepts higher than CD-quality file formats, most services (aggregators) accept (and request) the CD format (16 bit, 44.1 kHz). These files will be used to create the file formats needed for both downloading and streaming content providers. Delivering uncompressed audio, whether at the CD standard or higher, will always be preferable to any compressed file standard. If I am creating files for an artist or record company at something less than CD quality, I always try to also deliver the audio in the CD format, so that the client has this on file for reference or for later use in applications that use higher quality audio.

Film/Video

Audio for film and video is much more complex than music-only masters, owing to the addition of sound effects, foley, dialog, and so on. There may be some kinds of master processing of certain elements along the way, but they will be to a different standard and processes for doing so vary considerably. Making the final mixes is usually referred to as "re-recording" of the elements (instead of mixing) and includes some additional mastering-type processing, but there isn't usually a separate mastering stage after the mixing. Stems are sometimes remixed for CD or DVD release, and then a more traditional mastering may be done. Because of the complexity of audio for film or video, it is essential that you are in close communication with those working on the other elements and have clear directions from those responsible for the final mix.

Video Games

Formats for delivery of the audio for video games may vary, but it is likely that you will be asked to deliver a stereo mix, stems (described below and in section 8.1), and possibly a 5.1 surround mix. Because video games require so much music to accompany the many hours of game play, each audio element may get used in different versions at different times. To facilitate this, stereo stems are made from the final stereo mix. (A stem is simply a smaller element taken from the larger mix; stems can be recombined to form the original composition and mix, as well as new compositions and arrangements that do not include all of the elements from the full mix.)

A typical group of stems might be broken down as drums, percussion, bass, guitars, and keyboards, thereby making five stems. More complex compositions may yield more stems, such as drums, high percussion, low percussion, bass, rhythm guitars, lead guitars, horn section, piano, keyboards, lead vocal, and harmony vocals, for a total of 11 stems. Once the final mix is done, the stems are made simply by muting all the other tracks and running a "mix" of each stem element. In these collaborative projects that combine audio and other elements, you need to coordinate your work with those working on the other elements.

Chapter 13

Mastering Collaboration
The Mastering Team

Collaboration is at the heart of most recording projects. There are often many stakeholders involved in the mastering process; additionally, most people play some elements for friends and colleagues looking for feedback, even on projects where they might be pretty much wearing every hat. In this chapter I consider critical aspects of that collaboration process. I begin with an overview of how to talk about mastering, as this is generally the least understood aspect of the recording process. I then summarize the general practices and attitudes toward intervention and alteration of the mixed music during mastering. This is a topic that comes up repeatedly in the book when dealing with the specifics of mastering, but it's valuable to provide a comprehensive look at it here. Finally, since Internet connectivity has changed collaboration in every aspect of recording, I consider the particular challenges in regard to remote collaboration.

13.1 How to Talk About Mastering

I recently saw a posting on a heavily trafficked recording discussion group that was titled "The Difference Between Mixing and Mastering." I was reminded of how fuzzy these processes can be for many people, even those who have been handling such projects a few times. This is especially true for mastering—certainly it is the least understood part of the basic recording functions.

I think that part of the problem is that mastering engineers often assume that their collaborators understand the process, so they never explain it. Meanwhile, those involved in other aspects (recording, editing, and mixing) may be too embarrassed to admit that they don't understand what's going on. This is especially true when the mastering is done remotely—an increasingly common scenario. So, when I'm dealing with newbies and "experienced" collaborators alike, I take great care to be sure they understand the fundamental goals of mastering, as well as its limitations. I even do this as a reminder for established artists whom I have worked with previously.

I begin by laying out the primary objectives of the mastering session, and I mention the major aspects for which I will be looking for feedback. These points are outlined in the following section. Also, I make sure these points are clear before I delve into some of the more complex (and rarer) types of work that may also be part of the mastering. The only requirement of mastering that people are generally familiar with, and may have given some thought to, is the creation of the final sequence. Therefore, I ask for a sequence when I receive the files, though I explain that I don't actually *need* the sequence until the very end and that changing the sequence is one of the simpler tasks.

The Primary Goals of Mastering

Here are the primary goals of a typical mastering section followed by explanations of each and descriptions of how I communicate these goals. I call each element a "song" because that's usually what it is, but if you're handling something else, just substitute *element* or *selection*.

- Balance levels from song to song
- Balance frequencies from song to song
- Set overall level for the project
- Sequence and set spaces between songs

Balance Levels from Song to Song

As stated in chapter 10, job number one of mastering is to *balance levels from element to element.* I explain to my collaborators that because mixing typically happens over an extended period of time, and because songs often contain different dynamics (from ballads to rockers, for example), it isn't possible for the mix engineer to keep track of overall level from song to song. Yet, on the CD (or streaming, or wherever), these songs are going to play one right after the other, so it is important (now that they are mixed) to adjust the levels from song to song so that they sound reasonably balanced.

I explain that level balancing is not an exact science—that it can be very subjective—but that I will do my best to give each element an equivalent level. I usually save the more involved discussion of how to do this until we start to listen together. If we are collaborating remotely, I usually summarize the process I've used to set level (see section 10.1) in an email at the same time as I send a master for review. Remember: this is an overview, so you want to keep all four elements relatively simple so that your collaborators can understand the overall mastering concept.

255

Balance Frequencies from Song to Song

The primary goal of EQ'ing in mastering is to *match the frequency balance of all the elements*. As with level setting, in mastering I focus on getting all the songs to sound like they belong together as they play one right after the other. I explain that I might subtly rebalance the EQ of a song so that it is in better balance with the other songs, even though if I were listening to the song on its own I might not think it needed any EQ at all. The goal is to have each element feel reasonably balanced with each other in low, mid-, and high-frequency content. I mention that I might apply subtle EQ with the intention of enhancing the sound of a mix as well, creating the optimal balance on the frequency spectrum, but that primarily the use of EQ serves the overall goal of balancing all the songs.

Set Overall Level for the Project

Once I feel that the level and frequency balancing is clear, I have "the discussion" about overall level. I put "the discussion" in quotes here because it has become a critical moment in music mastering. Your collaborators need to understand the principles behind brickwall limiting, the reasons for its use, and its relative benefits and pitfalls. I explain how brickwall limiting on the final master has become an essential part of virtually every commercial recording, and how the negative effects of extreme limiting have led to listener protests and the existence of what has come to be called the "loudness war."

Although the collaborators may have opinions about the extent of overall limiting they want on the recording, more frequently it's not a matter that they've given any thought to. I suggest that I use a moderate amount of brickwall on their master—enough to be "competitive" but probably a bit less than many big-budget, mainstream recordings—and that they can make a judgment about what they want for their record after they've heard the effects of the limiting and compare their recording to others.

I have had collaborators come back and say that they want their record louder, so it would be right up there with commercial recordings. Unfortunately I can't say that I've ever had the response that they want less limiting so the record could retain a greater dynamic range. I hope that I've been a force to gently reverse the trends of the loudness war, but I recognize the collaborators' perspective: they want their recordings to stand up to most other recordings. So, at least a moderate amount of brickwall limiting helps them feel more comfortable with the final product.

I now also try to discover the extent of brickwall limiting that was used on the mixes, so that I know what my collaborators have been listening to. It is increasingly apparent that the limiting used on mixes plays an important role in applying brickwall limiting in mastering. Expectations set by the limiting used in mixing probably need to be adjusted in the mastering. (I explore this topic in appendix B.)

Sequence and Set Spaces Between Songs

Putting the songs in order (sequencing) and setting the spaces (or gaps, or spreads) between the songs are typically the final pieces in assembling a CD master. I covered the technical and creative aspects of setting the spaces in section 12.1, but right off I share the three most important points with my collaborators: (1) the default value is 2 seconds but anything from cross-fades to long silences can be done, (2) the playback volume can dramatically affect the perception of the space, and (3) there are different philosophies regarding spaces, but everyone is entitled to his or her own sense of what works best. I might also suggest that short spaces tend to keep listeners engaged as they move from song to song but that longer spaces can serve to "clear the air" between songs when the mood and/or tempo changes dramatically.

I have had collaborators who just say "put two seconds between each" and never consider anything different, and I've had others who spend a considerable amount of time fine-tuning the spaces in 1/10 of a second increments (and then send minute revisions after listening at home). I encourage collaborators to pay attention to the spaces so they can exercise their creative judgments if they care to.

For many projects, this is all that I do! If the project is well mixed and the collaborators are generally happy with what they have brought to me, then there is no reason to push the mastering process beyond these fundamental (and critical) goals.

13.2 Levels of Mastering Intervention

These primary goals of mastering encompass the standard interventions that a mastering engineer will take in creating the master. But there are further levels of intervention that come into play on certain projects. I generally run these possibilities by my collaborators so that they are aware of what might be done, but I suggest that in many instances the better solution is to turn to remixing when possible.

Changes in Volume on Selected Portions

Making changes to different sections of a mix, as opposed to global processing, is sometimes as simple as raising or lowering the level of an intro. For example, because the brickwall limiting will probably not kick in until the whole band enters, a single guitar intro may sound considerably louder relative to the band than it did in the original mix. This is why it's important to check your mixes with a brickwall limiter in place. Lowering the intro level is easy to do during mastering, so going back to the mix stage isn't necessarily an advantage (although you can run into problems if the instruments layer in until one of the entrances engages the limiter and changes the relative levels).

However, changing levels from section to section (louder chorus, quieter versus etc.) is likely to create some imbalances, especially in the rhythm section. This is rarely a successful mastering tactic, unless only very subtle changes are made. The case is similar if EQ'ing sections differently. Occasionally this kind of mastering intervention can be helpful, but the problem is usually better addressed in mixing.

Dealing with Noise

You may try to address problems with unwanted hums, buzzes, and hiss using notch filters and/or noise-reduction processors. However, because these problems are often not global but, rather, isolated in one or more of the original tracks, they are best tackled in the mix. If mastering has become the only option, it may be possible to provide some help; nevertheless, keep the benefits versus costs very much in mind. Often, processing used to reduce unwanted frequencies also reduces desirable elements. It's possible to become so focused on noise reduction that the reduced quality of the music goes unnoticed—and then the resulting master is less noisy but also sounds worse! It's important to A/B the effects of noise reduction by listening for the overall effect on the audio as well as the effect on the noise.

Fades, Edits, and other DSP

Adding or fine-tuning the end-of-song fades is relatively easy to do in a DAW and can certainly be an appropriate extension of mastering. Global edits can usually be done in mastering as well, if deemed desirable. Both fades and global edits are more easily accomplished during mixing, however, where there is the added ability to make adjustments on a track-by-track basis. Making these revisions in the mixing stage also allows folks to live with the changes before the finalizing process of mastering.

Other kinds of digital signal processing (DSP), such as compression and analog simulations, can be done subtly at the discretion of the mastering engineer. Mild processing can be helpful, but even that will involved some trade-off between initial impact and long-term musicality. Aggressive processing, however, significantly alters level and frequency balances and should be avoided unless the material is seriously lacking. More radical processing, such as modulating delays or amp distortion simulation, very rarely make sense on a project that is felt to be far along enough for mastering.

CREATIVE TIP

Do no harm.

The physicians' guidepost "Do no harm" can be applied to much of mastering and is too often lost in the zeal to "have an impact" (or more cynically, to justify the mastering engineer's fee). The "best" master is often the one which changes the original mixes the least, while satisfying the primary goals of mastering.

13.3 Managing Remote Mastering Projects

The key to any good collaboration is effective communication. Working remotely amplifies the need for clear communications, thereby averting problems. As the mastering engineer, you need to explain the various goals and techniques in a timely manner so that your collaborators stay focused on the issues and have some idea of the capabilities and constraints of mastering.

Delivery of the Master

Because you are working remotely, you can't get the kind of immediate feedback as you could if working side by side in the mastering room together. Instead, you need to prepare the master and send it to all involved (artist, producer etc.).

WHAT NOT TO DO

Don't send a master to anyone without proper permission.
As with mixes (see section 7.1), it is important to respect boundaries in regard to music production. These boundaries include not sending or giving material to other people (friends, clients, industry contacts, etc.) without first obtaining permission from the artist and/or record company (in many cases, the "record company" is a self-release by the artist).

Sometimes the artist will ask you to send a master to industry contacts or others who might be help with the release, but unless you've been given permission it is inappropriate to allow these masters to circulate until after the project has been released. I usually ask the artist to send me several copies of the final product, and then I give those to anyone I think might be able to help, but only after official release or with the permission of the artist and record company.

259

It used to be that delivering a physical CD-R master was the only viable way of providing a master for review. Even if you posted all the elements on an ftp site or other cloud storage (such as Dropbox or Gobbler) for download, the collaborators would have to assemble the elements and they still wouldn't have the correct spaces between songs unless they had the same software and burned the project to CD or you sent them the timing for each space for them to insert in their burning program.

Generally it is still easiest to mail or overnight-deliver the physical CD to the collaborators for review. With the advent of the DDP protocol, you now have a single set of files that can be used to reassemble masters anywhere and that can be shared via cloud storage or through an ftp site. I'm starting to see some software companies offering DDP reader software that you can provide your collaborators (send them the link), which allows them to load the DDP files and use the files to create a CD for review.

Getting Feedback

Once the preliminary information about goals and techniques has been communicated with your collaborators, and I have a master for their review, I send a note along, usually via email, that asks three questions:

1. How are the volume relationships between the songs?
2. How is the overall volume of the CD, file, or group of files?
3. How is the space (or spread) between elements?

I might ask for "any other comments as well," but I generally do not make a specific request that my collaborators consider other possible revisions, such as EQ or processing. I don't want them to be distracted from the primary areas they need to review.

Their responses range from acceptance of the master "as is" to requests for revisions on any or all of the main points. Occasionally I get questions regarding EQ or other processing choices, but those are rare. In regard to overall level, I try to convince them to keep the brickwall limiting to a reasonable level—more than I'd like but not so much as to crush the life out of the music. However, this does mean that most of my masters are slightly under the average gain of mainstream commercial releases. I do get collaborators who sometimes come back to me and say that they've compared the master to other CDs and they need it to be louder.

I try to determine if they want a little bit more gain, a medium amount, or a lot more (very subjective, but at least I get some direction). Then I simply lower the threshold on the brickwall limiter for each track in order to add x number of dBs to the limiting level (something like 1 dB for a little, 2 dB for a moderate amount, and 3 dB for a lot). (I cover these complexities concerning volume in appendix B.)

Thanks to complete and easy recall when working in the box, most revisions are quick and easy, so I encourage collaborators to be critical and to make sure they are completely happy with the final product. The biggest obstacle to the kind of easy back and forth that happens on remote projects is the delivery date, so if you can get the free DDP software working for your clients and deliver over the Internet, that promotes the collaborative process. (I expect to see more options in this regard appearing over the next few years.)

Mastering has the bonus of being the last step in most audio projects, so getting the final sign-off means letting go of the project and, though that can be difficult for some, it is also cause for celebration. A most gratifying conclusion—even if it is done remotely!

Appendix A

Notes on Surround Mixing and Mastering

Surround audio remains primarily a film and video format. While there are a large number of surround systems in American homes, they are almost exclusively part of a home theater and the surround audio is used only for movies. I include some introductory information on surround mixing and mastering in this appendix, but I do not cover the subject thoroughly because it still represents a very small segment of music delivery formats.

A.1 Surround Formats and File Setup

There are various formats for a surround system, primarily based on the scale of the listening environment. There are also various ways to set up DAW files for effective surround mixing, including DAWs that are limited to stereo output configurations.

Surround Formats

The most common surround format is 5.1. This number refers to a six-channel system that consists of five full-frequency channels and one low-frequency channel reproduced with a subwoofer. The five channels are front left, center, front right, rear left, and rear right—with the two rear speakers generally referred to as the surround speakers. The sixth or subwoofer channel is referred to as the low-frequency extension, or LFE, channel. See diagram A.1.

Many newer and larger movie theaters now boast a 7.1 surround system that simply adds a second level of rear or surround speakers—a greater distance from the front speakers—extending the range of potential for surround-sound placement farther back into the auditorium, as shown in diagram A.2.

File Setup

There are various ways to set up for a surround mix, and a lot depends on the capabilities of your DAW. To have full surround functionality you need to have surround features in your program, but it is possible to make surround mixes using DAWs without dedicated surround channels or complete surround panning capabilities. However, to work in surround at all, you will need a system with at least six separate outputs and a speaker and subwoofer system that can play back the 5.1 audio. If the speakers are powered, you can route directly from

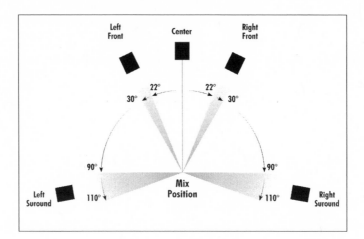

Proper 5.1 surround
speaker system setup.

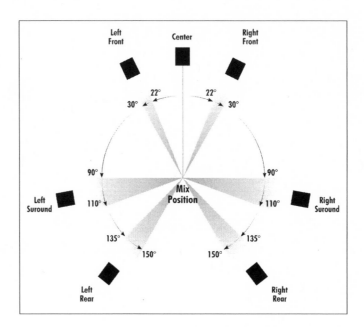

Proper 7.1 surround
speaker system setup.

264

you DAW outputs, but if they're not, you need separate amplification for each speaker and the subwoofer.

There are some home theater receivers with this capability, but for audio mixing you need one that has individual analog inputs for each of the channels and a DVD-multi function for handling those inputs. Many receivers can play back 5.1 surround audio, but they require a digital input that most DAW interfaces cannot output.

If your DAW has surround routing, you can simply route each channel to the 5.1 output matrix and send audio from the channel to any one of the six channels, controlling the level independently as needed. Screenshot A.1 shows a few tracks headed toward different 5.1 channels. The surround panning matrix is shown as dots in a box, with the relative front/back and left/right placement indicated by the position in the box.

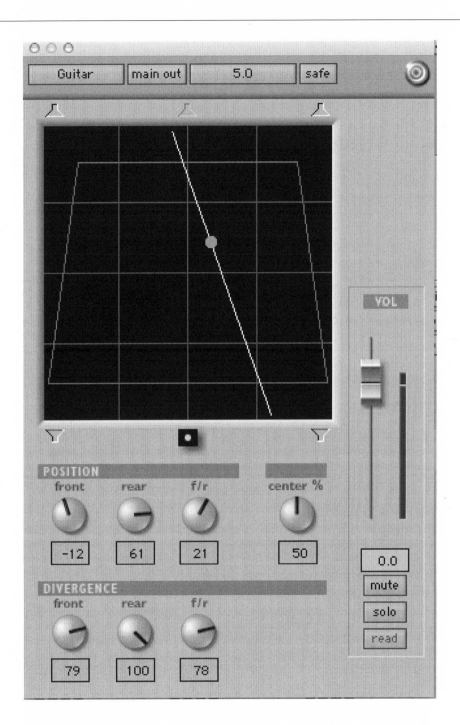

SCREENSHOT A.1

Routing for some surround
sound channels.

If you are using a stereo system to create a 5.1 mix, you will need to use your busses to send audio to channels other than to the front left and right that output to the stereo buss. One possible setup is shown in screenshot A.2. By creating an aux track that routes to each of the six 5.1 channels, you can use processing on each master send to the six channels. Six aux sends can then be used to feed the other six channels (front L/R, center, LFE, and surround L/R). The sends feed the aux tracks from each track and then the aux submasters feed the audio tracks for each of the 5.1 channels.

Surround setup in a stereo environment.

The six analog outputs feed the six speakers (five plus subwoofer) in your surround playback system. This is especially helpful when using some mastering functions such as brickwall limiting on the five audio channels or steep low-pass filtering on the LFE channel. I also show two separate reverbs—one feeding front L/R and the other rear L/R. You will notice that I'm also sending the center channel audio to the front L/R reverb.

In this model, when you are ready to create your final mix, you simply record each of the 5.1 audio tracks that you have been mixing and monitoring. You will probably need to convert those final channel files to create the proper format for delivery (see later for details on final surround-sound file delivery). You may need to study the screenshot carefully to grasp the full routing scheme used.

This setup gives full functionality for surround mixing, although some of the more elaborate surround panning moves are cumbersome. For example, sweeping in real time from the front speakers to the back speakers requires more elaborate automation than with a system that has a 5.1 matrix output configuration. Joystick panning, which gives you complete control over routing to the five main channels, can be duplicated only with many complex automation moves in a two-channel system with individual outputs for surround and no direct access to the surround matrix. However, many projects are unlikely to use joystick panning, so this limitation may be minimal.

A.2 Surround Panning and Perspective

The additional speakers in a surround system provide expanded capability in regard to placement of audio. Not only is there a much broader range of panning options, but the addition of a center speaker adds a whole new quality to the experience of what we are familiar with as center-panned audio. The three-dimensional quality of the speaker setup provides opportunities to give listeners different perspectives on their relationship to the ensemble. The way that mixes might take advantage of this expanded palette is partly a function of the nature of the program material—studio recordings, audio for live performance (e.g., concert DVDs), or audio for videos or films—and partly a function of the creative aesthetic of those who create the mixes.

Static versus Dynamic Panning

There are two basic approaches to surround panning: static and dynamic. The static model means that the sound is placed in the surround field, but it doesn't move (isn't panned dynamically) over the course of the mix. Audio for music concert DVDs or webcasts is often done using the static approach, as any movement of audio may be distracting and feel unrealistic. Dynamic panning involves moving the sound through the surround field in real time. Dynamic panning is sometimes used in movie soundtracks to follow the action, such as with the movement of sound from a radio as someone enters or leaves a room. See later in this appendix for more on panning practices and perspectives.

Center Channel versus Phantom Center

One of the most striking differences in working with surround mixing is the ability to utilize a center speaker. Working in stereo, as you do the majority of the time, you have become accustomed to achieving a "mono" effect by center-panning an element so that it comes out of the two speakers at equal volume. You perceive these sounds as "coming from the center," or at least that's how you have come to interpret the sound of center panning. The reality is, of course, that the sound is coming from sources on either side of your head! If you are listening in the mix position—hearing each speaker in equal balance—then center-panned sounds do sound somewhat "centered" (referred to as "phantom center"). However, as soon as you move closer to one speaker or the other, center-panned sounds sound like they're coming from that closer side of the room.

A center speaker provides true center listening. When you get the chance to use it in mixing, you discover how different that is from the phantom center that you've become used to in stereo mixing. Not only does center-panned sound remain center as you move toward one side of the room or the other, but even in the mix position the sound from the center speaker has a much more concrete, much more obvious point of origin. It is then that you realize exactly how "phantom" the phantom-center sound is in the stereo speaker configuration. Sound from the center speaker has a stability that is radically different from the perceived center quality of mono signals in stereo speakers. Access to rear (surround) speakers makes surround mixing really fun, but access to the center

267

speaker also transforms your ability to place sounds and radically changes the listening experience.

Center speakers for surround were developed largely to provide better sound placement for movie dialog. When their use is limited to stereo sound, anyone who isn't sitting in the center hears all the dialog as coming primarily from the speaker on his or her side of the theater. Center speakers place the dialog in the center of the screen, which is usually close to where we see the actor speaking. Of course, there are many instances when the speaker in a movie is not center-framed, and occasionally the mixer pans the dialog to the side the speaker appears on, but camera movement might disrupt that perception and so it is not frequently used.

It's similar with something like panning a lead vocal across the front (in stereo or surround) as the singer runs from one side of the stage to the other. This can be effective and fun, but it can also be distracting. We are used to hearing vocals emanate from a more consistent and stable place; even in a live situation when the singer is moving across the stage, his or her voice is not because the audience hears it from the loudspeakers.

Audience, Participant, or Camera POV

In regard to the point of view (POV) the surround mixer might adopt for the listener in a live music mix, there are two basic static approaches possible. The first point of view is that of an audience member, whereas the second places the listener in the middle of the music ensemble, as though one of the musicians. The audience POV puts all the direct sound in the front three speakers, typically recreating the panning of the stage setup; the musicians who are center stage are panned center and the musicians who are stage right or stage left are panned into the left or right speakers (using the audiences perspective on left and right). The surround speakers are used for ambience, through added reverb and/or reverb from room or audience mikes that capture the ambience of the performing hall. Using ambience in the rear speakers gives the sense of a three-dimensional space. This approach offers the listener the most realistic portrayal of "being there" in the most traditional setting, with the performers separated from and in front of the audience. The experience is greatly enhanced with additional ambience coming from behind the audience.

The second approach places the listener on stage, in the midst of the performers. The listener position could be in the middle of the orchestra, for example, surrounded by the instruments in a typical orchestra setting; or amid the instruments of a rock band, arrayed in whatever aesthetic seems best. For example, in the rock band setting, you might mimic a stage setup and put the vocals and rhythm instruments across the front speakers, and put the bass and drums in the rear (surround) speakers. Alternatively, you might abandon a realistic setup and array the instruments around the listening position based more on prominence, by putting the lead vocal, bass, drums, and rhythm guitar across the front speakers and the percussion, keyboard, and background vocals in the rear speakers.

However, if you don't adopt a static perspective, the placement possibilities become unlimited. You might use dynamic panning and have a guitar solo fly around from speaker to speaker, creating a wildly energetic effect. Unlike the stereo perspective that has been so thoroughly explored over the years (see section 4.2), creative surround placement and movement options are still in their infancy and there are no widely accepted standards.

The camera perspective is another approach to surround placement that can be used for creative panning choices. I saw one music video during which the camera traced a 360° circle around the drummer, and as it did the mixer panned the entire drum set in a corresponding 360° dynamic pan. This was somewhat disruptive, but also fun and inventive. It was also a reminder of how important it is to be mixing to picture when creating audio for use with video or film. You may want to have the guitar solo or the singer pan from left to center to right as he or she runs across the stage, even though the sound isn't actually moving at the concert.

You may not want to follow the camera movement at all, but you probably will want the panning to reflect the setup: if the keyboard player is on the left (stage right) in the video, you probably want them panned on the left. Of course, when the camera perspective switches to a shot from the back of the stage, the keyboard player will appear on the other side of the image; you probably wouldn't want to flip the panning on the piano for that shot, though you could. Again, both static and dynamic panning protocols are wide open, with little standardized techniques to draw from.

A.3 Surround Mixing Strategies

There are many ways to create a surround mix—there is even software that will create a surround mix from your stereo mix automatically ("unwrap" it). The most common procedure is to create a stereo mix first (you are almost certainly going to need one along with the surround mix) and then allow a surround mix to evolve from that stereo mix. The surround mix might be a simple extension of the stereo mix, or it might develop in a way that ultimately makes it quite different.

Software-Generated Surround Files

Software-generated files process the stereo files and extract ("unwrap") the audio into a surround format. Some of this software provides considerable control over how much information is fed to the center, surround, and LFE channels and whether the stereo channels are to be left intact or altered in the process. While this can be a quick solution for supplying a surround mix when you don't

269

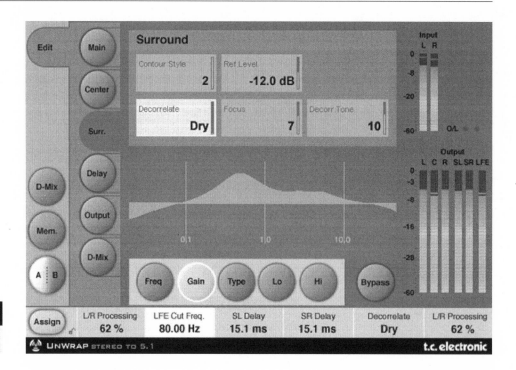

SCREENSHOT A.3

Unwrap interface.

have time, budget, or facility to create one properly, it can never achieve the aesthetics produced by creating the surround mix on your own. See screenshot A.3.

There is also software that will "down-mix" the 5.1 mixes back to stereo, and some of these programs are built into consumer receivers and systems that have surround playback capabilities. If you are playing a DVD, for example, and the audio output on the DVD player is set to surround, but the receiver is set to playback in stereo, the receiver might down-mix the surround mix for you (often with disastrous results regarding the mix). This is why DVDs should be set to default to the stereo mix unless surround output is specifically chosen from the audio setup menu. Unfortunately, DVDs are not always set up this way.

The more center and rear surround channel processing you employ, the more severe the problems that are likely to occur on a down-mix; however, those are the elements that can make surround mixing the most dramatic. Having software that will down-mix your surround mix can be helpful for you to hear and possibly avoid the worst problems if your surround mix does get down-mixed at the consumer level. See screenshot A.4.

Blowing up a Stereo Mix

Starting from the stereo mix means that much of the mixing work for surround sound has already been done. It's likely that the EQ, compression, panning, and even automation will move from your stereo mix and be appropriate to your surround mix. In fact, for much of the surround work I do, I maintain the stereo mix as is and simply augment it by feeding various elements to the center, surround left and right, and LFE channels. I generally need to add additional pro-

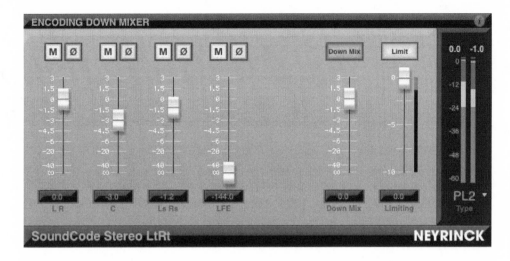

cessors for an expanded ambience palette as part of the augmentation from the stereo mix, but I do not alter the stereo mix or its original effects.

In this scenario, I might take essential center-panned information, such as vocals, snare drum, kick drum, and bass, and add them to the center speaker to provide more presence and stability. If I'm using the audience perspective, I create reverbs and delays to feed to the rear speakers to start the three-dimensional surround environment. Some reverb processors have 5.1 surround algorithms that can be used to feed all the channels, but you can produce similar results by using various reverbs for the center and surround speakers. One tactic would be to use the same reverb preset for the surround reverb as you are using for the front left/right, but make the reverb time slightly longer—simulating the greater distance from the source of the rear speakers. If you use the same reverb in both front and rear speakers, you will not get the sense of depth that the surround speakers are intended to produce.

If I'm using the using the listener perspective, placing the listener within the ensemble (which I tend to prefer), I might take peripheral elements that I want to feature, such as horns or percussion, and feed them to the rear speakers along with a different (but related) amount of ambience processing. I tend to maintain panning position (if sent to the surround speakers, then elements in front left will also appear rear left), but any configuration can work depending on how far from the world of the "realistic" you care to stray.

Building a Surround Mix from Scratch

One of the most interesting parts of creating surround mixes is the lack of precedent. Unlike stereo mixes, where many widely accepted protocols have taken root (vocals, kick, snare, and bass dead center or very close; drums panned to reflect the typical drum set setup, etc.), the world of 5.1 positioning is still very much wide open. While certain practices are pretty intuitive and well established, like putting extra ambience in the rear speakers, I hear all kinds of new approaches to surround mixing. Certainly the idea of maintaining the stereo mix in the front left/right speakers is not necessary, and there are surround mixes where certain elements—even critical elements like background vocals—have been taken completely out of the front speakers and are heard coming from the surround speakers.

If you're building a surround mix without concern for the stereo version, your options are extensive. You could rely heavily on the center speaker and create a lot of separation between elements by having them come from only one of the front and rear left/right speakers. You could create a constantly shifting mix using dynamic panning to move elements from left to right and front to back slowly, quickly, or both. You could build a mix that was mostly dry in the front, with heavy reverbs and audible delays in the rear speakers. Or, you could incorporate all those ideas in a more limited way in your mix. For me, the temptation is strongest to build a really full, rich, three-dimensional mix that's built on traditional approaches to placement and processing, but the potentialities to stretch the aesthetic are equally compelling.

The unfortunate aspect of surround mixing is that it hasn't achieved much commercial acceptance with music-only releases. Most of us who are primarily music mixers have little opportunity to create surround mixes except when we work on music intended for live concert DVDs. And with those, we are generally constrained to fairly static mixes and a certain faithfulness to reality, whether taking the audience's or the performer's perspective. Surround audio is now prevalent in film, television, and video game releases, but these are all media that combine sound and picture; in the world of music-only production, we're still waiting for surround sound to arrive.

A.4 Making a Surround Master

Mastering a surround mix may conform to many of the same standards as for mastering a stereo mix, but the process may be different when part of a film or video production. For example, live concert mixes for DVD may be one continuous sound file, requiring continuous processing; or they may be a series of separate files, more similar to a CD. Final surround mixes for film (which are beyond the scope of this book) require mastering all the mixed elements—dialog, effects, and music—into one continuous file (an enormously complex process).

Balance of all elements (level and frequency) over the entire program is just as essential in a surround master as in a stereo master. However, overall level considerations may vary more, again depending on the final destination. Level protocols for film and video delivery used to conform to a standard, but with the advent of digital audio, these standards have broken down. Because of the limitations of older film formats and film playback systems, audio was typically delivered with peaks resting at about –18 dB. New digital standards find mastered film, Internet, game, and DVD music achieving similar brickwall lim-

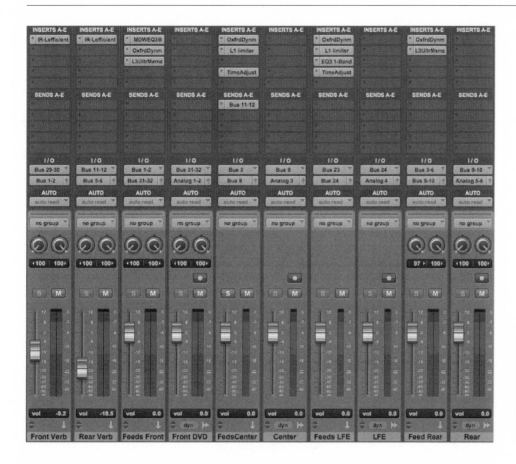

SCREENSHOT A.5

Routing to the 6 channels for a 5.1 mix in a stereo system using aux sends to route audio to all of the surround channels.

ited levels approaching digital zero, with considerable limiting adding impact (if reducing musicality).

Each aux track feeding the 5.1 tracks in screenshot A.5 has a brickwall limiter, so that mastering-type processing can be done to the final files. This also allows you to set the output to something lower that the typical −.02 dB used for CD or general music-track mastering. If you are delivering for DVD, film, video, or video game use, it's best to consult with the person doing the final assembly regarding the maximum output level.

If you are mixing and mastering one continuous audio program (live DVD or film, for example), there isn't the same need for a separate mastering session, since there aren't the problems that otherwise arise in balancing individual mixes created at different times and in different files. When you run your final mix, you are hearing everything that is a part of your final program, so the mastering is part of that final mix run. This can be done using dedicated surround channels if your DAW supports that (as in screenshot A.6), but it can also be done using six individual channels as long as you have the proper monitoring capabilities for referencing your surround mix.

By applying EQ, compression, and/or brickwall limiting on each feed to the 5.1 matrix, you can handle the mastering as a part of the end processing of your mix. Although you will have mixed each part of the program, processing

SCREENSHOT A.6

Routing for a 5.1 mix using dedicated surround channels.

individual tracks and sections in the process, you may find that you want to automate certain parts of the mastering on various segments. As different portions of the program vary, you may want to adjust certain parameters feeding the final tracks, such as the threshold on the buss compress to accommodate lengthy louder and quieter passages. Note the variety of processing plug-ins on the aux tracks that feed the final mixed tracks in screenshot A.5 (including brickwall limiting).

A.5 Delivering Surround Files

As noted earlier, surround comes in various formats, but the dominant format is 5.1 surround, made up of left, right, center, rear left, rear right, and LFE channels. The rear channels are often referred to as the "surround" channels—they feed the "surround" speakers in back or to the sides of the listener. The LFE channel is, in fact, a distinct channel so there are actually six channels of audio. Because it is not full frequency (carrying only subwoofer information, typically from about 90 Hz and below), the last is referred to as the .1 channel of 5.1.

Format requirements for delivering 5.1 audio may differ, but the standard for the digital audio files is 48 kHz, 16-bit AIFF files, as this is what is used in the most prominent authoring programs. It is essential that you communicate with the person assembling the final program to see what format is optimal (or essential). If you are using "bounce to disc" to create the mixed files, you can set those file format parameters as part of the bounce. If you record onto tracks within your DAW session, you will probably need to convert those files to the desired format; generally you'll be working at 24 bit and may well be using the BWF format, so you may need to convert those to 16 bit AIFF files.

Surround for DVD will be encoded as an AAC file for Dolby or some other codec for a different surround format, such as DTS. Usually the audio person supplies the 48 kHz, 16-bit AIFF files and the encoding is taken care of at the DVD authoring stage. If you are required to supply encoded files, you will need to get either a program that does the encoding or an add-on for your DAW that allows you to do this encoding within the DAW.

The standard encoded order for 5.1 surround files is as follows:

Channel 1: Front left
Channel 2: Front right
Channel 3: Center
Channel 4: LFE
Channel 5: Rear left
Channel 6: Rear right

It is critical that the files be in this order for them to encode properly, though you may be just delivering the individual files and it will be up the person assembling the master to create the proper encoded file.

Appendix B

Why Mixing and Mastering Can No Longer Be Separated

Recent Project #1

As I was finishing this book, I had an interesting mastering project come in that prompted this final appendix. The circumstances were as follows. The mixing had just been completed, and I was sent the final mixes for mastering. The engineer may not have had a lot of experience sending mixes for mastering (although the mixes were quite good), because I was first sent mixes that included the brickwall limiting, but at the last moment he realized that I might want the mixes without the limiting, so those were sent as well. Of course, as clearly explained at various points in this book, I definitely did want the mixes without the brickwall limiting for mastering purposes.

The problem that arose was that the artist, listening to the mixes without the brickwall limiter for the first time, was struck by how open and dynamic they felt. He told me that he now understood that the mix engineer may have been using too much limiting, and he wanted to regain some of that open quality that he heard in the mixes without the limiter.

I set about to master the record, and started by comparing the mixes with and without limiting to gauge the extent of limiting. I discovered that the mixes that had originally been approved were heavily limited, upwards of 10 dB or more at the peaks. As discussed in this book, one of the primary results of the limiting is the suppression of the kick and snare levels (because they often drive the limiter with their transients), so the mixes without the limiter had a disproportionate drum level. I did send one of the mixes back because I just couldn't get it to sound reasonable without killing it with the brickwall limiter, and the mix engineer created a new version with a lower drum level. The other mixes I mastered using a bit more limiting than I liked, and a multi-band compressor on a few tunes to tame some drum levels.

The artist liked the results, but also missed the impact of the mixes he had been hearing. He even said that he was sorry he'd heard the mixes with so much limiting, but having heard those, he missed the loss of impact on first listening. Plus there were level problems that emerged as a result of the more dynamic nature of these new masters. I received extensive notes and set about to correct the issues.

The only solution was to hit the tracks harder with the limiter, while at the same time making level moves to smooth over some of the problems created by the greater dynamic range. In the end I was able to master the record with less limiting than the original mixes, though more than I like. By using some of the techniques I describe in this book that can be done in mastering I was able to correct some of the broader level problems. Ultimately, the artist was happy with the master and able to get past the slight loss in impact, and enjoy the gain in musicality and expressiveness.

The mix engineer, not surprisingly, preferred his limited mixes. Though he enjoyed the increase in clarity and openness in the high end, he felt that too much low end had been lost in the process. However, the loss of perceived low end and the added clarity at the top are part of the same process (or unprocess, in this case!). The limiter had suppressed and flattened the transients while it had added impact through compression of the low frequencies. Backing off the limiting regained some transients and the sense of a more open top end, but that reduced the impact (or "relentlessness," to put a different spin on things) of the low end.

Recent Project #2

Reflecting on the experience described above, I was reminded of another recent project. This one I had mixed, and it was sent for mastering to an engineer whom I was unfamiliar with. As I always do, I provided the mixes without the brickwall limiter, but I also provided the limited mixes that the artist had approved as finals so that the mastering engineer would know what the artist had been hearing. When I received the final master, I was appalled at the results because the mixes had been smashed with what I considered to be excessive brickwall limiting. The mixes were dramatically altered as a result.

However, the artist was happy with the final master. He was swayed by the newly created impact and didn't seem bothered (or maybe didn't notice) how the balances had been altered (especially in the drums) and how the high end had been diminished and the low end muddied as a result. I held my tongue, knowing how hard it is to retreat from that sense of power created by heavily limited mixes.

The New Era of Mixing and Mastering

Issues around the use of brickwall limiting—now enshrined as part of the loudness war—have been with us for some time, but the extent to which this controversy has altered the basic relationship between mixing and mastering has yet to be fully acknowledged.

It is now impossible to consider mixing and mastering as separate activities. Yes, they have different goals and outcomes, but they have become completely intertwined, bound together with brickwall limiting. If the artist, producer, mixing engineer, and mastering engineer are not all in agreement on the approximate level of brickwall limiting that is going to be used in the final version, there will be great deal of creative and technical energy put into making great mixes that will then be subverted in the mastering. Or, conversely, the mastering engineer will be highly constrained by the amount of brickwall limiting used in the approved version of the mixes.

In this book I have emphasized the importance of clear and consistent communication among all collaborators. Failure to do so will result in a significant disconnect between the original mixes and the mastered versions. More specifically, *there should be agreement in the very early stages of the mixing process on the extent of brickwall limiting that will be used in final mastering,* so that the mixes meet that standard and the mastering engineer has clear direction regarding the limiting. In short, there needs to be agreement on one of the five following standards, so as to integrate the mixing and mastering processes.

1. Very light brickwall limiting (no more than 1 dB at the peaks). Will be the most dynamic and open sounding, but will be considerably quieter than almost everything commercially released.

2. Light to moderate brickwall limiting (2 to 3 dB at the peaks). Will remain open and dynamic, but will still be quieter than most commercial releases.

3. Moderate brickwall limiting (4 to 6 dB at the peaks). Will be somewhat reduced in dynamic range, but retain some openness and musicality. On the quieter side of many commercial releases but close enough to sound like it fits in most cases.

4. Moderate to heavy brickwall limiting (7 to 9 dB at the peaks). Significantly squashed, suppressing transients (especially drums)—listenable and impactful but relentless and not particularly musical. Competitive with most commercially released material.

5. Heavy brickwall limiting (10 dB and above at the peaks). High on the wow factor, very low on long-term listenability. Consistent with the loudest commercial releases.

279

It's clear that this would be a better musical world if the music were mastered to the standard of number 2 or 3 (number 1 is not realistic for most releases). But if that is going to be the case, it is critical that the mix engineer does not use a higher level (4 or 5) on the mixes than the artist is reviewing. By the same token, if the final release is going to be mastered to the level of 4 or 5, it is critical that the mix engineer use a similar level of limiting to finalize the mixes and prevent their being subverted by the mastering process. Sure, plans could change as the project progresses, but at least the work would be done with an acknowledgment of the effect that the loudness war is having on the relationship between mixing and mastering.

Audio Sources

The following audio examples are available for streaming at the book website:

Artist: Dave Murrant
CD: *Goodbye Kiss*
Track: "Ben Bean"

Artist: Acoustic Son
CD: *Cross the Line*
Track: "Google Me"

Artist: John Nemeth
CD: *Name The Day!*
Track: "Tough Girl"

Artist: Rachel Margaret
CD: *Note to Myself*
Track: "Right Between the Eyes"

Artist: Claudette King
CD: *We're Onto Something*
Track: "Too Little Too Late"

Artist: Acoustic Son
CD: *Cross the Line*
Track: "Back from the Edge"

Artist: Laurie Morvan Band
CD: *Fire It Up!*
Track: "Testify"

Artist: The Blues Broads
CD: *The Blues Broads Live*
Track: "Mighty Love"

Artist: Sista Monica
CD: *Sweet Inspirations*
Track: "You Gotta Move"

Artist: Acoustic Son
CD: *Cross the Line*
Track: "Better Days"

Artist: Cascada de Florees
CD: *Radio Flor*
Track: "Collar de Perlas"

Artist: Mike Schermer
CD: *Be Somebody*
Track: "Corazon"

Artist: Claudette King
CD: *We're Onto Something*
Track: "Can I Walk You to Your Car?"

Artist: Sista Monica
CD: *Can't Keep a Good Woman Down*
Track: "Cookin' With Grease"

Artist: Sista Monica
CD: *Can't Keep a Good Woman Down*
Track: "Cookin' With Grease"

Artist: Rick Hardin
CD: *Empty Train*
Track: "Next Best Thing"

Artist: Laurie Morvan
CD: *Fire it Up!*
Track: "Lay Your Hands"

Artist: Dave Murrant
CD: *Goodbye Kiss*
Track: "Snow Angel"

Artist: Rachel Margaret
CD: *Note to Self*
Track: "Right Between the Eyes"

Artist: Sista Monica
CD: *Can't Keep a Good Woman Down*
Track: "Crockpot"

Artist: Bonnie Hayes
CD: *Love in the Ruins*
Track: "I Can't Stop"

Artist: Bonnie Hayes
CD: *Love in the Ruins*
Track: "I Can't Stop"

Artist: Mike Schermer
CD: *Be Somebody*
Tracks: "Over My Head"

Artist: The Blue Devils
Track: "Current Year 2011"

Index

Note
- Page numbers followed by (2) indicate two references.
- Page numbers followed by *dg* indicate diagrams.
- Page numbers followed by *ss* indicate screenshots.
- Page numbers followed by +*dg* indicate discussions plus diagrams.
- Page numbers followed by +*ss* indicate discussions plus screenshots.

Printed in the USA/Agawam, MA
August 25, 2016

639327.004